Professional and Ethical Issues in Counseling and Psychotherapy

Gerald Corey is Professor in Human Services at California State University, Fullerton, and a licensed counseling psychologist. He has been named a Diplomate in Counseling Psychology by the American Board of Professional Psychology. Dr. Corey's previous books include Theory and Practice of Counseling and Psychotherapy, Manual for Theory and Practice of Counseling and Psychotherapy, Groups: Process and Practice, *and* I Never Knew I Had a Choice.

A licensed marriage, family, and child counselor, Marianne Schneider Corey co-authored Groups: Process and Practice *and collaborated with Gerald Corey on* I Never Knew I Had a Choice.

Patrick Callanan is a licensed marriage, family, and child counselor in private practice.

The three authors frequently work as a team co-leading residential growth groups. They also serve as consultants in the training and supervision of group leaders and offer continuing-education workshops in group process.

Professional and Ethical Issues in Counseling and Psychotherapy

Gerald Corey
California State University, Fullerton

Marianne Schneider Corey
Private Practice

Patrick Callanan
Private Practice

Brooks/Cole Publishing Company
Monterey, California
A Division of Wadsworth, Inc.

Printed in the United States of America

10 9 8 7 6 5 4

Library of Congress Cataloging in Publication Data
Corey, Gerald F.
    Professional and ethical issues in counseling and psychotherapy.
    Bibliography: p. 222
    Includes index.
    1. Psychotherapy ethics. 2. Counseling ethics.
I. Corey, Marianne Schneider, joint author.
II. Callanan, Patrick, joint author. III. Title.
RC455.2.E8C66   174'.2   79-9762
ISBN 0-8185-0326-2

Acquisition Editor: *Claire Verduin*
Production Editor: *John Bergez*
Interior and Cover Design: *Katherine Minerva*
Typesetting: *David R. Sullivan Company, Dallas, Texas*

To the significant people in our lives;
to our friends and colleagues

Preface

Professional and Ethical Issues in Counseling and Psychotherapy is primarily written for undergraduates and beginning graduate students in the helping professions. It is suitable for courses in any field involving human-services delivery, from counseling psychology to social work. It can be used as a core textbook in courses such as practicum, internship, field work, and ethical and professional issues, or as a supplementary text in courses teaching skills and theory. Since the issues we discuss are likely to be encountered throughout one's professional career, we have tried to use language and concepts that will be meaningful both to students who are doing their field work and to professionals who are interested in sharpening their skills through continuing-education seminars or in-service workshops.

Throughout this book we attempt to engage the reader in a struggle with the professional and ethical issues that most affect the actual practice of counseling and therapy—a struggle that we hope will span the reader's professional career. To this end we raise such questions as these: What is the influence of the character and personality of the therapist on the outcomes of therapy? How do the therapist's theoretical assumptions affect the course of therapy? Do the therapist's values have a place in therapy? What are the rights and responsibilities of clients and therapists? What are the unique problems associated with group work?

In raising these and many other questions, our goal is not merely to provide a body of information but to teach students a process of raising and thinking about the basic issues they will face as practitioners. On- many issues we present a number of viewpoints to stimulate discussion and reflection. We also present our own views when it seems appropriate to do so, because we believe that our readers will be better able to formulate their own positions if we are open with ours.

We don't mean to suggest that professionals are free to formulate any "ethics" they choose. In the text, we do cite the ethical codes of various professional organizations, which offer some guidance for professional practice. However, these guidelines leave many questions unanswered. We believe that students and professionals alike ultimately must struggle with many issues of responsible practice, including the question of how accepted ethical standards apply in the specific cases they encounter.

We have tried to make this book a personal one that will involve our readers in an active and meaningful way. To this end we have provided our readers with many opportunities to respond to our discussions and to draw upon their experiences in field work, volunteer work, or professional practice. Each chapter begins with a self-inventory designed to help readers focus on the key topics to be discussed in the chapter. Within the chapters, we frequently ask readers to think about how the issues apply to them and to write brief responses on the blanks provided. Open-ended cases and situations are presented to stimulate thought and assist readers in formulating their own positions. Finally, the activities, exercises, and ideas for thought and discussion contain many suggestions for expanding on the material and applying it in concrete ways, both inside and outside of class.

This book is thus a combination of textbook, student manual, and instructor's resource manual. Instructors will find an abundance of material and suggested activities, surely more than can be covered in a single course. We decided to retain the many questions, exercises, issues, and cases so that instructors and students can select the material that is most relevant to the teaching style of the instructor, the nature of the course, and the level and interests of the students. We would like to emphasize once again that this book is intended to stimulate an ongoing process of serious reflection on ethical and professional issues. In this sense, it is designed to raise many more questions than it will neatly answer.

Several colleagues were most helpful in reviewing this book. We would like to thank John Brennecke, Mt. San Antonio College; Randall Corliss, Pomona Valley Mental Health Center; Bill W. Hillman, University of Arizona; Bruce Fretz, University of Maryland; Kenneth Newton, University of Tennessee; and C. H. Patterson, University of Illinois. In addition, we are indebted to three people who have had a significant influence on this book in both direct and indirect ways: J. Michael Russell of California State University, Fullerton, with whom we have spent many hours in lively and fruitful dialogue on issues covered in this book; William H. Lyon of Chapman College, who has influenced our thinking in many areas of professional practice; and Chris Rubel, who has helped us in many ways, particularly by challenging us on the most fundamental issue in counseling and psychotherapy: Who has the right to counsel another person?

Gerald Corey
Marianne Schneider Corey
Patrick Callanan

Contents

4

Theoretical Issues in Counseling and Psychotherapy   58

5

Values and the Therapeutic Process   84

Professional and Ethical Issues in Counseling and Psychotherapy

Introduction ⠀⠀ 1

HOW THIS BOOK CAME INTO BEING

For a number of years the three of us have worked together as a team co-leading therapy and personal-growth groups. During this time we have watched each other grow and change personally and professionally. Although we have developed our own therapeutic styles and sometimes challenge one another's ideas, we do share a common philosophy in the way we view people and the nature of helping relationships.

Over the years we have worked independently in our own counseling practices as well as with one another, and during this time we have had to confront many professional and ethical issues that do not have clear-cut solutions. Exchanging our ideas and exploring our concerns together has helped each of us find increasing clarity as we formulate and revise our positions on these issues. Our interactions with students and fellow professionals have shown us that others wrestle with similar questions. It has become clear to us that students in the counseling field should confront the issues that will be a large part of their professional experience and would benefit by giving serious thought to their positions on these issues before they begin practicing.

Some of the issues we are referring to involve the fact that counselors, no less than clients, are *people*; they have their own personalities, private lives, strengths, and personal struggles. In Chapter 2, for instance, we point out that it's impossible to separate the kind of person a counselor is from the kind of help the counselor will be able to provide. Whether or not a counselor is willing and able to form honest and caring relationships with his or her clients is one particularly significant issue. To take another example, in Chapter 3 we talk about the problem of counselor "burn-out." How can we, as people who have our own limitations of energy and emotional resources and who have our own lives to think of, stay alive as therapists both to our own feelings and to those of our clients?

Other issues involve the nature of the therapeutic process and the helping

1

relationship. What theoretical stance should we choose, and how important is it to have a clear theoretical approach to counseling? What role do our personal values play in the counseling relationship? What ethical responsibilities and privileges do clients and counselors have? What special ethical and professional problems are involved in group counseling? What is the counselor's role in the community and in the institutional structure within which he or she must work?

In considering these kinds of questions, we found no books that were devoted exclusively to a treatment of professional and ethical issues in counseling and psychotherapy. We therefore decided to write such a book, one that would be meaningful to experienced practitioners as well as to students about to embark on their professional careers. Many of the issues that are relevant to beginning professionals surface again and again and take on different meanings at the various stages of one's professional development.

Just as we have found no easy answers to most of the issues that have confronted us in our professional practice, we have attempted to write a book that does not fall into the trap of dispensing prescriptions or providing simple solutions to complex issues. Our main purpose is to provide you with the basis for discovering your own guidelines within the broad limits of professional codes of ethics and divergent theoretical positions. We raise what we consider to be central issues, present a range of diverse views on these issues, discuss our own position, and provide you with many opportunities to refine your own thinking and to become actively involved in developing your own positions.

In making the statement that you are the one who will ultimately discover your own guidelines for responsible practice, we are not endorsing a position of absolute freedom. We're not implying that students are free to choose any set of ethics merely on the basis that it "feels right." The various human-services professions have developed codes of ethics that are binding upon the members of professional organizations. Any professional should, of course, know the ethical code of his or her specialty and should be aware of the consequences of practicing in ways that are not sanctioned by the appropriate professional organization. Even within the broad guidelines of ethical codes, responsible practice implies that professionals base their practice on informed, sound, and responsible judgment. To us, this implies that professionals should consult with colleagues, keep themselves current in their specialties through reading and periodic continuing-education activities, and be willing to engage in an honest and ongoing process of self-examination. Codes of ethics provide general standards, but these guidelines are not sufficiently explicit to deal with every situation. Often it is difficult to interpret them in practice, and there are differences of opinion concerning their application in specific cases. Consequently, counselors retain a significant degree of freedom and will meet many situations that demand the exercise of sound judgment. They will face issues in which there are no obvious answers, and they will have to struggle with themselves in an honest way to decide how they should act in order to further the best interests of their clients.

It is worth emphasizing that the issues dealt with in the text need to be periodically reexamined throughout your professional life. Even if you thought-fully resolve some of these issues at the initial stage of your professional development, there is no guarantee that everything will be worked out once and for all. They may take on new dimensions as you gain more experience, and questions that are of relatively minor importance at one time may become major concerns at another time as you progress in your profession. In addition, it may not be possible or even desirable to have solutions for all the professional concerns you will encounter. Many students burden themselves with the expectation that they should resolve all possible issues before they are ready to begin practicing, but we see the definition and refinement of the issues we raise as being an evolutionary process that requires a continually open and self-critical attitude.

SOME SUGGESTIONS FOR USING THIS BOOK

If you're like many students, you've probably found some textbooks difficult to relate to in a personally meaningful way, because you found them dry and abstract. Perhaps you have frequently found yourself reading passively just to acquire information, without being challenged to make a real synthesis of the ideas in the text with your own ideas and experiences or to formulate your own positions. Because we believe that this passive relationship of the reader to the material in a textbook is unfortunate, we've tried to write a book that will involve you in a personal and active way. This book deals with the central professional and ethical issues that you are likely to encounter in your work with clients, and we have made every effort to make it a practical book without making it a source of ready-made answers. Our aim has been to provide a context within which you can actively formulate your own positions.

In writing this book, we frequently imagined ourselves in conversations with our students, and we hope you will find it informal, personal, and designed to elicit your reactions to what we discuss. Whenever it seems appropriate, we state our own thinking and discuss how we came to the positions we hold. We think it's important to openly state our biases, views, convictions, and attitudes so that you can critically evaluate our stance rather than assume the validity of our views without a process of serious reflection. On many issues we present a diverse range of viewpoints so that you'll have material to use in formulating your own thoughts. Our hope is that you will give constant attention to ways of integrating your own thoughts and experiences with the issues we explore, so that you will not only absorb information but also deepen your understanding.

The format of this book is therefore different from that of most traditional textbooks. It is intended to be a personal manual that can be useful to you at various stages in your professional development. There are many questions and exercises interspersed in the text that we hope will stimulate you to become an active reader and learner. If you take the time to do these exercises and complete the surveys and inventories, the book will become both a challenge to reflect personally on the issues and a record of your reactions to them.

You should know that we have intentionally provided an abundance of exercises in each chapter, more than can be expected to be integrated in one semester or in one course. We invite you to look over the questions and other exercises and to decide which of them have the most meaning for you. At a later reading of the book, you may want to consider questions or activities that you omitted on your initial reading.

We'd like to make several other specific suggestions for getting the most from this book and your course, many of which have come from students who have been in our classes. In general, you'll get from the experience of this book and course whatever you're willing to invest of yourself, so it's important to clarify your goals and to think about ways of becoming actively involved. The following suggestions may help you to become more active as a learner.

1. *Preparation.* You can best prepare yourself to become active in your class by spending time outside of class reading and thinking about the questions we pose. Completing the exercises and responding to the questions and open-ended cases will help you focus on where you stand on some controversial issues.

2. *Dealing with your expectations.* Often students have unrealistic expectations of themselves. Even though they have had very little counseling experience, they may think that they should have all the right answers worked out once and for all before they begin to work with people, or they may feel that they lack appropriate experiences. If you haven't had much experience in counseling clients, you can begin to become involved in the issues we discuss by thinking about situations in which friends have sought you out when they were in need of help. You can also reflect on the times when you were experiencing conflicts and needed someone to help you gain clarity. In this way, you may be able to relate the material to events in your own life even if your counseling experience is limited.

3. *Pretest and posttest.* At the end of this chapter there is a multiple-choice survey designed to help you discover your attitudes concerning most of the issues we deal with in this book. We encourage you to take this inventory before you read the book to see where you stand on these issues at this time. You may want to take the inventory in more than one sitting so that you can give careful thought to each question. We also encourage you to take the inventory again after you complete the book, this time as a posttest. You can then compare your responses to see what changes have occurred in your attitudes as a result of the course and your reading of the book.

4. *Pre-Chapter Self-Inventories.* Each chapter begins with a self-inventory designed to stimulate your thinking about the issues that will be explored in the chapter. You might want to bring your responses to class and compare your views with fellow students. You may also find it useful to re-take the inventory after you finish reading the chapter to see whether your views have changed.

5. *Examples, cases, and questions.* Many examples are given in this book that are drawn from actual counseling practice in various settings with different types of clients. We frequently ask you to consider how you might have worked with a given client or what you might have done in a particular counseling situation. We hope you'll take the time to think about these questions and briefly respond to them in the spaces provided.

6. *End-of-chapter exercises and activities.* Each chapter ends with exercises and activities intended to help you integrate and apply what you've learned in the chapter. They include suggestions for things to do both in class and on your own, as well as ideas for thought and discussion that you can consider alone in a personal way or use for small-group discussions in class. The purpose of these aids is to make the issues come alive and to help you apply your ideas to practical situations. We think the time you devote to these end-of-the-chapter activities can be most useful in helping you achieve a practical grasp of the material treated in the text.

7. *The journal idea.* Many students have found it very valuable to keep an ongoing journal for the duration of the course in which they can do some more extensive writing about their positions on the issues discussed in class. A spiral notebook is ideal for keeping a record of some of your thoughts and experiences.

Some students have found it most valuable to read their journals a year or two later, because in this way they achieve a sense of how their thinking has evolved as they have gained more experience.

8. *The tape-recorder idea.* Some of our students use a tape recorder as an alternative to writing a journal. After a number of sessions with several clients, they think aloud about the concerns and issues that have come up. For instance, they may ask themselves: "Am I doing most of the talking in our sessions?" "Am I really listening to what my clients are saying?" "How can I know whether my clients are getting anything from our sessions?" By talking into a tape recorder (and dating your conversations), you may achieve some clarity and be able to focus on the issues that tend to be ongoing. Then, by listening to the recordings you've made over a period of time, you might find that new issues have replaced earlier ones or that you're facing again at a later period in your development some of the struggles or questions you faced when you began counseling.

9. *Selected outside reading.* At the end of the book you'll find an annotated reading list of additional sources you might want to consult. By developing the habit of doing some reading on issues that have meaning to you, you can gain new insights that you can integrate with your own frame of reference.

Most of all, we encourage you to use this book in any way that assists you to become involved in the issues. We hope you'll feel free to focus selectively on the questions and activities that have the most meaning for you at this time and that you'll remain open to new issues as they assume importance for you.

SOME SUGGESTIONS FOR GETTING THE MOST OUT OF YOUR PROFESSIONAL EDUCATION

In the preceding section we urged you to become an active learner as you use this book. Now we'd like to broaden this idea to include your entire program of training or professional preparation. Even though it may not be in your power to alter your program substantially, you can do more than simply meet an external set of requirements; you can choose to play an active role in making your education meaningful for yourself. To do so, you need to give some thought to the kind of education *you* need and want.

Although the nature of counselor-education programs is a vital professional issue, the scope of this book does not permit us to discuss it here. Instead we'll offer suggestions for getting the most out of whatever program you happen to be in. If you want to read about diverse approaches to the education and training of mental-health professionals, we recommend the following sources, all of which can be found in the annotated reading list at the end of the book: Arbuckle (1975), Brooks (1977a, 1977b), Danish et al. (1978), Egan (1975), Goldenberg (1973), Hatcher, Brooks, and associates (1977), Ivey and Authier (1978), Lewis (1978), and Wrenn (1973).

Self-Screening and Ongoing Self-Appraisal

People preparing for professional careers in counseling-related fields ordinarily undergo various types of screening, selection, and evaluation. Depending on the kind and level of program, greater or lesser weight may be given to such factors as grades, course work completed, personality tests, personal interviews, and the like. Even if these measures were perfectly appropriate and efficient, however, they could not take the place of your own self-screening and self-appraisal. Assuming that you meet some standard of suitability for a mental-health career, you must still decide, on an ongoing basis, whether your interests, wants, and abilities make this the right career for *you*.

Of course, this kind of self-evaluation would be important in any career choice, but it is particularly essential if you're considering a career in which you will have a direct, intimate impact on the lives of others. As we discuss in the next chapter, the personal needs and motivations of counselors can significantly influence the therapeutic relationship, and a high degree of self-awareness on the part of counselors is therefore indispensable. Yet many people are attracted to a career in the helping professions for reasons they haven't thought through. Consequently, we urge you to ask yourself such questions as these:

- What were some of my reasons for entering or considering a counseling program? What appeals to me about this kind of work?
- What led me to choose or consider a particular program rather than some other one?
- What abilities and traits do I have that I think would help me to be a good counselor?

One way to focus on the question of your suitability for a counseling career is to look at the screening and evaluation procedures used by your program or institution. If you're in an advanced program, why were you selected? What do the screening procedures imply about the abilities and traits considered important in the kind of work you're contemplating? If *you* were in charge of screening or evaluating students, what changes would you make in these procedures? What importance would you attach to such factors as grade-point average, academic preparation, personality tests, and personal screening by faculty or peers? What kinds of motivations would you look for in students? How would you evaluate the progress of students in your program? Returning to these questions from time to time in the course of your training might help you to determine the kinds of qualities you think are important in a good counselor and the extent to which you feel this kind of career and the particular program you're involved in are right for you.

Your self-appraisal shouldn't stop with your initial choice of a counseling career. At each step in your professional preparation, you can ask yourself how much you're satisfied with your progress and what kinds of development you still feel you need. Indeed, this kind of self-appraisal will be important to you throughout your professional career.

Taking Responsibility for Your Own Education

It's easy to criticize a program as boring or irrelevant, to find fault with the courses, the requirements, or the instructors. However, if at times you feel dissatisfied with your education, it would perhaps be more honest—and certainly more profitable—to look at yourself and at what *you* can do to make your professional preparation more meaningful. How much of yourself are you investing in your courses? Is your academic preparation merely something to tolerate, or is it an opportunity to learn new material and apply it to your own needs? Are you willing to take the personal risk of talking with your instructors and giving your own ideas? In short, if you see deficiencies in your education and training, what are you doing to fill in the gaps?

To take responsibility for your education, you need to have a grasp of your own needs and wants. You might begin by asking yourself such questions as these:

- Which courses in my program do I value most? Why?
- Which courses are least meaningful to me? Why?
- What kind of practical experience should I have? What kind of training and supervision would I like to receive?
- What kinds of personal, experiential opportunities would I like to have as a part of my preparation? What kinds of life experiences would it be valuable to have before I begin working?
- What value do I place on experiencing my own therapy, both individual and group, as a part of my program?

One very important way of taking responsibility for your education is to work on obtaining the kinds of practical experience that will be most helpful to you in your future work. In writing on "directions for tomorrow," Brooks (1977) asserts that students can no longer be expected to emerge from "traditional" training programs with the confidence and competence demanded by the new roles of the mental-health professional. In Brooks' view, these roles will require greater emphasis on interdisciplinary training, the development of consulting skills, and the encouragement of professionals to be change agents in the community. Extensive practicum placements will be especially important—ones "that get trainees out of the university and into the community, where they are closer to the human needs and issues of the majority of the population" (p. 366).

Observations of practicing professionals and supervised work with clients are invaluable parts of your training. We agree with Wrenn (1973) that students should have contact with clients as soon as possible and continue to have practical experience for the duration of the program. Wrenn maintains that this procedure enables students to get a realistic idea of what counseling is like and to relate their learning to "flesh-and-blood realities." In Wrenn's words, "Early and parallel contact with human realities must be introduced if candidates are not to turn into cognitive skeletons as counselors" (p. 276).

We encourage you, therefore, to explore the opportunities you have for early practical experience. In addition, we'd like to offer some suggestions for choosing practicum placements.

First, consider obtaining your field work in a variety of settings, with various types of clients. Although you may feel most comfortable in working with adolescents, for instance, you might consider broadening your experience to include working with young adults, the middle-aged, and the elderly. There is also much to be learned about the problems and procedures encountered in different types of agencies. Over a period of several semesters you might work at a community clinic, a state hospital, a school, and a mental-health center.

Second, consider exposing yourself to several different types of professional work to test your area of interest and help you decide on your area of specialization. For example, at different times you might counsel individuals, work with families, and co-lead a group.

Third, try to arrange for adequate on-the-job supervision, including individual meetings with your supervisor as you need them. In addition, if there is no provision for regular meetings of the student counselors, you might get together with fellow students on a weekly basis to discuss your experiences and receive feedback on different ways of working with your clients. An ongoing training and supervision group can give you the opportunity to discuss the issues you're struggling with, to share insights, and to learn about your own dynamics in your relationships with clients.

In this chapter, we've encouraged you to become active in your education and training. We'd also like to suggest that you try to keep an open mind about the issues you encounter during this time and throughout your professional career. An important part of this openness is a willingness to focus on yourself as a person and as a professional, as well as on the questions that are more obviously related to your clients. We hope this book will assist you in developing this openness to self-examination and growth as a person and as a counselor.

PRETEST/POSTTEST: A SELF-INVENTORY OF ATTITUDES AND BELIEFS RELATED TO PROFESSIONAL AND ETHICAL ISSUES IN COUNSELING AND PSYCHOTHERAPY

Directions: The purpose of this inventory is to survey your thoughts on various professional and ethical issues in the field of counseling and psychotherapy. Most of the items relate directly to topics that are explored in detail later in the book. The inventory is designed to introduce you to these issues and to stimulate your thought and interest. You may want to complete the inventory in more than one sitting, so that you can give each question your full concentration.

This is *not* a traditional multiple-choice test in which you must select the "one right answer." Rather, it is a survey of your basic beliefs, attitudes, and values on specific topics related to the practice of therapy. For each question, write in the letter of the response that most clearly reflects your viewpoint at this time. In many cases the answers are not mutually exclusive, and you may choose more than one response if you wish. In addition, a blank line is included for each item. You might want to use this line to provide another response more suited to your thinking or to qualify a chosen response.

Notice that there are two spaces before each item. Use the spaces on the left for your answers at the beginning of the course (the pretest). At the end of the course, you can re-take this inventory using the spaces on the right and covering your initial answers so that you won't be influenced by how you originally responded. Then you can see how your attitudes have changed as a result of your experience in this course.

You may want to bring the completed inventory to your beginning class session so that you can compare your views with those of others in the class. Such a comparison might stimulate some debate and help get the class involved in the topics to be discussed. In choosing the issues you want to discuss in class, you might go back over the inventory and circle the numbers of those items that you felt most strongly about as you were responding. You may find it instructive to ask others how they responded to these items in particular.

——— —— 1. The personal characteristics of counselors are
   a. not really that relevant to the counseling process.
   b. the most important variable in determining the quality of the counseling process.
   c. shaped and molded by those who teach counselors.
   d. not as important as the skills and knowledge the counselors possess.

   e. _____

——— —— 2. Which of the following is the most important personal characteristic of a good counselor?
   a. willingness to serve as a model for clients
   b. courage
   c. openness and honesty
   d. a sense of being "centered" as a person

   e. _____

——— —— 3. Concerning self-disclosure on the part of counselors to their clients, I believe that
   a. it is essential if a relationship is to be established.
   b. it is inappropriate and merely burdens the client.
   c. it should rarely be done and only when the therapist feels like sharing.
   d. it is useful for counselors to reveal how they feel toward their clients in the context of the therapy sessions.

   e. _____

——— —— 4. A client/therapist relationship characterized by warmth, acceptance, caring, nonjudgmentalness, empathy, and respect is
   a. a necessary and sufficient condition of positive change in clients.
   b. a necessary but not sufficient condition of positive change in clients.
   c. neither a necessary nor a sufficient condition of positive change in clients.

   d. _____

——— —— 5. Of the following factors, which is the most important in determining whether or not counseling will be effective?
   a. the kind of person the counselor is
   b. the skills and techniques the counselor possesses
   c. the motivation of the client to change
   d. the theoretical orientation of the therapist

   e. _____

——— —— 6. Of the following, which is the most important attribute of an effective therapist?
   a. knowledge of the theory of counseling and behavior
   b. skill in using techniques appropriately
   c. genuineness and openness

      d. ability to specify a treatment plan and evaluate the results

      e. _____

___ ___ 7. I believe that, for those who wish to become therapists, personal psychotherapy
      a. should be required by law.
      b. is not an important factor in developing the capacity to work with others.
      c. should be encouraged but not required.
      d. is needed only when the therapist has *real* problems.

      e. _____

___ ___ 8. I believe that, in order to help a client, a therapist
      a. must like the client personally.
      b. must be free of any personal conflicts in the area in which the client is working.
      c. needs to have experienced the very same problem as the client.
      d. needs to have experienced feelings similar to those being experienced by the client.

      e. _____

___ ___ 9. In regard to the client/therapist relationship, I think that
      a. the therapist should remain objective and anonymous.
      b. the therapist should be a friend to the client.
      c. a personal relationship, but not friendship, is essential.
      d. a personal and warm relationship is not essential.

      e. _____

___ ___ 10. I should be completely open, honest, and transparent with my clients
      a. when I like and value them.
      b. when I have negative feelings toward them.
      c. rarely, if ever, so that I will avoid negatively influencing the client/therapist relationship.
      d. only when it intuitively feels like the right thing to do.

      e. _____

___ ___ 11. I expect that I will experience professional "burn-out" if
      a. I get involved in too many exciting and demanding projects.
      b. I must do things in my work that aren't personally meaningful.
      c. my personal life is characterized by conflict and struggle.
      d. my clients complain a lot and fail to change for the better.

      e. _____

___ ___ 12. I think that professional burn-out
      a. can be avoided if I'm involved in personal therapy while working as a professional.
      b. is inevitable and that I must learn to live with it.
      c. can be lessened if I find ways to replenish and nourish myself.

d. may or may not occur, depending on the type of client I work with.

e. _____

_____ _____ 13. I feel that I will be a *professional* when I
a. join several professional organizations.
b. get an advanced degree or license.
c. get my first paying job.
d. feel competent to practice without supervision.

e. _____

_____ _____ 14. Of the following, my greatest fear when I think about beginning professional counseling is
a. that I'll make mistakes.
b. that my clients won't change fast enough.
c. that I'll identify too much with my clients' problems.
d. that I won't know enough or be skillful enough in using techniques.

e. _____

_____ _____ 15. If I had strong feelings, positive or negative, toward a client, I think that I would most likely
a. discuss my feelings with my client.
b. keep them to myself and hope they would eventually disappear.
c. discuss my feelings with a supervisor or colleague.
d. accept my feelings as natural unless they began to interfere with the counseling relationship.

e. _____

_____ _____ 16. I won't feel ready to counsel others until
a. my own life is free of problems.
b. I've experienced counseling as a client.
c. I feel very confident and know that I'll be effective.
d. I've become a self-aware person and developed the ability to continually reexamine my own life and relationships.

e. _____

_____ _____ 17. If a client evidenced strong feelings of attraction or dislike for me, I think that I would
a. help the client work through these feelings and understand them.
b. enjoy these feelings if they were positive.
c. refer my client to another counselor.
d. direct the sessions into less emotional areas.

e. _____

_____ _____ 18. Of the following motivations, the one that best expresses my reason for wanting to be a professional helper is
a. my desire to help people find their answers within themselves.

b. my hope of changing the world in some way.
c. my need to straighten other people out.
d. the prestige and status that I associate with being a professional helper.

e. _____

19. When I consider being involved in the helping professions, I value most
a. the money I expect to earn.
b. the security I imagine I will have in the job.
c. the knowledge that I will be intimately involved with people who are searching for a better life.
d. the personal growth I expect to experience through my work.

e. _____

20. I see counseling as
a. a process of reeducation for the client.
b. a process whereby clients are taught new and more appropriate values to live by.
c. a process that enables clients to make decisions regarding their own lives.
d. a process of giving advice and setting goals for clients.

e. _____

21. With respect to value judgments in counseling, therapists should
a. feel free to make value judgments about their clients' behavior.
b. actively teach their own values when they think that clients need a different set of values.
c. remain neutral and keep their values out of the therapeutic process.
d. encourage clients to question their own values and decide upon the quality of their own behavior.

e. _____

22. Counselors should
a. teach desirable behavior and values by modeling them for clients.
b. encourage clients to look within themselves to discover values that are meaningful to them.
c. reinforce the dominant values of society.
d. very delicately, if at all, challenge clients' value systems.

e. _____

23. As a counselor, I expect that my values will affect the counseling process
a. when I deal with clients who hold values very divergent from my own.
b. when I feel convinced that the client is living by inappropriate values.
c. only if I attempt to impose my values on my clients.

d. in every counseling session, since I believe that I will counsel clients in accordance with my beliefs and attitudes.

e. _____

____ ____ 24. If a client came to me with a problem and I could see that I would not be objective because of my values, I would
a. accept the client because of the challenge to become more tolerant of diversity.
b. tell the client at the outset about my fears concerning our conflicting values.
c. refer the client to someone else.
d. attempt to influence the client to adopt my way of thinking.

e. _____

____ ____ 25. A therapist's primary responsibility is to
a. the client.
b. the therapist's agency.
c. society.
d. the client's family.

e. _____

____ ____ 26. I would tend to refer a client to another therapist
a. if I had a strong dislike for the person.
b. if I didn't have much experience working with the kind of problem the client presented.
c. if I saw my own needs and problems getting in the way of helping the person.
d. if the client seemed to distrust me.

e. _____

____ ____ 27. My ethical position regarding the role of values in therapy is that, as a therapist, I should
a. never impose my values on a client.
b. expose my values, without imposing them on the client.
c. teach my clients what I consider to be proper values.
d. keep my values out of the counseling relationship.

e. _____

____ ____ 28. The main criterion of whether I'm competent to practice counseling is
a. whether I have a state license to do counseling.
b. whether I've had training, supervision, and experience in the areas I am practicing in.
c. whether my clients feel they are being helped.
d. whether I feel confident and secure in what I'm doing.

e. _____

____ ____ 29. Of the following, I consider the most unethical form of therapist behavior to be
a. promoting dependence in the client.

    b. becoming sexually involved with clients.

    c. breaking confidentiality without a good reason to do so.

    d. accepting a client who has a problem that goes beyond the therapist's competence.

    e. _____

___ ___ 30. Regarding the issue of counseling friends, I think that

    a. it is seldom wise to accept a friend as a client.

    b. it should be done rarely and only if it is clear that the friendship will not interfere with the therapeutic relationship.

    c. friendship and therapy should not be mixed.

    d. it should be done only if it seems appropriate to both the client and the counselor.

    e. _____

___ ___ 31. Regarding confidentiality, I believe that

    a. it is ethical to break confidence when there is reason to believe that the client may do serious harm to himself or herself.

    b. it is ethical to break confidence when there is reason to believe that the client will do harm to someone else.

    c. it is ethical to break confidence when the parents of a client ask for certain information.

    d. it is ethical to inform authorities when a client is breaking the law.

    e. _____

___ ___ 32. Therapists should terminate therapy with a client when

    a. the client decides to do so and not before.

    b. they judge that it is time to terminate.

    c. it is clear that the client is not benefiting from the therapy.

    d. the client reaches an impasse.

    e. _____

___ ___ 33. A sexual relationship between a client and therapist is

    a. ethical if the client initiates it.

    b. ethical if the therapist decides it is in the best interests of the client.

    c. ethical only when client and therapist discuss the issue and agree to the relationship.

    d. never ethical.

    e. _____

___ ___ 34. Concerning the issue of physically touching a client, I think that touching

    a. is unwise, because it could be misinterpreted by the client.

    b. should be done only when the therapist genuinely feels like doing it.

    c. is an important part of the therapeutic process.

d. is ethical when the client requests it.

e. _____

_____ _____ 35. Regarding the place of theory in counseling, I think that therapists should
   a. ignore it, since it has no practical application.
   b. select *one* theory and work within its framework.
   c. borrow something from most of the theories of therapy.
   d. select a theory on the basis of the client's personality and presenting problem.

e. _____

_____ _____ 36. I believe that a therapist should be
   a. active and directive.
   b. relatively nondirective, allowing the client to direct the course of the counseling.
   c. whatever the client needs or requests.
   d. directive or nondirective, depending on the client's capacity for self-direction.

e. _____

_____ _____ 37. Concerning my role as a counselor, I believe that
   a. my role is determined by my theoretical framework.
   b. my role should be defined by the agency I work for.
   c. I should be role-free, because roles interfere with effective counseling.
   d. my role will be defined largely by the type of clients I work with.

e. _____

_____ _____ 38. The most important function of a therapist is
   a. to encourage a client to face reality.
   b. to interpret the meaning of a client's symptoms.
   c. to simply be with clients, so that they will have the courage to look at aspects of their lives they might not otherwise be able to look at.
   d. to give specific instructions concerning what the client should do outside the therapy sessions.

e. _____

_____ _____ 39. Regarding the issue of who should select the goals of counseling, I believe that
   a. it is primarily the therapist's responsibility to select goals.
   b. it is primarily the client's responsibility to select goals.
   c. the responsibility for selecting goals should be shared equally by the client and therapist.
   d. the question of who selects the goals depends on what kind of client is being seen.

e. _____

____ ____ 40. Concerning the role of diagnosis in counseling, I believe that
   a. diagnosis is essential for the planning of a treatment program.
   b. diagnosis is counterproductive for therapy, since it is based on an external view of the client.
   c. diagnosis is dangerous in that it tends to label people, who then are limited by the label.
   d. whether or not to use diagnosis depends on one's theoretical orientation and the kind of counseling one does.

   e. _____

____ ____ 41. Concerning the place of testing in counseling, I think that
   a. tests generally interfere with the counseling process.
   b. tests can be valuable tools if they are used as adjuncts to counseling, particularly when a client requests them.
   c. tests are essential for people who are seriously disturbed.
   d. tests can be either used or abused in counseling.

   e. _____

____ ____ 42. Regarding the issue of psychological risks associated with participation in group therapy, my position is that
   a. clients should be informed at the outset of possible risks.
   b. these risks should be minimized by careful screening.
   c. this issue is exaggerated, since there are no real risks.
   d. careful supervision will offset some of these risks.

   e. _____

____ ____ 43. Concerning the counselor's responsibility to the community, I believe that
   a. the counselor should educate the community concerning the nature of psychological services.
   b. the counselor should attempt to change patterns that need changing.
   c. community involvement falls outside of the proper scope of counseling.
   d. counselors should become involved in helping clients to use the resources available in the community.

   e. _____

____ ____ 44. On the issue of marketing psychological services, I believe that the professional counselor should
   a. teach the public how to be wise consumers.
   b. allow clients to discover for themselves what services are available.
   c. provide guidelines for consumers so that they will learn how to evaluate psychological services.
   d. help members of the community overcome their fears about asking for professional assistance.

   e. _____

—— —— 45. As an intern, if I thought my supervision was inadequate, I would
    a. talk to my supervisor about it.
    b. continue to work without complaining.
    c. seek supervision elsewhere.
    d. feel let down by the agency I worked for.

    e. _____

—— —— 46. My view of supervision is that it is
    a. something that I could use on a permanent basis.
    b. a threat to my status as a professional.
    c. valuable to have when I reach an impasse with a client.
    d. a way for me to learn about myself and to get insights into how I work with clients.

    e. _____

—— —— 47. When it comes to working within institutions, I believe that
    a. I must learn how to survive with dignity within a system.
    b. I must learn how to subvert the system so that I can do what I deeply believe in.
    c. the institution will stifle most of my enthusiasm and block any real change.
    d. I can't blame the institution if I'm unable to succeed in my programs.

    e. _____

—— —— 48. If my philosophy were in conflict with that of the institution I worked for, I would
    a. seriously consider whether I could ethically remain in that position.
    b. attempt to change the policies of the institution.
    c. agree to whatever was expected of me in that system.
    d. quietly do what I want to do, even if I must be devious about it.

    e. _____

—— —— 49. I think that an ethical therapist is one who
    a. always follows the ethical codes of the profession.
    b. always puts the welfare of the client first.
    c. continually raises questions concerning his or her practice.
    d. has all the answers to difficult questions and issues.

    e. _____

—— —— 50. I believe that one of the most pressing ethical and professional concerns in counseling is
    a. the encouragement of client dependence on therapists.
    b. how professionals deal with community change.
    c. the way counseling can be a self-serving activity.
    d. finding ways to offer psychological services to those who most need it but cannot afford it financially.

    e. _____

The Counselor As a Person and the Therapeutic Relationship

2

The purpose of the pre-chapter self-inventories is to assist you in identifying and clarifying your attitudes and beliefs concerning the issues to be explored in the chapter. Keep in mind that the "right" answer is the one that best expresses your thoughts at this time. We suggest that you complete each inventory before reading the chapter; then, after reading the chapter and discussing the material in class, you can re-take the inventory to see whether your positions have changed in any way.

Directions: For each statement, indicate the response that most closely identifies your beliefs and attitudes. Use the following code: A = I strongly agree; B = I slightly agree; C = I slightly disagree; D = I strongly disagree.

_____ 1. Therapists' attitudes are more important than their theoretical orientations in terms of initiating positive personality changes in clients.

_____ 2. The personal qualities of therapists are at least as important as their knowledge and skills in effecting client change.

_____ 3. Therapists should remain relatively anonymous and avoid disclosing much of themselves, so that they don't unduly influence their clients.

_____ 4. For therapy to be successful, the relationship between client and therapist must be characterized by acceptance, trust, and personal warmth.

_____ 5. Part of the counselor's task is to serve as a model for clients, because clients learn a great deal by imitating the behavior of the therapist.

_____ 6. The ability of a therapist to establish a good personal relationship with a client is essential, but it is not sufficient by itself to bring about behavioral change.

---- 7. Unless therapists have a high degree of self-awareness, there is a real danger that they will use their clients to satisfy their own needs.

---- 8. Before therapists begin to practice, they should be free of personal problems and conflicts.

---- 9. Counselors or therapists should be required to undergo their own therapy before they are licensed to practice.

---- 10. Counselors who actually are satisfying personal needs through their work are behaving unethically.

INTRODUCTION

One of the most basic issues in the counseling profession concerns the significance of the counselor as a person in the therapeutic relationship. Since counselors are asking people to take an honest look at themselves and to make choices concerning how they want to change, it seems critical to us that counselors themselves be searchers who hold their own lives open to the same kind of scrutiny. Counselors should repeatedly ask themselves such questions as the following: What makes me think I have a right to counsel anyone else? What do I personally have to offer others who are struggling to find their way? Am I doing in my own life what I urge others to do?

Counselors and psychotherapists can acquire an extensive theoretical and practical knowledge and can make that knowledge available to their clients. But to every therapeutic session they also bring themselves as persons. They bring their human qualities and the life experiences that have molded them. It is our belief that professionals can be well-versed in psychological theory and can learn diagnostic and interviewing skills and still be ineffective as helpers. It seems obvious to us that, if counselors are to promote growth and change in their clients, they must be willing to promote growth in their own lives by exploring their own choices and decisions and by striving to become aware of the ways in which they can ignore their own potential for growth. This willingness to attempt to live in accordance with what they teach and thus to be positive models for their clients is what makes counselors "therapeutic persons."

Surely, counselors have more to offer their clients than themselves as persons. They have some knowledge of the dynamics of behavior and possess intervention skills that are invaluable tools for helping others. However, we believe that such knowledge and skills are most effective in the hands of counselors who apply them to themselves as well as to others.

THE IMPORTANCE OF THE COUNSELOR'S PERSONALITY AND CHARACTER: SOME THEORETICAL PERSPECTIVES

In this section, we describe how various theoretical perspectives assess the significance of the therapist's personal characteristics and the quality of the client/therapist relationship in determining the outcomes of therapy. Although there are extreme viewpoints on this issue, most theoretical models are based on the assumption that the client/therapist relationship must be characterized by caring, trust, acceptance, understanding, and respect if therapy is to have a positive outcome. Most theorists also agree that the kind of person a therapist is crucially influences the kind of relationship that develops between the client and the therapist.

Two Opposing Views: Carl Rogers versus Albert Ellis

The range of viewpoints on the importance of the therapist as a person is well represented by the opposing views of Carl Rogers and Albert Ellis. For Rogers (1961), the attitudes and feelings of the therapist are more important than techniques and theoretical orientation. He lists three personal characteristics of therapists that form the core of a positive therapeutic relationship: (1) congruence or genuineness, (2) unconditional positive regard for the client, and (3) accurate empathic understanding. Rogers claims that communicating these attitudes to clients releases inherent growth forces and enables clients to drop facades and begin a deeper exploration of their defenses. If, by virtue of the persons they are, therapists succeed in creating an accepting and caring climate, then clients will move in these directions:

- they will experience and understand aspects of themselves that they previously repressed;
- they will become better integrated and able to function more effectively;
- they will increasingly become the persons they would like to be;
- they will become more self-directing and self-confident;
- they will move toward an internal locus of evaluation;
- they will become more accepting and understanding of others;
- they will move away from pleasing others, away from oughts and shoulds, away from lives based on the expectations of others, and away from pretenses; and
- they will become more open to new experiences.

For Rogers, then, the most significant contributions of therapists to positive change in their clients are their personal attributes and the relationships these attributes enable them to establish with their clients. Within this perspective, who therapists are as persons is far more important than what they do or what techniques they use in counseling.

At the other end of the spectrum from Rogers' view of the importance of the therapeutic relationship is the view of therapy espoused by Albert Ellis, the founder of rational-emotive therapy (RET). In *Humanistic Psychotherapy*, Ellis (1973) has this to say about the role of the client/therapist relationship in personality change:

> Actually, quite effectual therapy, leading to a basic personality change, can be done without any relationship whatever between client and therapist. It can be accomplished by correspondence, by readings, and by tape recordings and other audiovisual aids, without the client having any contact with, or knowing practically anything about, the person who is treating him [p. 140].

Ellis maintains that clients can make positive changes even when they feel lectured at and think their therapists dislike them. They can blindly follow exercises prescribed by their therapists and maintain unpleasant relationships with them and still show evidence of behavioral change. Thus, for Ellis, personal warmth, affection, and caring are secondary; good therapy can be done without them.

Between the opposing views of Rogers and Ellis, there are various degrees of emphasis placed on the importance of the person of the counselor and the quality of the therapeutic relationship. We will briefly review some of these viewpoints.

The Psychoanalytic View

Orthodox analysts avoid sharing much of their feelings and experiences with their clients in order to encourage the process of *transference*—the projection onto the analyst of feelings the client has had toward the significant people in his or her life. In psychoanalysis, the transference phenomenon is thought to be crucial to therapy and to be promoted by the neutrality, objectivity, anonymity, and relative passivity of the therapist.

Psychoanalytic theory also assumes that analysts will have feelings toward their clients. When the occurrence of these feelings stems from the analyst's own unfinished business or distortions, it is called *countertransference.* The feelings of the analyst can range from extreme dislike to excessive attachment and involvement. Because such feelings are seen as obstacles to successful therapy, analysts are required to undergo their own extensive analysis as part of their training. In this way, their unresolved needs and conflicts will not interfere with the progress of therapy. Moreover, analysts are expected to be constantly alert for the possible reappearance of countertransference; if it occurs, they must submit themselves to further analysis. Clearly, although psychoanalysis does not encourage the sharing of feelings on the part of the therapist, it does place great emphasis on the therapist's self-awareness.

The Existential-Humanistic View

Existentially oriented therapists emphasize the person-to-person encounter in therapy. Therapy is seen as a shared journey in which both the therapist and the client strive for authenticity. The client is seen as a partner in this endeavor rather than as an object to be diagnosed and analyzed.

Two writers representative of this viewpoint are Sidney Jourard and James Bugental. In *The Transparent Self,* Jourard (1971) suggests that therapists can invite clients to live authentically by the example they provide of authentic and self-disclosing behavior. According to Jourard, therapists should work toward a person-to-person relationship fostered by self-disclosure: "Manipulation begets manipulation. Self-disclosure begets self-disclosure" (p. 142). This kind of therapeutic relationship can change the therapist as much as it does the client; consequently, "those who wish to leave their being and their growth unchanged should not become therapists" (p. 150). After all, Jourard maintains, therapists who conceal their real selves in the therapeutic session are engaging in just the kind of behavior that generated problems for their clients in the first place.

In his book *The Search for Existential Identity,* Bugental (1976) reveals how his own struggles and search for identity have been highlighted through his work as a psychotherapist. He considers that his openness to his own experiencing is the key variable in the establishment of an authentic relationship with a client. The authenticity of the relationship then inspires the client to look within and discover his or her own center and inner being.

A special form of the existential-humanistic approach is Gestalt therapy. The leading Gestalt writers all underscore the importance of the therapist as a person in fostering client growth (see Kempler, 1973; Perls, 1969; Polster & Polster, 1973). In *Gestalt Therapy Verbatim,* for example, Perls (1969) cautions against thinking of Gestalt therapy as a bag of tricks. A therapist who practices in this way becomes a mere technician who only encourages inauthentic behavior on the part of the client. As Perls puts it, "One of the objections I have against anyone calling himself a Gestalt Therapist is that he uses a technique. A technique is a gimmick. A gimmick should be used only in the extreme case. We've got enough people running around collecting gimmicks, more gimmicks and abusing them." Perls believes that the overuse of techniques keeps therapists hidden as persons, so that they practice a "phony therapy that *prevents* growth" (p. 1).

For existential-humanistic therapists, then, the authenticity of the therapeutic relationship is an essential condition of genuine and effective therapy. Although techniques can be useful, they can also be obstacles to the establishment of such a relationship if the therapist remains aloof or hidden.

The Behavioral View

The stereotypic picture of behavioral therapists is that they are more concerned with employing techniques to effect specific behavioral changes than with developing personal relationships with their clients. Sometimes therapists who follow a behavioral orientation are viewed as being mechanical, manipulative, and highly impersonal.

To a large extent, these views are based on a misconception of what behavioral therapists actually do. Although they don't place the same weight on either the personal characteristics of the therapist or the client/therapist relationship as the existential-humanistic writers do, most behavioristic writers contend that the establishment of a good interpersonal relationship is an essential part of the therapeutic process. However, even if these writers agree that such factors as warmth, empathy, and authenticity are necessary for behavioral change, they do claim that they are not sufficient. In addition to such personal characteristics, the skills and competencies of a therapist are critical in determining successful outcomes.

This point of view is represented by Goldstein (1973), who contends that a working relationship is a prerequisite of effective psychotherapy but not sufficient in itself for "maximally effective therapy" (p. 220). Since therapists cannot impose conditioning techniques on clients unless the clients are motivated to change and willing to cooperate, techniques can only be used effectively within the context of the working relationship the therapist develops with the client. For Goldstein, a working relationship "is one in which the therapist and patient are working together toward a commonly agreed upon goal. If this is not accomplished, then, in the vast majority of cases, therapy will be ineffective" (p. 220).

Bandura (1969) gives another view of this issue in his description of the therapist as a role model for the client. He contends that most of the learning that occurs in clients is based upon imitation of the modeling provided by the therapist during the sessions. Clients typically view the therapist as worthy of emulation and often pattern attitudes and behaviors after those of the therapist. The therapist, *as a person,* thus becomes a significant role model for the client. In this way, the personality of the therapist has a critical effect on the therapeutic process.

A third perspective worth noting here is that of Glasser (1965), whose "reality therapy" is fundamentally a form of humanistic behavior modification based on nonrigorous operant-conditioning principles. Glasser developed this approach primarily for people in institutions. He succeeded in translating some concepts of behavior modification into relatively straightforward terms.

For Glasser, the basic role of the reality therapist is to become involved with clients and encourage them to face reality. He maintains that an involvement between the client and therapist must be established before effective therapy can occur. Clients need to know that the therapist cares about them, as evidenced by the therapist's warmth, understanding, acceptance, and belief in the capacity of the client to succeed. Through personal involvement with the therapist, the client learns that there is more to living than focusing on failures and irresponsible behavior.

Reality therapists demonstrate their caring and respect for their clients by refusing to accept blaming and excuses. They care enough about their clients to view them in light of what they can do if they face up to reality.

Summary of Various Theoretical Perspectives

Although the various theories we have reviewed make different evaluations of the importance of the therapist as a person and the resulting client/therapist relationship, most of them agree that the quality of the therapeutic relationship is an important variable in successful therapy. Similarly, most therapeutic approaches emphasize the therapist's ability to be an integrated, mature, caring, honest, and growing person in the therapeutic encounter. Most also stress the value of providing a safe and trusting environment that allows the client to engage in significant self-exploration. Some theorists, however, as represented by Albert Ellis, place little importance on the quality of the client/therapist relationship.

At this point, pause a moment to consider how you view the importance of the therapist as a person by answering the following questions.

1. To what extent do you think the counseling process is affected by the kind of person the counselor is?

   _____

   _____

   _____

   _____

2. If, after considering various viewpoints on the issue of the counselor as a person, you are still unclear about your own position, what steps might you take to clarify your thinking on this issue?

   _____

   _____

   _____

   _____

PERSONAL CHARACTERISTICS OF EFFECTIVE COUNSELORS

In the previous section, we discussed several theoretical views of the importance of the counselor as a person. Our own position is that the personal characteristics and the behavior of counselors are vitally related to the formation of significant relationships that will stimulate clients to move forward. For this reason, we see the personal attributes of the therapist as the single most important determinant of successful therapy. In this section we examine some of the characteristics that we think are important for effective counselors to have, and we ask you to think of the personal attributes *you* deem to be vital. Of course, no counselor is likely to fully possess all the attributes we mention; we're not contending that being a successful counselor is synonymous with being a model of perfection! We do believe, though, that counselors who are willing to continually look within themselves and struggle toward becoming more effective human beings are the ones who are most likely to make a positive difference in the lives of their clients.

The following is a list of personal traits and characteristics that we believe represent an ideal that counselors might aim for. As you read over our list, ask yourself whether you agree with each item and whether there are other traits that you think are important. Then you can use your list of significant personal characteristics as a starting-point for reflection on your own struggle to become a more effective person.

1. *Good will.* Effective counselors must have a sincere interest in the welfare of others. The way they relate to others shows that they respect, trust, and value other people. Caring about others doesn't necessarily imply merely showing warmth and giving support. It may involve challenging others to look at aspects of their lives they might just as soon ignore. It may involve a refusal to tolerate dishonest behavior and a corresponding willingness to encourage others to live without their masks and shields. Caring is perhaps best shown when counselors avoid using clients to meet their own needs.

2. *The ability to be present for others.* By the ability to be emotionally present for clients, we mean the ability and willingness to be with them in their experience of pain or joy. This ability stems from the counselor's openness to his or her own struggles and feelings. This is not to say that counselors must talk with their clients about their own experiences but rather that being in touch with their own emotions enables counselors to be compassionate and empathic with their clients.

3. *A recognition and acceptance of their personal power.* Effective counselors recognize their personal power, not in the sense that they dominate or exploit their clients but in the sense that they are in contact with their own strength and vitality. They feel confident and alive and have no need to diminish others or feel superior to them. They recognize that two people in a relationship can both be powerful, and they don't have to assume a superior role to feel competent. Indeed, one of their aims is to help clients discover their own autonomy and competence.

4. *The knowledge that they have found their own way.* Effective counselors strive to develop counseling styles that are expressions of their own personalities. They are open to learning from others and may borrow concepts and techniques from different schools of therapy, but their styles are ultimately their own.

5. *A willingness to be vulnerable and to take risks.* Ideally, counselors exemplify in their own lives the kind of courage and openness they hope to promote in their

clients. Thus, they are willing to take risks, to be vulnerable at times, to trust their intuitions even when they're unsure of the outcome, to be emotionally touched by others, to draw on their own experiences in order to identify with the feelings and struggles of other people, and to disclose what they think and feel about their clients when it is appropriate to do so.

6. *Self-respect and self-appreciation.* Counselors will be most effective if they feel like "winners." In other words, they should have a strong sense of self-worth that enables them to relate to others out of their strengths rather than out of their weaknesses.

7. *A willingness to serve as models for their clients.* One of the best ways to teach others is by example. Accordingly, effective counselors don't ask their clients to do things they aren't willing to do themselves. If they genuinely value risk taking, openness, honesty, self-examination, and so on, then they will exhibit some degree of these qualities in their own lives.

8. *A willingness to risk making mistakes and to admit making them.* Effective counselors realize that they will accomplish little if they rarely take the chance of failing. They know they will make mistakes, and they try to learn from them without burdening themselves excessively with self-recrimination.

9. *A growth orientation.* The most effective counselors remain open to the possibility of broadening their horizons instead of telling themselves they have "arrived." They question the quality of their existence, their values, and their motivations. Just as they encourage their clients to become more autonomous, they attempt to live by their own values and standards rather than by the expectations of others. They are committed to a continual search for self-awareness, and they know that an appreciation of their own limitations, strengths, fears, and vulnerabilities is essential if they are to facilitate this kind of self-understanding in their clients.

Now that we've listed some traits that we think are important for effective counselors to have, we'd like to give you the chance to reflect a moment on your reactions.

1. From our list of personal traits of effective counselors, select one or two that you think are most important, and state why. Are there other characteristics we haven't mentioned that you think are equally important? What are they?

   _____

   _____

   _____

   _____

   _____

2. If you worked with a colleague who lacked what *you* considered to be important characteristics of an effective counselor, what would you do?

   _____

   _____

   _____

3. At this point in your evolution as a counselor, what do you consider to be the major *personal strengths* that will be assets to you as a counselor?

_____

_____

_____

_____

4. Now list the personal areas that you see as being potential liabilities for you as a counselor.

_____

_____

_____

_____

THERAPIST SELF-AWARENESS AND THE INFLUENCE OF THE THERAPIST'S PERSONALITY AND NEEDS

Since counselors ask their clients to examine their behavior and lives in order to understand themselves more fully, it is incumbent upon them to be equally committed to self-awareness in their own lives. Moreover, without a high level of self-awareness, counselors will obstruct the progress of their clients. The focus of the therapy will shift from meeting the client's needs to meeting the needs of the therapist. Consequently, counselors and therapists should be aware of their own needs, areas of unfinished business, personal conflicts, defenses, and vulnerabilities—*and* how these may intrude on their work with their clients. In this section, we consider some specific areas that we think counselors need to examine.

Personal Benefits

One critical question that counselors can ask themselves is "What do I personally get from doing counseling?" There are many answers to this question. Many therapists experience excitement and a deep sense of satisfaction from being with people who are struggling to achieve self-understanding, who recognize that their lives aren't the way they want them to be, and who are willing to experience pain as they seek a better life for themselves. Some counselors enjoy the feeling of being instrumental in others' changes; others appreciate the depth and honesty of the therapeutic relationship. Still other therapists value the opportunity to question their own lives as they work with their clients. Therapeutic encounters can in many ways serve as mirrors in which therapists can see their own lives reflected. As a result, therapy can become a catalyst for change in the therapist as much as in the client.

Personal Needs

Therapeutic progress can be blocked when therapists use their clients, perhaps unconsciously, to fulfill their own needs. For example, out of a need to nurture others or to feel powerful, people sometimes need to feel that they have the answers concerning how others should live. The tendency to give advice and try to direct another's life can be especially harmful in a therapist, because it leads to excessive dependence on the part of clients and only perpetuates their tendency to look outside themselves for answers. Therapists who need to feel powerful or important may begin to think that they are indispensable to their clients or, worse still, make themselves so.

The goals of therapy can also suffer when therapists who have a strong need for approval focus on trying to win the acceptance, admiration, respect, and even awe of their clients. Some therapists may be primarily motivated by a need to receive confirmation of their value as persons and as professionals from their clients. It is within their power as therapists to control the sessions in such a way that these needs are continually reinforced. Because clients often feel a need to please their therapists, they can easily encourage therapists who crave continuous reinforcement of their sense of worth.

One of the goals of therapy, as we see it, is to teach the *process* of problem solving, not just to solve problems. When clients have learned the process, they have less and less need of their therapists. Therapists who tell clients what to do or use the sessions to buttress their own sense of self-worth diminish the autonomy of their clients and invite increased dependence in the future.

When therapists are not sufficiently aware of their own needs, they may abuse the power they have in the therapeutic situation. Some therapists and counselors gain a sense of power by assuming the role of directing others toward solutions instead of encouraging them to seek alternatives for themselves and choose among them. A solution-oriented approach to counseling may also spring from the therapist's need to feel a sense of achievement and accomplishment. Some therapists feel very ill at ease if their clients fail to make instant progress; consequently, they may either push their clients to make decisions prematurely or even make decisions for them. This tendency can be encouraged even more by clients who express gratitude for this kind of "help."

Of course, therapists *do* have their own personal needs, but these needs don't have to assume priority or get in the way of clients' growth. Most people who enter the helping professions do want to nurture others, and they do need to know that they are instrumental in helping others to change. In this sense, they need to hear from clients that they are a significant force in their lives. In order to keep these needs from interfering with the progress of their clients, therapists should be clearly aware of the possibility of working primarily to be nurtured by others instead of working toward the best interests of their clients. If they are open enough to recognize this potential danger, the chances are that they will not fall into using their clients to meet their own needs.

It's hard to find fault with therapists who find excitement in their work. The rewards of practicing psychotherapy are many, but one of the most significant rewards is the joy of seeing clients move from being victims to assuming control over their lives. Therapists can achieve this reward only if they avoid abusing their influence and maintain a keen awareness of their role as facilitators of others' growth. As you consider your own needs and their influence on your work as a therapist, you might ask yourself the following questions.

1. How can you know when you're working for the client's benefit and when you're working for your own benefit?

   _____

   _____

   _____

2. How much do you think you might depend on clients to tell you how good you are as a person or as a therapist? Are you able to appreciate yourself, or do you depend primarily on others to validate your worth and the value of your work?

   _____

   _____

   _____

3. How can you deal with feelings of inadequacy, particularly if you seem to be getting nowhere with a client?

   _____

   _____

   _____

Unresolved Personal Conflicts

We have suggested that the personal needs of a therapist can interfere with the therapeutic process, to the detriment of the client, if the therapist is unaware of their impact on his or her work. The same is true of personal problems and unresolved conflicts. This is not to say that therapists must resolve all their personal difficulties before they begin to counsel others; such a requirement would eliminate almost everybody from the field. In fact, it's possible that a counselor who has rarely struggled or experienced anxiety may have real difficulty in relating to a client who feels desperate or caught in a hopeless conflict. Moreover, if therapists flee from anxiety-provoking questions in their own lives, they probably won't be able to effectively encourage clients to face such questions. The important point is that counselors can and should be *aware* of their biases, their areas of denial, and the issues they find particularly hard to deal with in their own lives.

To illustrate, suppose that you're experiencing a rough time in your life. You feel stuck with unresolved anger and frustration. Your home life is tense, and you're wrestling with some pivotal decisions about how you want to spend the rest of your life. Perhaps you're having problems with your children or your spouse. You might be caught between fears of loneliness and a desire to be on your own, or between your fear and need of close relationships. Can you counsel others effectively while you're struggling with your own uncertainty?

To us, the critical point isn't *whether* you happen to be struggling with personal questions but *how* you're struggling with them. Do you see your part in creating your own problems? Are you aware of your alternatives for action? Do you recognize and try to deal with your problems, or do you invest a lot of energy in denying their existence? Do you find yourself generally blaming others for your problems? Are you willing to consult with a therapist, or do you tell yourself that you can handle it, even when it becomes obvious that you're not doing so? In short, are you willing to do in your own life what you encourage your clients to do?

If you're not working on being aware of your own conflicts, then you'll be in a poor position to pay attention to the ways in which your personal life influences your work with clients, especially if some of their problem areas are also problem areas for you. For example, suppose a client is trying to deal with feelings of hopelessness and despair. How can you intensively explore these feelings if, in your own life, you're busily engaged in cheering everybody up? If hopelessness is an issue you don't want to face personally, you'll probably steer the client away from exploring it. As another example, consider a client who wants to explore her feelings about homosexuality. Can you facilitate this exploration if you haven't been open to your own feelings about homosexuality? If you feel discomfort in talking about homosexual feelings and experiences, and you don't want to have to deal with your discomfort, can you stay with your client emotionally when she brings up this topic?

Since you'll have difficulty staying with a client in an area that you're reluctant or fearful to deal with, consider what present unfinished business in your own life might affect you as a counselor. What unresolved conflicts are you aware of, and how might these conflicts influence the way you counsel others?

_____

_____

_____

_____

_____

_____

THE ISSUE OF PERSONAL THERAPY FOR COUNSELORS

In the last section, we stressed the importance of counselors' self-awareness. A closely related issue is the value of personal therapy for those who wish to become counselors. There are several reasons why we think potential counselors should be encouraged to experience their own therapy.

First of all, we believe that those who expect to counsel others should know what the experience of being a client is really like. We don't assume that most potential therapists are "sick" and in need of being "cured," but then we don't make that assumption about most clients, either. Many clients are attracted to counseling because they want to explore the quality of their lives and the alternatives they have for a richer existence. Potential counselors can approach therapy in much the same way. Therapy can help us take an honest look at our motivations in becoming helpers. It can help us explore how our needs influence our actions, how we use power in our lives, what our values are, and whether we have a need to persuade others to live by them. We can look at our need to be recognized and appreciated, at painful memories and past experiences that have shaped our ways of living, and at the sources of meaning in our lives. In the process, we can experience first-hand what our clients experience in therapy.

Another reason for undergoing therapy is that all of us have blind spots and unfinished business that may interfere with our effectiveness as therapists. All of us have areas in our lives that aren't fully developed and that can keep us from being as effective as we can be, both as persons and as counselors. Personal therapy is one way of coming to grips with these and other issues.

Ideally, we'd like to see potential counselors undergo a combination of individual and group therapy, because the two types supplement each other. Individual therapy provides the opportunity to look at ourselves in some depth. Many counselors will experience a reopening of old psychic wounds as they engage in intensive work with their clients. For example, their therapeutic work may bring to the surface guilt feelings that need to be resolved. If they are in private therapy at the same time as they are doing their internship, they can productively bring such problems to their sessions.

Group therapy, on the other hand, can provide the opportunity to get feedback from others on how they experience us. It allows us to become increasingly aware of our personal styles and gives us a chance to experiment with new behavior in the group setting. The reactions we receive from others can help us learn about personal attributes that could be either strengths or limitations in our work as counselors.

Many training programs in counselor education recognize the value of having students involved in personal-awareness groups with their peers on an ongoing basis. A group can be set up specifically for the exploration of personal concerns, or such exploration can be made an integral part of training and supervision groups. Whatever the format, students will benefit most if they are willing to focus on themselves personally and not merely on their "cases." Unfortunately, many beginning counselors would rather focus exclusively on client dynamics. Their group learning would be more meaningful if they were open to exploring such questions as: How am I feeling about my own value as a counselor? Do I like my relationship with my client? What kinds of reactions are being evoked in me as I work with this client? In short, if counselors in training are willing to become personally invested in the therapy process, they can use their training program as a real opportunity for expanding their own awareness.

CHAPTER SUMMARY

In this chapter, we've discussed one of the most basic issues in the practice of therapy and counseling—the counselor's own personality as an instrument in therapeutic practice. We have stressed the idea that counselors might possess knowledge and technical skills and still be ineffective in significantly reaching clients. Our belief is that the life experiences, values, attitudes, and level of care that counselors bring to their therapy sessions are crucial factors in the establishment of effective therapeutic relationships.

In summarizing various theoretical perspectives on the importance of the kind of person the therapist is, we indicated that most theories agree that at least a good working relationship is essential for therapy to progress. Consequently, we explored how the therapist's needs and personality influence the client-therapist relationship, and we encouraged you to look at personal characteristics within yourself that you think would hinder or help you in forming effective relationships with your clients.

ACTIVITIES, EXERCISES, AND IDEAS FOR THOUGHT AND DISCUSSION

These activities and questions for thought and discussion are designed to help you apply your learnings to practice. Many of them can profitably be done alone in a personal way, or with another person; others can be done in the classroom as discussion activities, either with the whole class or in small groups. We suggest that you select those that seem most significant to you and do some writing on these issues in your journal.

1. In small groups in your class, explore the issue of why you're going into the helping profession. This is a basic issue, and one that many students have trouble putting into concrete words. What motivated you to seek this type of work? What do you think you can get for yourself? What do you see yourself as being able to do for others?

2. You may want to do additional reading on the role of the counselor's personality and character and the importance of the client/counselor relationship in various theoretical approaches. This topic is a good one for a panel discussion, in which each participant can represent the position of a particular theorist. Some sources to consider include the following: Arbuckle (1975), Bugental (1976), Corey (1977a), Ellis (1973), Glasser (1965), Jourard (1971), and Rogers (1961).

3. In discussing the counselor's personality and behavior, we suggested a tentative list of personal traits and characteristics that we think are important for counselors. The following questions are based on this list. Attempt to answer them as honestly as you can. These questions would also make good material for small-group discussions.

   a. Do you have a sincere interest in the welfare of others?

   b. To what degree are you able to be emotionally present with clients and experience pain or joy with them?

   c. Do you feel a sense of personal power in your own right, or do you derive power from having others in an inferior position?

   d. To what degree do you think you're finding your own way? When are some times that you tend to follow others instead of being your own person?

   e. Do you see yourself as having courage? Can you think of times when you lacked courage? In what ways is courage important for counselors?

   f. How open are you to the viewpoints of others?

   g. In what ways do you respect and appreciate yourself?

   h. Do you see yourself as a model for clients? In what ways? Do you see yourself as doing in your own life what you hope your clients will do in their lives?

4. Make your own list of traits you think are important for counselors to have, and explain each item on your list.
5. Discuss the dangers of believing that you have to be the "perfect person" before you'll be ready to counsel others.
6. If you were interested in selecting a therapist for individual therapy, what kind of person would you look for? What personal traits or attributes would you consider most important?
7. In this chapter, we discussed some of the personal needs that can motivate therapists. Ask yourself to what degree each of the following is important for you:
   a. the need to nurture others
   b. the need to direct others' lives
   c. the need to win approval and respect from clients
   d. the need for power
   e. the need to feel that one is doing something worthwhile
8. What other personal needs do you have that may be met by counseling others? To what degree do you think that they might get in the way of your work with clients? How can you recognize and meet your needs—which are a real part of you—without having them interfere with your work with others?
9. After you've thought through the two preceding questions, form small groups in your class and discuss how counselors can take care of their needs without impinging on the welfare of their clients. Unfortunately, too many beginning counselors believe that it's wrong to have personal needs and try too hard to keep their needs out of counseling. Explore this issue with your fellow students.

The Counselor
As a
Professional 3

PRE-CHAPTER SELF-INVENTORY

For each statement, indicate the response that most closely identifies your beliefs and attitudes. Use the following code: A = I strongly agree; B = I slightly agree; C = I slightly disagree; D = I strongly disagree.

_____ 1. Most professionals in the counseling field will inevitably burn out because of the demands of their jobs.

_____ 2. Counselors who know themselves can avoid experiencing overidentification with their clients.

_____ 3. Strong feelings about a client are a sign that the counselor needs further therapy for himself or herself.

_____ 4. Feelings of anxiety as a beginning counselor indicate unsuitability for the counseling profession.

_____ 5. A competent counselor can work with any client.

_____ 6. I expect that I'll have difficulty making demands on my clients.

_____ 7. A professional counselor will avoid either getting involved socially with clients or counseling friends.

_____ 8. A major fear I have is that I'll make mistakes and seriously hurt a client.

_____ 9. Real therapy does not occur unless a transference relationship is developed.

_____ 10. A professional counselor will not withhold anything personal about himself or herself from a client.

INTRODUCTION

In this chapter we turn our attention to the counselor as a professional. Our decision to discuss this topic separately from that of the counselor as a person is in some ways an arbitrary one, because it's impossible to talk about the counselor "as a professional" without considering the personal qualities that influence the kind of professional he or she becomes. As we discussed in Chapter 2, we believe that a counselor's values, beliefs, personal attributes, life experiences, and way of living are intrinsically related to the way he or she functions as a professional. However, counselors do have a professional identity, and some issues are specifically related to their professionalism as counselors. Although some of the questions we discuss are of special concern to the beginning counselor, you'll probably find yourself struggling with most of these issues again and again throughout your professional career.

COMMON CONCERNS OF BEGINNING COUNSELORS

Many students in counselor-training programs tend to bring up the same fears, resistances, self-doubts, concerns, and questions. They may wonder whether they have what it takes to be professional counselors, or they may seriously question the nature of their impact on the people they counsel. Moreover, students inevitably discover that there is a gap between their formal, academic learning and the actual work they do when they come face to face with clients. The discovery that they have mainly themselves to work with—that, although techniques can be helpful, they must ultimately draw on themselves as persons—can be a frightening one. You should keep in mind, however, that these kinds of concerns are rarely resolved once and for all; even as an experienced counselor, you'll probably find yourself struggling from time to time with doubts and anxieties about your adequacy or the value of your work.

The following questionnaire is drawn from statements we frequently hear in practicum and internship courses; they represent a sampling of the issues faced by those who begin to counsel others. Apply these statements to yourself, and decide to what degree you see them as your concerns. If a statement is more true than false for you, place a "T" in front of it; if it is more false than true for you, place an "F" in front of it.

_____ I'm afraid that I'll make mistakes.

_____ My clients will really suffer because of my blunders and my failure to know what to do.

_____ I have real doubts concerning my ability to help people in a crisis situation.

_____ I demand perfection of myself, and I constantly feel I should know more than I do.

_____ I would feel threatened by silences in counseling situations.

_____ It's important to me to know that my clients are making steady improvement.

_____ It would be difficult for me to deal with demanding clients.

_____ I expect to have trouble working with clients who are not motivated to change or who are required to come to me for counseling.

_____ I have trouble deciding how much of the responsibility for the direction of a counseling session is mine and how much is my client's.

_____ I think that I should be successful with all my clients.

_____ I expect to have trouble in being myself and trusting my intuition when I'm counseling.

_____ Sometimes I'm concerned about how honest I should be with clients.

_____ I'm concerned about how much of my personal reactions and my private life is appropriate for me to reveal in counseling sessions.

_____ I tend to worry about whether or not I'm doing the proper thing.

_____ I sometimes worry that I may overidentify with my client's problems to the extent that they may become *my* problems.

_____ During a counseling session I would frequently find myself wanting to give advice.

_____ I'm afraid that I may say or do something that might greatly disturb a client.

_____ I can see myself trying to persuade clients to take certain actions.

_____ I wonder how much of my values I should reveal to clients.

_____ I'm concerned about counseling clients whose values are very different from my own.

_____ I would be concerned about whether or not my clients liked and approved of me and whether or not they would want to come back.

_____ I'm concerned about being mechanical, in my counseling, as though I were following a book.

Once you've gone through these statements, you might go back over them again and select the issues that represent your greatest concerns. You can then begin to challenge some of the assumptions behind these concerns. Suppose, for example, that you feel greatly afraid of making mistakes. You may be saying to yourself: "I should know more than I do, and I should have answers for my clients. If I were to get stuck and not know what to do with a given client, that would be terrible; it would completely erode my self-confidence. If I make mistakes, I might drive my clients away, and they would be far worse off than when they began counseling with me." If you burden yourself with these or similar expectations, you might begin to challenge your basic assumptions by asking yourself such questions as these:

- Why should I be all-knowing?
- Who told me that making mistakes would be fatal?
- Am I really expected to provide solutions for clients?
- Are my clients so fragile that they won't be able to survive my mistakes?

As we discuss some of the issues encountered by practicing counselors, ask yourself how you relate to these issues and whether you should begin to question some of your assumptions. You might also find it useful to write about other concerns you now have as you think about becoming a professional counselor. What issues are most pressing for you? What assumptions underlie your concerns? How valid are these assumptions?

ANXIETY

Many counselors experience some anxiety about their work, particularly if they have had little or no experience as counselors. As you think of facing your first clients, you may ask yourself: What will my clients want? Will I be able to give them what they want? What will I say, and how will I say it? Will they want to come back? If they do, what will I do then?

Although raising such questions can be part of a process of self-inquiry and growth for even an experienced counselor, it's possible to become so anxiety-ridden that you cannot deal with the questions effectively. Your anxiety may feed on itself, especially if you think that it's abnormal or tell yourself that you wouldn't be experiencing so much anxiety if you were really suited for the counseling profession. It may help to realize that a certain amount of anxiety indicates an awareness of the uncertainty that surrounds your work with clients. Although anxiety can get out of hand and freeze a counselor into inactivity, some anxiety is certainly to be expected. In fact, we become concerned when we encounter student counselors who never exhibit any kind of self-doubt or self-questioning, which we believe to be part of the evolutionary process of becoming a counselor. The experience of anxiety can lead to honest self-appraisal. We often hear students say that their peers seem so much more knowledgeable, skilled, and confident than they themselves feel. When such students have the courage to bring their feelings of inadequacy into the open, they frequently discover that they aren't alone and that those who appear the most self-confident also have doubts about their capabilities as counselors.

This is where regular meetings with your fellow students and your instructor are vitally important. There are no easy solutions to the kind of anxiety you are likely to experience; in any event, we think it's counterproductive to try to remove all anxiety. With your peers you can discuss your fears, worries, and questions, and you can gain a sense of how they deal with such feelings. You can also explore with them how much of your anxiety reflects a genuine appreciation of the uncertainties inherent in your chosen profession. This kind of exchange offers invaluable opportunities for personal and professional growth. And, since it takes courage to share your feelings, doing so may defuse some of the anxiety that is unrealistic.

Before you continue reading, pause a moment to list some of your current fears or worries concerning your professional work:

_____

_____

_____

_____

_____

_____

EXPECTING INSTANT RESULTS

Many beginning counselors become discouraged when they don't see immediate, positive results in their clients. These counselors may be assuming that their role is to solve any and all problems their clients bring to the sessions. Accordingly, they may ask: Is my client getting better or worse? How do I know if what I'm doing during our sessions is really worth anything?

The fact is that clients generally don't make immediate gains. Indeed, it's far more common for them to report an increase in anxiety in the early stages of counseling and at various points later on. In trying to be honest with their counselors and with themselves, they are giving up many of their defenses and are likely to experience an acute sense of vulnerability. Counselors therefore need to be able to continue working without knowing whether or not they're having positive effects on a client. They may not know the nature of their impact until months after the conclusion of a therapeutic relationship, if then.

DEALING WITH DIFFICULT CLIENTS

To a beginning counselor, almost every client seems difficult, in part because any counselor wants to succeed and needs to see signs of progress in the client. Even for experienced counselors, however, there are genuinely difficult clients. Some of these clients pose particular problems that tend to come up fairly often in a counseling practice. As we describe each of these clients, allow yourself to imagine that you are their counselor. What kinds of feelings and thoughts do they evoke in you? How do you imagine you would deal with each one?

Silent Clients

The silent client is particularly troublesome for beginning counselors, who may interpret a client's silence as evidence that they aren't using the "right technique." For some counselors, a silent moment in a therapeutic session may seem to last an hour. Out of their anxiety they may employ a barrage of questions in an attempt to get the client to open up. Or they may break silences with noisy chatter because of their own discomfort and fail to pursue what the silence means.

Although silence *may* be an indication that the sessions are not very fruitful, there are some distinct values to silence, and counselors need to learn that silence can have many meanings. The client may be waiting for the therapist to initiate a direction, particularly if the therapist has developed a style of asking many questions, making suggestions, or otherwise taking major responsibility for the sessions. The client may be quietly thinking or simply allowing himself or herself to experience some feelings aroused by the session. The client may feel stuck and not know what to say next or feel bored and anxious for the session to end. Both client and therapist may be resisting moving to a deeper level of interaction. Thus, silence may or may not be counterproductive, and it's important to explore the particular meaning of silence in each instance. You might ask yourself: How do I generally respond to long silences? Am I able to communicate with another person through silence as well as through words? What would I be likely to do if a client habitually said very little?

Overly Demanding Clients

Overly demanding clients are especially troublesome for counselors who feel that their function is to meet all the demands of their clients. Because they perceive themselves as helpers, they might convince themselves that they should give unselfishly, regardless of the nature of the demands made upon them. They may therefore have difficulty dealing with clients who call them at home to talk at length about ever-present crises, or who want to be seen more frequently, or who become so dependent that they need to be told what to do at every turn. Such clients may insist that, if their counselors really cared for them, they would be more "giving." Counselors can easily become entangled with such clients and not know how to extricate themselves. Out of a sense of guilt, or out of a failure to be assertive in setting realistic limits, they may allow themselves to be controlled by excessive demands.

If you've had some counseling experience, review any experiences you've had with overly demanding clients. What were some of the demands that were placed upon you? In what ways were these demands unrealistic or unreasonable? Do you find that you're able to set reasonable limits? Are you able to make demands for yourself?

In dealing with overly demanding clients, you may have to work through your own need to be needed. An extremely dependent client who continually tells you that you're indispensable is relating to you as a child to a parent. It's easy to keep this kind of client dependent on you, so that you can continue to feel needed. You might convince yourself that you're expected to be available to your clients at all times, while ignoring the benefit you obtain from being needed.

Unmotivated Clients

Some clients have little investment in their counseling or little motivation to change in any significant way. Perhaps their main motivation for being in counseling is that someone else thought it would be a good idea. Again, counselors need to be alert to the dangers of allowing themselves to be perpetually drawn into games with their clients. If you find that you're doing most of the work and that you seem to care more about some clients than they care about themselves, you have good reason to believe that your own needs, not those of your clients, are being served.

We have discussed only a few examples of clients who may pose special problems for you. What other kinds of clients might be "difficult clients" for you? How do you see yourself reacting to them?

_____

_____

_____

_____

_____

_____

LEARNING YOUR LIMITS

All counselors are faced with the task of learning their limits, which includes recognizing that they aren't going to succeed with every client. Even experienced therapists sometimes doubt their effectiveness with clients they just can't seem to reach. For new counselors, the inability to touch a client can be even more threatening, particularly since it's easy to believe at first that they should be able to work effectively with any client. Many beginning counselors tell themselves that they should like all the people who come to them for help or that they should be willing to work with anyone.

It takes courage as well as wisdom to admit that you can't work effectively with everyone. You might work well with children but have real problems in trying to understand adolescents. Or you might be very close to certain children but feel removed and distant from others. Some counselors find meaning in working with the elderly, while others become depressed and discouraged. At some point you may need to consider whether it's better to accept a client you feel you cannot relate to or to admit to the client that another counselor would be more suitable.

Ask yourself what kinds of clients you would most like to work with and what kinds of clients you would least like to work with. Then it might be useful to look honestly at some of your motivations for preferring certain clients over others. Do you want only those clients whom you feel comfortable with or who promise the greatest hope of success, or are you willing to endure some level of discomfort as you learn to work with a greater range of people? Are you able to admit to yourself and to your prospective clients that you don't *have* to succeed with everyone?

Clients I would most like to work with:

_____

_____

_____

_____

Clients I would least like to work with:

_____

_____

_____

_____

ON DEMANDING PERFECTION

Many counselors burden themselves with the belief that they must be perfect—that they must always know the appropriate thing to say or do, must never make mistakes, and must always have the skill needed to deal with any kind of counseling situation. Yet the fact is that all of us, new or experienced, are going to make mistakes. We fail to do our clients justice when we think of them as being so fragile that they will fall apart if we make mistakes. By overemphasizing the importance of avoiding mistakes, we diminish our clients' role in working toward their own decisions. Furthermore, if most of our energies go into presenting the image of the polished professional, we have little energy left for actually working with the client. Perhaps this is where the client is really cheated. It's hard to conceive of a genuine, therapeutic relationship growing from such a situation.

A practicum in which you're getting supervision and have an opportunity to discuss your work might be a good place to bring up the issue of perfection. Sometimes students involved in group supervision are reluctant to talk about their inadequacies for fear of what their peers or instructors will think. It can take a good deal of ego strength to be willing to share your mistakes and apprehensions. It isn't easy to say "I'd like some time to talk about the difficulties I'm having with one of my clients. Our relationship is stirring up a lot of feelings in me at this point, and I'm not sure how to proceed." Although it does take courage to ask for others' perceptions and feedback, this is an excellent way to learn not only about how to proceed with the client but also about your own dynamics. In this connection, you might ask yourself the following questions.

1. Am I reluctant to use my practicum (group supervision) sessions to talk freely about what I'm experiencing as I work with certain clients? If so, what is holding me back?

   _____

   _____

   _____

2. If I feel insecure about making mistakes and about how I'll be perceived by my instructor and my peers, am I willing to share my insecurities with them? If not, what is holding me back?

   _____

   _____

   _____

3. What are some specific insecurities that I'd be willing to explore with fellow students and an instructor or supervisor?

   _____

   _____

   _____

SELF-DISCLOSURE AND BEING YOURSELF

Many counselors, regardless of their years of experience, struggle with the issue of how much self-disclosure is appropriate in their counseling. It is not uncommon to fall error to either extreme—disclosing too little or disclosing too much.

Excessive Self-Disclosure: Denying Your Professional Role

Most beginning counselors (and many experienced ones) have a need to be approved of by their clients. It's easy for these counselors to engage in the sharing of intimate details so that their clients will perceive them as being human. They may talk about themselves a great deal, regardless of how appropriate their self-disclosure is for a given client, in the hope that their openness about their private lives will encourage their clients to trust them and share more of themselves.

Counselors who engage in excessive self-disclosure are often those who are trying to avoid getting lost in a professionally aloof role. Some of these counselors would rather be seen as a friend than as a professional with specialized helping skills, and some use the client/counselor relationship to explore their own needs. The danger of this approach is that a pseudo-realness can develop out of their need to be seen as human. Trying too hard to prove their humanness, they may not only fail to be authentic but also limit their potential effectiveness. When therapists disclose detailed stories about themselves, they take the focus away from the client. Although they are supposedly sharing their problems and experiences for the benefit of their clients, more often than not such sharing serves their own needs.

Van Hoose and Kottler (1977) admit that self-disclosure by the therapist has many values, but they caution that there is a fine distinction between appropriate, timely self-disclosure and self-disclosure that serves the therapist's own needs. They contend that, whenever therapists take the focus off their clients and put it on themselves, they are in danger of abusing their clients. They put the issue bluntly:

> Whenever the therapist engages in long-winded stories or anecdotes irrelevant to the client's pressing concern, he is keeping the focus on himself and acting unethically. Each and every time that the therapist takes the focus off the client and puts it on himself he is wasting valuable time in the interview and negating the client's importance [p. 61].

Self-disclosure on the part of the counselor need not be excessive, however. Facilitative disclosure, which is hard for many of us to learn, enhances the therapeutic process. It admits the client into the therapist's private world when to do so is relevant and timely within the context of the therapeutic relationship. Appropriate disclosure can focus on the reactions of the therapist to the client in the here-and-now encounter between them. With a few words, and sometimes even nonverbally, the therapist can express feelings of identification and understanding. The focus thus remains on the client, and the self-disclosure is not a contrived technique to get the client to open up. Appropriate self-disclosure is one way of being yourself without trying to prove your humanity to the point of being inauthentic or serving your own needs at the expense of the client. At this point, take some time to reflect on the following questions and on your own criteria for determining whether your self-disclosure is facilitative.

1. How important is it to you that your clients like you and perceive you as being human?

   _____

   _____

   _____

2. How much of your outside life are you willing to make known to your clients? For what reasons would you reveal your personal life?

_____

_____

_____

3. How might your clients be helped or hindered when you talk about yourself?

_____

_____

_____

4. How do you decide whether to share your personal reactions and feelings, positive and negative, concerning the client and your relationship?

_____

_____

_____

5. Would you tell a client that you were finding it difficult to concentrate on him or her during a particular session if you were in turmoil over some personal matter of your own? Why or why not?

_____

_____

_____

Too Little Self-Disclosure: Hiding behind Your Professional Role

While some counselors go the extreme of denying their professional role in order to be seen as friendly and human, some go to the opposite extreme: hiding themselves behind professional facades, becoming so caught up in maintaining stereotyped role expectations that they let little of themselves show in their interactions. Perhaps out of a fear of appearing unprofessional or otherwise losing the respect of their clients, they tend to keep their personal reactions out of the counseling session. Consider for a moment whether it's possible to perform your functions as a professional without being aloof and impersonal. Is it possible that the more insecure, frightened, and uncertain you are in your professional work, the more you will tend to cling to the defense afforded by a professional image?

We believe that "professional" aloofness may stem from unrealistic expectations some counselors have concerning their role in therapy. Trying to live up to these expectations neither helps clients nor fosters our own growth. Consider the following statements, and check the ones that describe your expectations of yourself.

____ I should always know what to say and do in a counseling session, for I need to appear competent if I am to earn the trust of my clients.

____ I should always care for my clients, and I should care for all of them equally.

____ I should like and enjoy my clients; I must be all-accepting, all-understanding, and fully empathic.

____ To be an effective counselor, I must have everything "together" in my own life; any indication that I have personal problems diminishes my effectiveness.

____ I should be able to figure out what my clients want and need, even if they don't know themselves or don't reveal their wants and needs to me. Further, I should be able to provide them with solutions to their problems.

____ I must remain neutral and objective at all times and avoid having personal feelings and reactions toward my clients.

We believe that these kinds of notions concerning what it means to be a professional lead counselors to hide behind professional facades instead of being themselves in a nonmechanical and real way. By accepting these and other lofty standards, counselors end up playing roles that aren't always congruent with the way they feel. In moments of uncertainty with clients, they may act all-knowing; if they find it difficult to care about or like certain clients, they may deny their feelings by focusing on positive ones; if they feel disinterested or bored, they may try to force themselves to pay attention. If you find that you tend to adopt an inauthentic professional role, you might ask yourself whether you can realistically expect your clients to shed inauthentic behavior and become increasingly genuine with themselves and with you. After all, what kind of behavior are you modeling for your clients if you fail to be authentic with them?

Sidney Jourard (1971) makes a helpful distinction between hiding behind professional roles (which is undesirable) and being a person who plays many roles (which is inevitable). He points to the fact that, when we get lost in our roles, we become alienated from ourselves. For Jourard, one of the major roles of therapists is to be transparent with their clients, at least with respect to their experiences in the counseling relationship. This kind of authenticity is basic to effective psychotherapy, he argues, because it offers the possibility of a genuine encounter between therapist and client. Clients will not be fooled if therapists attempt to hide their basic feelings by resorting to expert techniques: "Patients are seldom that insensitive. Moreover, if a therapist thus hides his being, he is engaging in the same inauthentic behavior that generated symptoms in the patient, and supposedly, he is trying to undo this self-alienating process" (p. 148).

Pause a moment now to list specific kinds of feelings that you would *not* be willing to disclose to your clients. Why would you be unwilling to make these disclosures?

_____

_____

_____

_____

_____

What kinds of feelings can you see yourself sharing with your clients?

_____

_____

_____

SELF-DECEPTION

Even with the best of intentions and motives, both counselors and clients can fall prey to the phenomenon of self-deception. Self-deception occurs in subtle ways and is not to be confused with conscious lying. The client and the therapist both want to see productive results come out of the therapeutic relationship, and both may convince themselves that what they are doing is worthwhile, regardless of the reality. Let's consider client self-deception first.

It's safe to assume that people who are clients by choice have an investment in experiencing positive changes. They are committing themselves financially and emotionally to a relationship in the hopes that they will experience less conflict, feel better about themselves, get along with others better, and feel more in charge of their own lives. Given these kinds of expectations and the personal investment involved, there is always the possibility that clients will overestimate what they are really getting from counseling. Some may have to feel they are benefiting in order to justify the personal sacrifices they are making to obtain counseling. In failing to be open to the reality of the situation, however, they render the counseling experience less effective.

Counselor self-deception sometimes operates in subtle ways to reinforce the self-deception of clients. Counselors, too, have an investment in seeing their clients make progress. Less experienced counselors, in particular, may find it very hard to tolerate periods in which their clients seem to make little progress or actually seem to regress. Counselors whose egos are heavily invested in a successful outcome may not want their clients to talk about their ambivalent feelings concerning the value of their counseling. Similarly, if counselors need to feel that they are solving problems and "straightening out" their clients, they are likely to be less skeptical than they should be in evaluating therapeutic outcomes. Although there is no sure-fire method of avoiding self-deception, being aware of the hazard may lessen the chance that you'll "see" nonexistent results in order to satisfy your expectations and those of your clients. As a way of exploring how self-deception can arise in counseling, consider the following questions.

1. How would you feel if several of your clients complained that they weren't really getting anywhere? How would you respond?

_____

_____

_____

_____

2. How would you feel if you couldn't detect any signs of progress with a client? Would you tend to blame the client? Yourself?

_____

_____

_____

DEALING WITH TRANSFERENCE AND COUNTERTRANSFERENCE

As you become involved in the practice of counseling or psychotherapy, you will inevitably have to come to grips with issues relating to transference and countertransference, even though you may not use these terms. It is beyond the scope of this book to deal with these topics in great detail, but we do encourage you to think about how you can deal with the feelings clients may direct toward you and the feelings you may have toward certain clients. We believe that counselors' handling of these feelings has a direct bearing on therapeutic outcomes.

Transference

Transference refers to the usually unconscious process whereby clients project onto their therapists past feelings or attitudes toward significant people in their lives. The concept of transference stems from psychoanalysis, which stresses clients' unrecognized or unresolved feelings concerning past relationships, but the phenomenon is not restricted to psychoanalytic therapy.

In transference, a client's "unfinished business" produces a distortion in the way he or she perceives the therapist. The feelings that are experienced in transference may be positive or negative; they may include love, anger, affection, hate, dependence, ambivalence, and others. The essential point is that they are connected with the past but are now directed toward the therapist.

The therapeutic value of transference is that it allows clients to express distorted feelings without getting the response they expect. This is the crucial difference between the therapy and their past experience. If a client is treating the therapist as a stern and rejecting father, the therapist does not respond with the expected defensive and negative feelings. Instead, the therapist accepts the client's feelings and helps the client understand them. As Brammer and Shostrom (1968) explain, "The general principle here is that the counselor should not fit himself into the client's projections, so as to satisfy the client's neurotic needs. If the counselor fulfills the client's expectations, there is the possibility they will be perpetuated by virtue of having been reinforced" (p. 239).

There are various viewpoints on the place of transference in therapy. Some therapeutic approaches view transference as the very core of the process, while others tend to ignore it as an issue. From the psychoanalytic perspective, transference is an essential part of the therapeutic process. Thus, Alexander (1956) writes, "The principal therapeutic tool is transference, in which the patient relives, in relationship to the therapist, his earlier interpersonal conflicts. Regression to the dependent attitude of infancy and childhood is a constant feature of the transference, and in the majority of cases, the central one" (p. 193). For psychoanalysts, transference allows clients to relive their past in therapy, using the therapeutic relationship to work through unresolved emotional conflicts. In this way, they can counteract the effects of early painful experiences and achieve insight into how the past interferes with their present functioning.

In contrast to the psychoanalytic view, Rollo May (1967) warns that too much emphasis on transference as a reenactment of past relationships can detract from the meaning of the client's present encounter with the therapist. Transference, May argues, can become an intellectualized notion that therapists hide behind in order to avoid the intensity of personal encounters with their clients.

For Corlis and Rabe (1969)—who, like May, are humanistically oriented—transference is a special case of resistance. They argue that, if it does occur and is worked out, a new and different relationship develops between client and therapist. After transference feelings are explored, the client no longer treats the therapist as a "repository of past experiences" but as a separate human being that he or she is discovering anew: "The distortions of past conditioning drop away, and the interpersonal relationship begins to rest on existential grounds" (pp. 95–96).

Carl Rogers (1951) contends that transference, in the psychoanalytic sense of the term, does not tend to develop in the client-centered therapy he espouses. As Rogers puts it, "if the definition being used is the transfer of infantile attitudes to a present relationship in which they are inappropriate, then very little if any transference is present" (p. 200).

In writing on the place of transference in Reality Therapy, William Glasser (1965) also rejects the psychoanalytic view that the relationship between client and therapist should involve a reexperiencing of past attitudes and feelings. For Glasser, the client's relationship with the therapist is based on the here-and-now: "Psychiatric patients are not seeking to repeat unsuccessful involvements, past or present; they are looking for a satisfying human involvement through which they can fulfill their needs now" (p. 52).

Some writers argue that concepts such as transference can be used by therapists to protect and control their clients. Steinzor (1967), for example, cites the tendency of many therapists to deflect a client's criticism by formulating elaborate concepts to explain it as a manifestation of the client's irrational and unconscious aggression. In this context, he makes a point that anyone involved in the helping professions should consider: "Any approach to a patient is potentially wicked which places the person in an inferior position and constantly emphasizes his weakness and relative lack of power" (p. 138).

Even if transference is viewed as a real and significant phenomenon in therapy, it should be recognized that it is not a catch-all intended to explain every feeling that clients express toward their therapists. For example, if a client expresses anger toward you, it may be justified. If you haven't been truly present for the client, responding instead in a mechanical fashion, your client may be expressing legitimate anger and disappointment. Similarly, if a client expresses affection toward you, these feelings may be genuine; simply dismissing them as infantile fantasies can be a way of putting distance between yourself and your client. Of course, most of us would probably be less likely to interpret positive feelings as distortions aimed at us in a symbolic fashion than we would negative feelings. It is possible, then, for therapists to err in either direction—to be too quick to explain away negative feelings or too willing to accept whatever clients tell them, particularly when they are hearing how loving, wise, perceptive, or attractive they are. In order to understand the real import of clients' expressions of feelings, therapists must actively work at being open, vulnerable, and honest with themselves. Although they should be aware of the possibility of transference, they should also be aware of the danger of discounting the genuine reactions their clients have toward them.

We will now present a series of brief, open-ended cases in which we ask you to imagine yourself as the therapist. How do you think you would respond to each client? What are your own reactions?

Your client, Sharon, seems extremely dependent upon you for advice in making even minor decisions. It is apparent that she doesn't trust herself and often tries to figure out what you might do in her place. She asks you personal questions about your marriage, how you get along with your children, and so forth. Evidently she has elevated you to the position of one who has it "all together" and is trying to emulate you in every way. At other times Sharon tells you that, whenever she tries to make her own decisions, they turn out badly. Consequently, when faced with a decision, she vacillates back and forth and becomes filled with self-doubt. Although she claims to realize that you cannot give her "the" answer, she keeps asking you what you think about her decisions.

1. Would you be inclined to give Sharon advice by telling her what you think she should do? If not, what would you say to her?

   _____

   _____

   _____

2. How much would you reveal to Sharon about your private life? How would you respond to her personal questions?

   _____

   _____

   _____

3. Do you think you would explore Sharon's past reactions to important people in her life in order to determine how she developed her dependence and lack of self-trust? Why or why not?

   _____

   _____

   _____

4. How would you feel about Sharon's desire to emulate you? If many of your clients expressed this desire, do you think you might come to believe that what they say about you is true? How might this belief affect your counseling?

_____

_____

_____

_____

Carl seems to treat you as an authority figure. He once said that you were always judging him and that he was reluctant to say very much because you would consider everything he said to be foolish. Although he has not confronted you directly since then, you sense many digs and other signs of hostility. On the surface, however, Carl seems to be trying very hard to please you by telling you what he thinks you want to hear. He seems convinced that you will react negatively and aggressively if he tells you what he really thinks.

1. How would you feel toward a client like Carl?

_____

_____

_____

2. How do you think you would deal with Carl's indirect expressions of hostility?

_____

_____

_____

3. What therapeutic value, if any, do you see in directly expressing your feelings toward Carl, particularly anger and frustration?

_____

_____

_____

4. How might you encourage Carl to express and work through his feelings?

_____

_____

_____

Gayle expresses unrealistic expectations about what you "should" be for her. She tells you that you should be more available to her, that you should give more than you're giving, that you don't care for her in the way that she would like you to, and that you should be far more accepting of her feelings.

1. How would you feel if you received these messages, even if you knew
   they were unrealistic?

   _____

   _____

   _____

2. Would you reassure Gayle that you *do* care for her and then try to
   convince her that she is making unrealistic demands on you? If not, how
   would you respond to her?

   _____

   _____

   _____

Countertransference

So far we have focused on transference and the feelings of clients toward their
therapists, but therapists also have emotional reactions to their clients, some of
which may involve their own projections. *Countertransference* occurs when a
therapist's own needs become entangled in the therapeutic relationship, obstruct-
ing or destroying his or her objectivity. Countertransference can be manifested in a
number of ways, some of which we will now discuss.

1. *The need for constant reinforcement and approval* can be a source of
countertransference. Just as clients may develop an excessive need to please their
therapists in order to feel liked and valued, so too therapists may have an
inordinate need of reassurance concerning their effectiveness. Albert Ellis (1973)
contends that therapists must be willing to let go of the irrational idea that their
clients must think well of them. They need to challenge and confront their clients'
irrational and self-defeating thinking, and they can do so only if they are willing to
risk their clients' disapproval.

1. Do you feel you need to have the approval of your clients? How willing
   are you to confront them even at the risk of being disliked?

   _____

   _____

   _____

2. If you have some counseling experience, what is your style of confronting
   a client? Do you tend to confront certain kinds of clients more than
   others? What does this tell you about you as a therapist?

   _____

   _____

   _____

2. *Seeing yourself in your clients* is another form of countertransference. This is not to say that feeling close to a client and identifying with that person's struggle is necessarily an instance of countertransference. However, one of the problems many beginning therapists have is that they identify with clients' problems to the point that they lose their objectivity. They become so lost in their clients' worlds that they are unable to separate their feelings from those of their clients. Or they may tend to see in their clients traits that they dislike in themselves.

1. Have you ever found yourself so much in sympathy with others that you could no longer be of help to them? What would you do if this were to happen with a client?

    _____

    _____

    _____

2. From an awareness of your own dynamics, list some personal traits clients might have that would be most likely to elicit overidentification on your part.

    _____

    _____

    _____

3. One of the common manifestations of transference or countertransference is the development of *sexual or romantic feelings* between clients and therapists. When this kind of transference occurs, therapists can exploit the vulnerable position of their clients, whether consciously or unconsciously. Seductive behavior on the part of a client can easily lead to the adoption of a seductive style by the therapist, particularly if the therapist is unaware of his or her own dynamics and motivations. On the other hand, it's natural for therapists to be attracted to some clients more than to others, and the fact that they have sexual feelings toward some clients does not have to mean that they cannot counsel these clients effectively. More important than the mere existence of such feelings is the manner in which therapists deal with them. Feelings of attraction can be recognized and even acknowledged frankly without becoming the focus of the therapeutic relationship. The possibility that therapists' sexual feelings and needs might interfere with their work is one important reason why therapists should experience their own therapy when starting to practice and should continue to be willing to consult another professional when they encounter difficulty because of their feelings toward certain clients.

1. What do you think you would do if you experienced intense sexual feelings toward a client?

    _____

    _____

    _____

2. What are some specific ways in which you might behave seductively or flirtatiously with a client?

_____

_____

_____

4. Countertransference can also take the form of *compulsive advice giving*. Many nonprofessionals and even some professionals equate counseling with giving advice. A tendency to give advice can easily be encouraged by clients who are prone to seek immediate answers to ease their suffering. The opportunity to give advice places therapists in a superior, all-knowing position—one that some counselors can easily come to enjoy—and it isn't difficult for therapists to delude themselves into thinking that they do have answers for their clients. They may also begin to give advice because they feel uncomfortable if they're unable to be prescriptive or because they find it difficult to be patient with their clients' struggles toward autonomous decision making.

In all these cases, the needs of the therapist are taking priority over those of the client. Even if a client has asked for advice, there is every reason to question whose needs are being served when therapists fall into advice giving.

1. Do you generally find it hard to refrain from giving advice? What do you think giving advice does for you?

_____

_____

_____

2. What kind of advice do you think you would be most tempted to give clients? Why? Would you give yourself your own advice?

_____

_____

_____

5. *A desire to develop social relationships with clients* may stem from countertransference, especially if it is acted upon while therapy is taking place. Occasionally clients let their therapists know that they would like to develop more of a relationship than is possible in the limiting environment of the office. They may, for instance, express a desire to get to know their therapists as "regular people." Even experienced therapists sometimes must struggle with the question of whether to blend a social relationship with a therapeutic one. When this question arises, therapists should assess whose needs would be met through such a friendship and decide whether effective therapy can coexist with a social relationship. Some questions you might ask yourself in this context are:

• If I establish social relationships with certain clients, will I be as inclined to confront them in therapy as I would be otherwise?

- Will my own needs for preserving these friendships interfere with my therapeutic activities and defeat the purpose of therapy?
- Am I sensitive to being called a "cold professional," even though I may strive to be real and straightforward in the therapeutic situation?

It is impossible to deal adequately here with all the possible nuances of transference and countertransference. In this section we have called attention to some of the ways in which either of these phenomena can militate against good therapeutic outcomes. Although transference can be used to help the client achieve insight, both transference and countertransference can work against the best interests of the client. Certainly, therapists must be prepared to recognize and deal with the occurrence of these phenomena. A high degree of self-awareness and a relative freedom from unfinished business are the therapist's best protection against the intrusion of transference and countertransference on the therapeutic relationship.

COUNSELOR BURN-OUT

Counselor burn-out is a topic that is currently receiving a great deal of attention at professional conferences and conventions. Many people in the helping professions find that they grow tired and lose the energy and enthusiasm they once experienced in their work. They talk of feeling drained, empty, and fragmented by the pull of many different projects. Since burn-out is an occupational hazard that most professional helpers face at one time or another, it is important to be prepared for it. Burn-out can rob you of the vitality you need if you are to communicate hope and provide healthy modeling for your clients.

Professional helpers need to see that what they do is worthwhile; yet the nature of their profession is such that they often don't see immediate or concrete results. This lack of reinforcement can have a debilitating effect as counselors begin to wonder whether anything they do makes a difference to anyone. The danger of burn-out is all the greater if they practice in isolation, have little interchange with fellow professionals, and fail to seek an explanation of their feelings of deadness.

To offset this hazard, many professionals find other ways to experience a sense of productivity and freshness. At a recent conference on counselor burn-out and self-renewal, professionals from the audience shared some of the ways in which they kept their sense of aliveness. Some found satisfaction in making things with their hands. Some taught special-interest courses at local colleges or offered workshops. Others found renewal in writing about their professional interests or in attending conventions and workshops where they had a chance to share ideas and experiences with colleagues. Still others reported that they needed to separate themselves completely from their work at times, perhaps by traveling to new and different places.

In a workshop on death and dying, Dr. Elisabeth Kübler-Ross indicated that she found working with dying patients to be demanding and draining. Consequently, instead of devoting herself full-time to this work, she spent part of her time giving lectures and workshops for other professionals. Sharing her specialized talents with others in the field provided her with a sense of freshness and vitality and kept her from becoming overly taxed emotionally by the demands of her specialty.

Occasionally, cutting back on professional involvements can help prevent burn-out. For example, a while back the three of us discovered that we were approaching our group work, which we did as a team, with less than our usual enthusiasm. We didn't look forward to it as much as we had before, and we felt that we weren't as creative as we had been. Moreover, many of our groups during this period seemed less involved and less inclined to invest themselves in therapeutic work. Once we became aware of these problems, we began to question what was happening with us. One of our discoveries was that we had offered a lot of intensive workshops in a rather short period of time. Reducing the number of these workshops gave us the chance to be more selective of group members and also gave us more time for ourselves between group sessions. The result of this strategy was that we found ourselves much more excited and enthusiastic, and the group members in turn seemed much more committed to their work. We were fortunate that the three of us were able to focus quickly on our lack of enthusiasm and energy and to find the source of our difficulty in ourselves rather than in the group members. Had we continued at our old pace, the quality of our professional work would have suffered, and we could easily have become victims of burn-out.

Professionals who limit their work to one type of activity are particularly susceptible to burn-out. Many therapists who work alone in their own practice report that they often get caught in the routine of seeing client after client. They find it increasingly difficult to be fully present for their clients, especially when it seems that they are dealing with the same kind of problem over and over again. After a while they may well find themselves responding almost mechanically. It may be very difficult to deal with this kind of situation if one's livelihood seems to depend on maintaining one's own private practice. Nevertheless, therapists can question whether sticking to one kind of practice is worth the price they're paying in deadness and lack of excitement.

Of course, professionals in agencies such as mental-health clinics, counseling centers, and community institutions are not immune to a similar sapping of energy. If they find themselves putting a lot of their energies into various projects but getting little in the way of positive feedback, they may reach the point where they feel they have nothing more to give. Sometimes people working in such institutions report that much of their time and energy is spent in dealing with conflicts within the agency. This kind of drain on one's personal resources can have a most deadening effect.

Professionals in public agencies and institutions have adopted various ways of lessening the pressures inherent in their environments. Some vary their activities by teaching, supervising and training interns, doing public-relations work in the community, consulting with other colleagues or agencies, or working on their own special projects. Exchanging positions with someone from a different agency is another way of generating new vitality. Counselors from different agencies can trade places with one another for periods varying from a week to several months. This procedure allows counselors to share their special talents with another staff and to work with new people for a time. It can thus benefit both the counselors who make the exchange and the staffs that host the visiting counselors.

Since professional burn-out is an internal phenomenon that becomes obvious to others only in its advanced stages, you should take special care to recognize your own limits. How you approach your tasks and what you get from doing them are more important than how much you're doing. Some people are able to put much more of themselves into a project than others without feeling drained. One person, for example, may feel exhausted after conducting a group-therapy session, while another may come out of it energized and excited. One helpful suggestion is to find what Jourard (1971) calls a "check out" place where you can briefly meditate and experiment with different ways of living without pressure from others. Ultimately, whether you experience burn-out depends on how well you monitor your own responses to the stresses of your work and the effects these stresses have on you and on the quality of your counseling.

We encourage you now to look at the factors that are most likely to cause burn-out in you. A common denominator in many cases of burn-out is the question of *responsibility*. Counselors may feel responsible for what their clients do or don't do; they may assume total responsibility for the direction of therapy; or they may have extremely high expectations of themselves. How does this apply to you? In what ways could your assumption of an inordinate degree of responsibility contribute to your burn-out?

_____

_____

_____

There are other causes of burn-out besides an excessive sense of responsibility. Consistently working with clients you don't like, or who are unmotivated and yet demanding, or who don't appreciate or value you, are just a few factors that can cause burn-out. How would working with such clients affect you? What other factors can you think of that would lead to your burn-out?

_____

_____

_____

_____

Now think of some ways of *preventing* burn-out or regaining your vitality should you experience the burn-out syndrome. The following is a list of suggestions for dealing with burn-out. Of course, counselors need to find their own way of remaining vital as professionals; our purpose in presenting this list is simply to stimulate you to think of your own ways of preventing or treating burn-out. After you think about each suggestion, rate each one by using the following code: A = this approach would be very meaningful to me; B = this approach would have some value for me; C = this approach would have little value for me.

_____ Think of ways to bring variety into my work.
_____ Become involved in peer-group meetings where a support system is available.
_____ Find other interests besides my work.
_____ Attend conferences, conventions, and workshops where I can share ideas with colleagues.

_____ Attend to my health and take care of my body by exercising and eating well.

_____ Take stock of what I'm doing to determine whether it is meaningful or draining.

_____ Do some of the things now that I plan to do when I retire.

_____ Take time for myself to do some of the things that I enjoy doing.

_____ Refuse to get caught in the trap of assuming an inordinate amount of responsibility.

_____ Attend a personal-growth group or some type of personal-therapy experience to work on my level of vitality.

_____ Engage in travel or seek new experiences.

_____ Read stimulating books and do some personal writing.

_____ Exchange jobs for a time with a colleague.

_____ Find nourishment with family and friends.

_____ Find a person who will confront and challenge me and who will encourage me to look at what I'm doing.

Now list some other personal solutions to the problem of burn-out.

_____

_____

_____

_____

_____

FRAGMENTATION

Fragmentation is a problem that is closely related to burn-out. People may feel that they're doing too much in too little time and not doing justice to any of their activities. Or they may feel as if they're here, there, and everywhere but at the same time nowhere. Some of the factors that can lead to a sense of fragmentation are: driving great distances to and from work or from one appointment to another; never taking a break between involvements in different activities; taking on diverse and sometimes conflicting commitments; being swamped with paper work; and attending innumerable meetings. Although we suggested earlier that a way to prevent burn-out is to introduce some diversity into your work, there is also the danger of becoming overextended—pulled in so many different directions that you lose all sense of yourself. At such times you may feel that there is little time between activities and that one experience seems to blur into the next.

Counselors who begin to feel fragmented should stop to ask themselves such questions as these: What effect is my work having on me? Am I merely doing chores that have been assigned to me and that give me little sense of accomplishment? If I'm in an administrative position, how willing am I to delegate responsibility to others? Do I need to have a finger in every pie?

Fragmentation is especially likely to be a problem in institutional settings, where many demands are made on professionals that have little to do with counseling expertise. Counselors in such settings who begin to feel fragmented might need to ask questions like the following:

- Am I so conscious of my security in the system that I never make any waves?
- Am I so convinced that I'm the only one capable of doing the work that I never delegate any of it?
- Do I take on work that is beyond my ability to do?
- Do I ever ask myself whether I'm doing what I really want to do?
- Do I ever say no?

Fragmentation is often a problem for beginning counselors, who may spread themselves thinner than they might wish in order to make a living. However, like burn-out, fragmentation is an issue that can be handled only by therapists themselves. They are their own monitors; they need to pay attention to their internal workings and decide on their own limits.

CHAPTER SUMMARY

In this chapter we have discussed a broad range of issues related to the professional identity of counselors. They do not by any means represent an exhaustive list. However, by reflecting on these issues now, you may be better able to recognize and struggle with these and related questions as you grow in your chosen profession. We have tried to emphasize that you may need to review your resolutions of these issues periodically throughout your career. This kind of openness and honest self-appraisal is an essential quality of those who wish to be effective helpers.

ACTIVITIES, EXERCISES, AND IDEAS FOR THOUGHT AND DISCUSSION

Most of the following activities and discussion questions lend themselves well to small-group interaction in class. Some of them can be done in dyads, others in groups of three to seven people. The purpose of the subgroups is to give you a chance to share your ideas with fellow students. Many of these exercises will also help you get to know others in your class on a more personal basis.

1. What are some of the major problems you expect to be faced with as a beginning counselor? What are some of your most pressing concerns?
2. Do you experience anxiety when you think of working with clients? Do you worry about what you will say or do or whether you'll be of any help to your client? How do you deal with your anxiety?
3. Do you demand perfection from yourself? Can you risk making mistakes, or do you play it safe for fear of seeming incompetent?
4. What kind of results would you look for in working with clients? How would you determine the answers to such questions as: Is the counseling doing any good? Is my intervention helping my client make the changes he or she wants to make? How effective are my techniques?
5. Do you demand instant results? What happens to you if you don't get immediate feedback?

6. Think of the type of client you might have the most difficulty working with. Then become this client in a role-playing fantasy with one other student. Your partner attempts to counsel with you. After you've had a chance to be the client, change roles and become the counselor. Your partner then becomes the type of client you just role-played.

7. In dyads, explore the reasons you would have for experiencing a client as difficult. For instance, if you would find it hard to work with a hostile and aggressive client, explore the feelings that you imagine you'd experience in working with such a client. Have your partner give you feedback; then switch roles.

8. In subgroups explore the issue of how willing you are to be self-disclosing to your clients. Discuss the guidelines you would use to determine the appropriateness of self-disclosure. What are some areas you would feel hesitant about sharing? How valuable do you think it is to share yourself in a personal way with your clients? What are some of your fears or resistances about making yourself known to your clients?

9. In subgroups discuss some possible causes of professional burn-out. Then examine specific ways that you could deal with this problem. After you've explored this issue in small groups, reconvene as a class and make a list of the causes and solutions your groups have come up with.

10. Try the following role-play in dyads. One person assumes the role of the therapist, the other of a client whom the therapist doesn't like. Role-play a session in which the therapist informs the client of his or her feelings. Afterwards, discuss how each of you experienced the interaction. The purpose of the exercise is to give you practice in dealing with *your own* feelings when you work with clients you don't like.

11. In small groups, discuss how you might behave toward a client who evoked strong feelings in you. For example, how might you deal with a client who reminded you of your father? Your mother? A sibling? A former spouse?

12. Do you see it as a danger that you could be lulled into self-deception by believing everything that your clients see in you? For instance, if clients keep telling you that you have it "all together," might you begin to see yourself in ways that you'd like to be but actually are not?

Theoretical Issues in Counseling and Psychotherapy

4

For each statement, indicate the response that most closely identifies your beliefs and attitudes. Use the following code: A = I strongly agree; B = I slightly agree; C = I slightly disagree; D = I strongly disagree.

_____ 1. I have settled on a definite theory of counseling.

_____ 2. I would rather combine insights and techniques derived from various theoretical approaches to counseling than base my practice on a single model.

_____ 3. My view of people is basically positive.

_____ 4. What happens in counseling sessions is more my responsibility than it is my client's.

_____ 5. I would find it difficult to work for an agency if I was expected to perform functions that I didn't see as appropriate counseling functions.

_____ 6. I have the power to define my own role and professional identity as a counselor.

_____ 7. Clients should always select the goals of counseling.

_____ 8. I'd be willing to work with clients who didn't seem to have any clear goals or reasons for seeking counseling.

_____ 9. Giving advice is a legitimate part of counseling.

_____ 10. Enhancing a client's social adjustment is a legitimate goal of counseling.

_____ 11. A diagnosis is helpful, if not essential, when a client begins counseling.

_____ 12. There are more dangers than values associated with diagnosis in counseling.

_____ 13. Testing can be a very useful adjunct to counseling.

_____ 14. I think the medical model of mental health can be fruitfully applied in counseling and psychotherapy.

___ 15. There is a real danger that counseling techniques can be used to keep the therapist hidden as a person.

___ 16. Skill in using a variety of techniques is one of the most important qualities of a therapist.

___ 17. Theories of counseling can limit counselors by encouraging them to pay attention only to behavior that fits their particular theory.

___ 18. Counselors should develop and modify their own theories of counseling as they practice.

___ 19. A theory should be more than an explanation of disturbed behavior; it should challenge my world view.

___ 20. Counselors can identify their theoretical preferences by paying attention to the way they actually practice.

INTRODUCTION

Professional counselors should be able to conceptualize *what* they do in their counseling sessions, as well as *why* they're doing it. Too often practitioners are unable to explain why they use certain counseling procedures. For example, when you meet a new client, what guidelines should you use in structuring your first interview? What do you want to accomplish at this initial session? Which of the following are you interested in knowing about your client? Why?

- the presenting problem (the reason the client is seeking counseling)
- the client's present style of coping with demands, stresses, and conflicts
- the client's early experiences as a child, particularly in relationship to parents and siblings
- the client's ego strength
- the client's history of successes and failures
- the client's developmental history
- the client's struggle with current choices
- the client's goals and agenda for counseling

During your initial session, what are some of the interventions you might make in getting to know your client? How would you want to structure your future sessions? Consider the following questions, and briefly write your responses.

1. Would you want to begin with a detailed case history? Why or why not?

_____

_____

_____

2. Do you consider diagnosis a necessary prerequisite to counseling? Why or why not?

_____

_____

_____

3. Are tests important as a prerequisite to counseling? Would you decide whether to test, or would you allow your client to make this decision?

_____

_____

4. How much would you structure the session to obtain *current* information about your client's life? How much would you want to know about the client's past?

_____

_____

_____

5. Would you do most of the talking? Why or why not?

_____

_____

_____

6. Who would set the goals of the therapy? Who would be primarily responsible for what was discussed? Why?

_____

_____

_____

7. Who would take the greater responsibility for *directing* the session? At the initial session, would you ask many questions? Would you encourage your client to structure the session?

_____

_____

8. Would you develop contracts with your clients specifying what they can expect from you, what they want from counseling, and what they are willing to do to meet their goals? Why or why not?

_____

_____

_____

9. Would you be inclined to use directive, action-oriented techniques, such as homework assignments? Why or why not?

_____

_____

_____

10. What aspects of the client's life would you stress?

_____

_____

_____

In this chapter we focus on how your theoretical positions and biases influence your actual practice. Ideally, theory should help you to make sense of what you do in your counseling sessions. Since your answers to the preceding questions depend on your view of personality and of counseling, looking at how you responded to these questions is one way to begin clarifying your theoretical approach. Another way of thinking about this issue is to imagine a client asking you to explain your view of counseling in clear and simple terms. Would you be able to tell your client *what* you most hoped to accomplish and *how* you would go about it?

BASIC THEORETICAL ASSUMPTIONS: A SELF-INVENTORY

Students often conceive of a theory as a rigid formula that prescribes, step by step, what to do in given counseling situations. In contrast, we see a theory as a general guide for practice, not a set of rigid procedures. A theoretical approach provides a direction so that we can question what we do and make sense of the various dimensions involved in counseling relationships. It challenges us to look at our basic assumptions about human beings, to ask what we most expect to occur through counseling, to clarify our role and function in the therapeutic relationship, and to provide a framework for evaluating the outcomes of counseling.

The various models of counseling and psychotherapy are each based on a set of assumptions about the nature of persons and of therapy. These assumptions significantly influence the ways in which counselors view their role and interact with clients. Although a full treatment of counseling theory falls outside the scope of this book, the following self-inventory may help you to review the most significant models of therapy and to pinpoint some of the elements of your own theoretical orientation. (For an extended survey of the various approaches to counseling, see Corey, 1977a, 1977b.)

The following statements summarize core ideas of nine different approaches to therapy. Indicate your agreement or disagreement with each statement by using the following code: A = I strongly agree; B = I slightly agree; C = I slightly disagree; D = I strongly disagree.

Psychoanalytic Therapy

_____ 1. Human beings are basically determined by unconscious motivation, irrational forces, sexual and aggressive impulses, and early-childhood experiences. Understanding the unconscious is the key to understanding human behavior.

_____ 2. Normal personality development is based on a successful resolution of conflicts at various stages of psychosexual development. Early development is thus a crucial determinant of personality.

_____ 3. Clients have developed stubborn defense systems to ward off anxiety, and they resist recognizing experiences that are out of their awareness. Insight, understanding, catharsis, and the working through of repressed material are the essential core of the therapy process.

_____ 4. Therapists should remain relatively anonymous and encourage clients to project onto them the feelings they have had toward the significant people in their lives (transference). The analysis and interpretation of transference leads to insight and personality change.

_____ 5. For therapy to be effective, clients must be willing to commit themselves to an intensive, long-term process.

Existential-Humanistic Therapy

_____ 1. Human beings define themselves by their own choices. Although there are factors that restrict their choices, ultimately their self-determination is the basis of their uniqueness as individuals.

_____ 2. Anxiety can be the result of recognizing one's ultimate aloneness and responsibility to choose for oneself.

_____ 3. The central issues in counseling and therapy are freedom and responsibility, the necessity of making one's own choices, and the search for identity and self-actualization. Emphasis should be placed on such themes as meaning in life, guilt, anxiety, responsibility, death, and one's ultimate aloneness.

_____ 4. Since the goal of therapy is to help clients become responsible for the direction of their own lives, what occurs in therapy is largely the client's responsibility.

_____ 5. Therapists' major tasks are to accurately grasp the subjective worlds of their clients and to establish authentic relationships in which clients can work on understanding themselves and their choices more fully.

Client-Centered Therapy

_____ 1. Clients have the potential for self-direction. They can become aware of their own problems and of the means of resolving them if they are encouraged to explore present feelings and thoughts.

_____ 2. People are basically trustworthy and are striving toward growth and wholeness.

_____ 3. Clients can make progress without the therapist's interpretations, diagnoses, evaluations, and directions. What they *do* need from therapists are warmth, acceptance, respect, empathy, and caring— what Rogers calls *unconditional positive regard.*

_____ 4. The therapist's role consists primarily of active listening, responding in ways that reflect and clarify the client's feelings and thoughts, and communicating an understanding of the inner world of the client.

_____ 5. The relationship between client and therapist is the heart of therapy. Techniques are less important than the attitudes of the therapist toward the client.

Gestalt Therapy

____ 1. People are responsible for their own feelings, and clients in therapy should be challenged to look at ways in which they avoid this responsibility.

____ 2. The client's awareness, in and of itself, is a curative factor in therapy. Clients should be encouraged to identify the unfinished business from the past that is interfering with their present functioning. By reexperiencing these conflicts as if they were occurring in the present, clients may learn to recognize and accept their inner polarities.

____ 3. The here-and-now of the client's experience is more important than an exploration of the past or future. Therapy should focus on the client's present feelings, body messages, and blocks to awareness.

____ 4. The therapist should avoid giving diagnoses, interpretations, and lengthy explanations of the client's behavior.

____ 5. The therapist may use a wide range of action-oriented techniques in assisting clients to experience and identify their own feelings.

Behavior Therapy

____ 1. People are basically shaped by learning and sociocultural conditioning.

____ 2. Since all behavior is the result of learning, the goal of clients in therapy is to eliminate maladaptive behaviors and learn constructive ones. Therapy should focus on overt behavior, the specification of treatment goals, and the evaluation of results. Therapy is not complete unless the new behaviors are actually practiced in real-life situations.

____ 3. Therapists should be active and directive. Their techniques should be based on principles of learning and geared toward changing behavior. Therapists should emphasize the manipulation of environmental variables rather than the client's past, unconscious material, or other internal states. The underlying cause of behavior need not be identified or treated for therapy to be successful.

____ 4. A good working relationship between client and therapist is a necessary but not sufficient condition of effective therapy. The client must be willing to experiment actively with new behaviors.

____ 5. Therapists can appropriately be regarded as experts in the diagnosis of maladaptive behaviors and the prescription of curative procedures.

____ 6. Reinforcing desired behaviors and serving as models for their clients are appropriate functions of therapists.

Transactional Analysis

____ 1. People often experience difficulty because of decisions they made about themselves early in life that are no longer appropriate.

____ 2. The verbal and nonverbal messages received from parents significantly influence people's views of themselves.

____ 3. Clients should be taught to recognize the ego states in which they function, the ways in which injunctions and messages they assimilated as children affect them now, and the life scripts that determine their actions. They should also be taught the basics of personal and interpersonal functioning so that they can understand the nature of their transactions with others.

_____ 4. Therapists should play an active role as teachers, trainers, and resource persons in therapy. At the same time, clients should be viewed as equal partners in the therapeutic endeavor.

_____ 5. For therapy to be effective, clients must carry out contracts to work on specific issues, rather than simply talk about problems in order to gain insight.

_____ 6. The goal of therapy is to liberate clients from past messages and enable them to redecide how they will live. Clients should be encouraged to become independent of the therapist as soon as possible so that they can be their own therapists.

Rational-Emotive Therapy

_____ 1. People's belief systems and evaluations of situations, not the situations themselves, are the causes of emotional disturbances.

_____ 2. People tend to incorporate irrational beliefs from external sources and then continue to indoctrinate themselves with these beliefs.

_____ 3. To overcome the self-indoctrination that has resulted in irrational thinking, therapists should use active methods of intervention, such as teaching, persuading, attacking faulty thinking, and giving homework assignments.

_____ 4. The goal of therapy is to substitute a rational belief system for an irrational one.

_____ 5. A warm personal relationship between client and therapist is neither necessary nor sufficient for effective therapy. Rather, the effectiveness of therapy depends on the therapist's skill in probing and confronting the client's belief system and persuading the client to practice activities that will lead to positive change.

Reality Therapy

_____ 1. All human beings have a need to develop a "success" identity, and one way to do so is by living realistically and accepting the responsibility for one's behavior.

_____ 2. Therapists who emphasize such concepts as unconscious motivation and who focus on the past as the determinant of present behavior actually provide people with excuses for avoiding reality and their responsibility for their own behavior.

_____ 3. Therapists should challenge clients to make value judgments about their own behavior. It is therefore appropriate for therapy to be concerned with judgments of right and wrong.

_____ 4. Therapy should focus on changing present behavior, not on achieving insights about the past or about the client's attitudes. Clients must be willing to commit themselves to a program of change, develop a plan of action, and follow through. Therapists should not accept any excuses from clients for failure to follow through on their commitments.

_____ 5. Although it is the client's responsibility to decide upon the goals of therapy, the therapist should be active and directive in encouraging the client to face reality and make value judgments about his or her behavior.

Adlerian Therapy

_____ 1. People are primarily social beings, shaped and motivated by social forces. However, consciousness, not the unconscious, is the center of personality. People are creative, active, choice-making beings, not victims of fate.

_____ 2. All people have basic feelings of inferiority that can motivate them to strive for mastery, superiority, power, and perfection. Feelings of inferiority can thus be the wellsprings of creativity. Perfection, not pleasure, is the goal of life.

_____ 3. People's styles of life are formed early on to compensate for a particular inferiority. These styles of life consist of people's views about themselves and the world and their distinctive behaviors and habits as they pursue their personal goals.

_____ 4. People can shape their own futures by actively and courageously taking risks and making decisions in the face of unknown consequences. By encouraging clients to live *as if* they were the people they want to be, therapists can challenge them to choose the life they want to live.

_____ 5. Therapists should encourage clients to become actively involved with other people and to develop new life-styles through relationships.

After you've finished rating the preceding statements, review them to determine which assumptions you believe are most valid as underpinnings of counseling practice. Which four or five assumptions do you consider to be *most* significantly related to effective counseling and therapy?

_____

_____

_____

_____

_____

_____

_____

How do you expect these assumptions to influence the way you practice?

_____

_____

_____

_____

_____

DEVELOPING A COUNSELING STANCE

Developing a counseling stance is more complicated than merely accepting the tenets of a given theory. We believe that the theoretical approach you use to guide you in your practice is an expression of your uniqueness as a person and an outgrowth of your life experience. Further, your counseling stance must be appropriate for the type of counseling you do and the unique needs of your clients.

We believe that a theoretical approach becomes more useful and meaningful after you've taken a critical look at the *theorist* who developed the theory, as well as its key concepts, since a theory of counseling is often an expression of the personality of the theorist. However, blindly following any single theory can lead you to ignore some of the insights that your life opens up to you. Of course, this is our bias, and many would claim that providing effective therapy depends on following a given theory.

A major consideration in developing or evaluating a theory is the degree to which that perspective helps you to understand what you're doing. Does your framework provide a broad base for working with diverse clients in different ways, or does it restrict your vision and cause you to ignore variables that don't fit the theory? We think there's a danger of forcing your clients to conform to your expectations if you are a "true believer" of one theory. For example, if you believe that a need for power is the underlying motive of most human behavior, your clients will tend to focus on aspects of their lives dealing with power and ignore other, perhaps equally important, aspects. If you stress body awareness, here-and-now awareness, recognizing games, remembering dreams, or working with past experiences, your clients are likely to focus on these issues and interpret much of their behavior in light of the constructs you use. It's important, therefore, to evaluate the dimensions you decide to pay attention to in your counseling work. The following questions can help you make this evaluation.

1. Where did you acquire your theory? Did you incorporate many of your views from your instructors or training supervisor? Has one theory intrigued you to the point that it is the sole basis for your orientation?

   _____

   _____

   _____

2. Do you embrace a particular theory because it is a justification of your own life-style, experiences, and values? For instance, do you adopt a theory that stresses an active, didactic role for the therapist because you see yourself as "straightening out" your clients? What does your approach stress, and why does it appeal to you?

_____

_____

_____

_____

_____

3. To what degree does your theory challenge your own previous frame of reference? Does your theory cause you to test your hypotheses, beliefs, and assumptions? Does it encourage you to think of alternatives? To what degree does your theory reinforce your present world view? Does your theory force you to extend your thinking, or does it merely support your biases?

_____

_____

_____

_____

_____

4. Is your theoretical approach open or closed? Does it allow for incorporating new ideas from other approaches?

_____

_____

_____

5. How do you see your own life experiences as an influence in your counseling style? In what ways have your life experiences caused you to modify your theoretical viewpoint?

_____

_____

_____

_____

THE USE OF TECHNIQUES IN COUNSELING AND THERAPY

Your view of the use of techniques in counseling and therapy is closely related to your theoretical model. The issue of techniques includes such questions as *what* techniques, procedures, or intervention methods you would use and *when* and *why* you would use them. Some counselors are very eager to learn new techniques, treating them almost as if they were a bag of tricks. Others, out of anxiety over not knowing what to do in a given counseling situation, may try technique after technique in helter-skelter fashion. However, counselors should have sound reasons for using particular methods of intervention, and we question the benefit to the client of an overreliance on technique.

It can be very illuminating to see yourself working with a client on videotape or to listen to a session you've tape-recorded. Instead of focusing your attention on what your client said or did, you can monitor your own responses and get some general sense of how you related to your client. We suggest that you review your sessions with several clients in this way, paying attention to questions such as the following:

- Do you ask many questions? If so, are the questions mainly to get information, or are they open-ended ones designed to challenge your client? Do you raise questions merely because you don't know what else to do and hope that your questions will keep things moving?
- Do you tend to give advice and work quickly toward solutions? Or do you allow your client to explore feelings in depth instead of focusing on solutions to problems?
- How much direction do you give to the sessions? Who typically structures the sessions?
- How much support and reassurance do you give? Do you allow your clients to fully express what they're feeling before you offer support? Do your attempts to give support tend to cut them off from what they're feeling?
- Do you challenge your clients when you think they need it? Do your interventions get them to think about what they're saying on a deeper level?
- Who does most of the talking? Do you hear yourself as preaching or persuading? Are you responsive to what your client is saying?
- How often do you clarify what you hear? Do you check whether you're hearing what your client means to express?
- Do you reflect back to your clients what you hear them saying? If so, is your reflection done mechanically, or does it encourage a deeper self-exploration?
- Do you interpret much, telling your clients what you think certain behaviors mean? Or do you leave it to them to discover what their behavior means from their own perspectives?
- Do you use techniques primarily to get clients moving, or do you wait until they express some feelings and then use a technique geared to helping them experience their feelings on a more intense level?
- Do you use techniques that "feel right" for you and that you're comfortable using? Have you experienced these techniques yourself as a client?
- Are the counseling procedures you use drawn from one counseling approach? Or do you borrow techniques from various approaches and use them when they seem appropriate?
- When you use a particular technique, does it seem mechanical to you? Or do you feel that your techniques are appropriate and unforced?
- How do your clients generally respond to the techniques you use? Do they react negatively to any of your counseling methods?

Monitoring your own work in the light of these questions can help you discover your counseling style, to ask yourself why you're making the interventions you make, and to evaluate the impact these counseling procedures have on your clients. This willingness to reflect on the effects your interventions have on clients is of the utmost importance.

We believe that the purpose of techniques is to facilitate movement in a counseling session and that your counseling techniques really cannot be separated from your personality and your relationship with your client. When counselors fall into a pattern of mechanically employing techniques, they become technicians and are not responding to the particular individuals they're counseling. You can lessen the chances of falling into a mechanical style by deliberately paying attention to the ways you tend to use techniques. Particular techniques may be better suited to some therapists' personalities and styles of counseling than to others'. At times you may try a technique that you've observed someone else using very skillfully, only to find that it fails for you. In essence, your techniques should fit your counseling style, and you should feel comfortable and real in using them.

We like Sidney Jourard's (1968) ideas on the issue of the role of techniques in psychotherapy. He views therapy as "a way of being with another person" rather than as a system of techniques. This is not to say that therapists shouldn't master techniques and have a grasp of theory; in fact, Jourard sees a willingness to learn theory and techniques as a sign of seriousness in one's work that distinguishes professional therapists from amateurs. His position is summed up well in the sentence "Effective psychotherapists, who succeed in inviting sufferers to change their previous ways of being, are not technicians, although they will have mastered their techniques" (p. 58).

THE DIVISION OF RESPONSIBILITY IN THERAPY

The question of who is primarily responsible for the direction and outcomes of psychotherapy is a controversial one that therapists often agonize over. As with many of the issues we've raised, there are extreme viewpoints. On one side are those who claim that the therapist is the expert and is therefore in charge. Whether clients succeed or fail is seen largely as a function of the knowledge and skill of the therapist. However, even in active-directive therapies, which tend to emphasize the therapist's responsibility, clients are not seen as passive; on the contrary, they must practice new behaviors outside of the sessions or carry out homework assignments. At the other extreme, some of the experiential therapies place the primary responsibility for the direction and outcomes of therapy on the client. The therapist's job is to be psychologically present and facilitate the client's utilization of his or her own resources. As we consider a few of these theoretical views on the issue of the division of responsibility in therapy, think about how you see this issue as it affects your own practice.

Theories Stressing the Therapist's Responsibility

A behavioral viewpoint. Many behavior therapists emphasize the therapist's role in structuring sessions in such a way that clients experience success and don't drop out prematurely. In their view, claims by therapists that clients have insufficient motivation or ego strength to continue with the demands of therapy are rationalizations. As Goldstein (1973) puts it, "Therapy is the therapist's responsibility. It is the therapist who at the very least implicitly establishes himself as the expert, and any failure is the therapist's failure." (p. 222).

The rational-emotive viewpoint. Albert Ellis (1973) views psychotherapy as an educative process in which the therapist teaches the client ways of self-understanding and changing. The therapist therefore assumes a great share of the responsibility for directing the session. The rational-emotive therapist employs a rapid-fire, highly directive, persuasive methodology that emphasizes the cognitive aspects of therapy.

Theories Stressing the Client's Responsibility

The client-centered viewpoint. Although Carl Rogers stresses the responsibility of the therapist to be authentic in the therapeutic relationship, he does see the client as responsible for directing the sessions. Clients should use the therapeutic relationship to explore areas that are deeply significant to them, and Rogers assumes that they have the best vantage point for deciding what these areas are. The therapist facilitates this process by creating a supportive climate in which clients eventually feel trusting enough to drop their defenses and find the resources for change within themselves.

Experiential viewpoints. Extreme claims that the full responsibility in therapy rests with the client have been expressed by the late founder of Gestalt therapy, Fritz Perls, and a leading figure in the encounter-group movement, William Schutz.

Perls (1969) assumed that most people become patients because of their unwillingness to accept responsibility for their own lives. Instead of relying on themselves, most people, he argued, look to external sources of support. Perls claimed that most people who seek therapy don't want to be cured; rather, they want to become "more adequate in their neurosis" (p. 75). Because of this belief, Perls used to begin his workshops with this declaration: "I am responsible only for myself and for nobody else. I am not taking responsibility for any of you—you are responsible for yourselves" (p. 74). He elaborated on this statement by saying "So if you want to go crazy, commit suicide, improve, get 'turned on,' or get an experience that will change your life, that's up to you. I do my thing and you do your thing" (p. 75). Schutz (1971) expresses a similar conviction to participants at the outset of a workshop: "If you want to resist instructions or group pressure, that is up to you. If you want to bow to pressure, it's your decision. If you want to be physically injured or go crazy, that, too, is up to you. You are responsible for yourself" (pp. 160–161).

Dimensions of the Therapist's Responsibility

As you consider the range of viewpoints on the division of responsibility in therapy, think about your own position on this issue. What do you see as your responsibility, both to your client and to yourself? What do you expect from your client? Do you burden yourself with the total responsibility for what happens in therapy?

We've observed that many beginning counselors tend to deprive their clients of their rightful responsibility for their experience in therapy, because they anxiously take so much of this responsibility on themselves. If clients don't progress fast enough, these counselors may blame themselves for not knowing enough, not having the necessary skill and experience, or not being sensitive or caring enough. They may worry constantly about their adequacy as counselors and transmit their anxiety to their clients. *If only* they were better therapists, their clients would be changing in more positive directions! Of course, this may be true, but overly anxious counselors frequently fail to see the role their clients play in the outcomes of their own therapy, whether for better or for worse.

We believe that counselors would do well to bring up the question of responsibility during their initial sessions with each client, so that clients can begin to think about their part in their own therapy. At this time the therapist should discuss the length of the sessions, the duration of the therapy, confidentiality, fees, general goals, methods, and any other matters that might affect the client's decision to enter this therapeutic relationship.

We see therapy as a joint venture of the client and the therapist. Both have serious responsibilities for the direction of therapy, and this issue needs to be clarified during the initial stages of counseling. In our view, counselors who typically decide what to discuss and are overdirective run the risk of perpetuating their clients' dependence. We'd like to see clients encouraged from the start to assume as much responsibility as they can. Even directive therapies such as Transactional Analysis, behavior therapy, Rational-Emotive Therapy, and Reality Therapy stress client-initiated contracts and homework assignments as ways clients can fulfill their commitment to change. These devices help to keep the focus of responsibility on the clients by challenging them to decide what *they* want from therapy and what *they* are willing to do to get what they want.

Although we have stressed the tendency of some therapists to take on too much responsibility, we do believe that therapists have responsibilities to their clients, including:

- being emotionally present for their clients,
- keeping themselves enthused and energetic,
- taking on only as many clients as they can handle effectively,
- being willing to live up to their contracts with their clients,
- being honest with clients,
- refusing to accept clients whom they are not personally or professionally competent to counsel,
- discussing any factors that may influence a client's decision to enter the relationship, and
- discussing and structuring the various dimensions of the therapeutic relationship.

As you consider your responsibilities to your clients, try to be as specific as you can. For example, you might ask yourself whether counselors have a responsibility to arrange for regular breaks in their day's schedule. Although counselors differ in their capacity to cope with intensity, we wonder how ethical it is for counselors to work with clients continuously without taking enough time to center themselves. How much investment will you have in the clients you see at the end of a long and full day of work? Can you be as present for these clients as you were for those you saw earlier in the day?

Before you continue, write down what you consider to be some of your responsibilities toward your clients and some of their responsibilities to themselves.

I'm responsible for:

_____

_____

_____

_____

_____

My clients are responsible for:

_____

_____

_____

_____

_____

ROLES AND FUNCTIONS OF COUNSELORS

The roles and functions of counselors depend on their theoretical perspectives, the type of counseling they do, where they work, and the kinds of people they counsel. We think that, to a large degree, counselors are responsible for defining their own roles and choosing their own functions as part of creating their professional identities. Too often counselors passively allow others to define their roles for them. Even if their positions involve job descriptions that limit their options, often they fail to exercise the freedom they *do* have in deciding on their job priorities.

When one of the authors was on an accreditation team visiting a high school, a counselor was asked "How do you spend most of your time? Would you like to be doing things as a counselor that you aren't doing now?" The counselor replied that he worked on scheduling, dealt with truancy and tardiness problems, and spent most of his time dealing with students who were sent to him by teachers for disciplinary reasons. This was the role assigned to him by the school administrators, and he seemed to be satisfied with it. He didn't feel comfortable with personal or social counseling, career counseling, or other work that would involve dealing with students on a more intimate basis. There were other counselors in the same school, however, whose view of counseling included being receptive to exploring intimate issues with students. Even though some of these psychologically oriented counselors sometimes faced conflict with their administrators, they were active in defining their own roles by developing a rationale for how they were spending their time. Because they had given careful thought to what they wanted to do, they were able to create, in part, their own professional roles.

Of course, the type of counseling you do will determine some specific functions. The functions performed by career counselors are different from those performed by crisis-intervention counselors. The roles of counselors who work primarily with severely disturbed people in institutional settings will differ from those of counselors who specialize in personal-growth approaches for people without major problems. Functions that are appropriate in some counseling situations, then, may be inappropriate in others.

You can begin to consider now what functions would be appropriate for you to perform in the kind of position you hope to obtain. How would you deal with being required to perform functions that you thought were inappropriate or interfered with your effectiveness as a counselor? Could you work in an agency that expected you to perform such functions? If you accepted such a job, would it be worth the price you would have to pay? Look over the following list of activities, and ask yourself whether you see each one as an appropriate part of a counselor's job and one that you can see yourself performing regularly. Rate each one, using the following code: A = I would accept this activity as part of my role; B = I'd have difficulty carrying out this function; C = I'm undecided.

_____ 1. administering discipline
_____ 2. reporting on a client's progress to a board, a judge, an administrator, or some other authority
_____ 3. doing clerical work
_____ 4. helping people obtain legal or financial aid
_____ 5. administering tests
_____ 6. interpreting test results
_____ 7. providing remedial instruction or tutoring
_____ 8. doing community work
_____ 9. supervising students during lunch
_____ 10. referring clients to community-service agencies
_____ 11. working with family members of clients
_____ 12. teaching grooming and personal hygiene
_____ 13. driving a person to and from work
_____ 14. writing reports based on problems of clients
_____ 15. doing research on the·incidence of certain types of problems

In considering these activities, you should realize that at times clients need services that aren't strictly counseling services. Thus, counselors may need to provide auxiliary helping services, such as teaching grooming, before they can do more direct counseling. Because basic physical and security needs must be met before attention can be devoted to higher-order needs (such as self-actualization), some counselors consider assisting clients to find ways of meeting basic needs to be part of their work. In the following space, write a succinct description of your view of your role as a counselor.

_____

_____

_____

_____

_____

_____

DECIDING ON THE GOALS OF COUNSELING

Aimless therapy is unlikely to be effective, yet too often practitioners fail to devote enough time to thinking about the goals they have for their clients and the goals clients have for themselves. In this section we discuss possible goals of therapy, how they are determined, and who should determine them. Counselors' answers to these questions are directly related to their theoretical orientations. In a self-inventory earlier in this chapter, we summarized key concepts and goals of nine approaches to therapy. You might refer back to the inventory to review the diversity of viewpoints concerning therapeutic goals.

Goals and Theoretical Approaches

When students think about what the central goals of therapy should be, they may feel perplexed by the broad range of goals specified by different theoretical approaches. Behaviorist theorists recommend specific, measurable goals, such as eliminating fears, learning how to be assertive in social situations, losing weight, curing disabling physical symptoms, reducing tensions and stresses, and coping more effectively with specific conflict situations. Relationship-oriented therapists stress such lofty goals as becoming full, autonomous, and free persons. For Rogers (1961), the general therapeutic goal is to become a fully functioning person; for Maslow (1968, 1970) the goal is to become a self-actualizing person; for May (1967) the goal is to accept one's freedom to create a unique existence and to understand one's "being-in-the-world." Frankl (1963) talks about the search for meaning and purpose, Bugental (1976) describes the search for authentic existence, and Jourard (1971) writes of the "transparent self." Unlike the specific, concrete goals of behaviorist therapists, these broad goals involve personal characteristics that are usually very difficult to measure.

Confronted with this theoretical diversity, you might conclude that no reconciliation is possible among the goals emphasized by different approaches. Yet some convergence of these goals is possible. Behavior therapists, for example, don't necessarily reject the general goals of the relationship-oriented therapists; rather, they insist that general goals should be translated into specific, short-term tasks that have observable results. These concrete goals can focus the counseling sessions, and they allow both the client and the therapist to make some assessment of the degree to which their objectives are being accomplished. In writing on this issue of the convergence of the behavioristic and humanistic view of goals, Wrenn (1966) notes that practicing counselors can integrate the "two psychological worlds" by using behavioristic techniques to accomplish humanistic goals.

Deciding on Your Goals As a Counselor

What are some of the basic goals that you would use to guide your work with clients? The following list presents ten therapeutic goals. Indicate how much you would emphasize each by using the following code: A = an extremely important goal; B = a somewhat important goal; C = a relatively unimportant goal.

_____ 1. that clients will take risks and open new doors that may result in increased awareness of themselves and others

____ 2. that clients will recall past events and work through emotions that are blocking their full enjoyment of living now

____ 3. that clients will come to recognize that they have the capacities within themselves to reshape their lives by making new choices

____ 4. that clients will begin to question their values and assumptions about life and determine the degree to which these beliefs are valid for them now

____ 5. that clients will reduce or eliminate specific behavioral problems and replace their faulty learning with more effective behavior

____ 6. that clients will learn the process of using their resources for solving their own problems

____ 7. that clients will become more conscious of their options and more willing to make choices for themselves and accept the consequences

____ 8. that clients will acquire the information necessary to make better choices

____ 9. that clients will experience the range of their own personal power so that they give up feeling and behaving like victims

____ 10. that clients will uncover the influence of the past on their present behavior

Now write what *you* consider to be the *most basic* and *significant* goal of counseling:

_____

_____

_____

Questionable Goals

In addition to clarifying what you consider to be the central goals of counseling, it is also well for you to formulate your ideas concerning goals that are of questionable value. For example, is solving problems for a client a worthwhile goal? Is it part of your job to provide answers for clients if you believe that they lack the resources to solve their own problems? Consider how you might counsel clients who came to you seeking advice. How does giving advice contribute to goals of counseling that you consider worthwhile?

Other questionable objectives in counseling include "straightening out" clients, trying to get clients to conform to expected patterns of socially acceptable behavior, and imposing goals on clients that they haven't chosen for themselves. For example, is it the counselor's task to help clients become "well adjusted," in the sense of conforming to social norms? Jourard (1968) answers in the negative: "At his worst, the psychotherapist is but one more agent of socialization, a 'trainer' who adds his technical know-how to that of parents, educators, and propagandists, to ensure that people will conform to institutional norms" (p. 38). Rather, Jourard believes, the therapist's goal should be to help clients understand and go beyond the situations that restrict their responsible exercise of freedom. Therapists function at their best when they guide clients "toward liberation from the clutch of the past" and from the "bewitching effects of social pressure" (pp. 37–38). If therapists become agents of the status quo, they hinder their clients' efforts to become healthy, growing persons. Jourard would therefore like to see therapists function as "responsible anarchists" who are "committed to an endless search for ways to live that fosters growth, well-being, idiosyncrasy, freedom, and authenticity" (p. 42).

If you critically examine possible goals of counseling, you'll be less likely to find yourself working toward goals you don't really believe in. On the following lines, list some possible counseling goals that you think are of questionable value:

_____

_____

_____

_____

_____

Who Determines Therapeutic Goals?

Most counseling approaches agree that the imposition of goals by the therapist does not lead to effective counseling and that goals should be set by the client and the therapist working together. However, some therapists believe that they know what is best for their clients and try to persuade their clients to accept certain goals. Others are convinced that the specific goals of counseling ought to be determined entirely by their clients and try to keep their own views out of their counseling.

One way to handle the issue of who sets counseling goals is to decide on the *general* goals you have for all your clients and then provide time in your sessions for exploring the *specific* reasons individual clients are in counseling. For example, as a general goal you may value developing clients' ability to decide for themselves and accept responsibility for their choices. This general goal can be applied to the concrete and specific goals of your clients, such as making a career decision, working on a school problem, understanding a relationship more fully, or learning to be more assertive. We believe that it's useful for counselors to share their general goals with their clients while stressing that the establishment of therapeutic goals will be an ongoing process that involves both the client and the counselor. Often clients have only vague notions about what it is they want from counseling. They may know only that they want to feel better or understand themselves better. Working on what specific things they want from counseling can itself be a crucial part of the therapeutic process.

Of course, the issue of who sets the goals of counseling must be seen in the light of the theory you operate from, the type of counseling you offer, the setting in which you work, and the nature of your clientele. If you work in crisis intervention, your goals are likely to be short-term and practical, and you may be very directive. If you're working with children in a school setting, you may aim at combining educational and therapeutic goals. As a counselor with institutionalized elderly people, you may stress teaching survival skills and ways of relating to others on their ward. What your goals are, and how actively involved your client will be in determining them, depend to a great extent on the type of counseling you provide.

DIAGNOSIS AS A PROFESSIONAL ISSUE

Psychodiagnosis refers to the analysis and explanation of a client's problems. Diagnosis may include an explanation of the causes of the client's difficulties, an account of how these problems developed over time, a classification of any disorders, a specification of preferred treatment procedures, and an estimate of the chances for a successful resolution. Whether diagnosis should be part of psychotherapy is a controversial issue. Some mental-health professionals see diagnosis as an essential step in any treatment plan, but others view it as an inappropriate application of the medical model of mental health to counseling and therapy. Even though you may not yet have had to face the practical question of whether to diagnose a client, you will most likely need to come to terms with this issue at some point in your work. In this section we briefly review some of the arguments for and against the use of diagnosis in therapy and ask you to consider how valuable diagnosis is from your viewpoint.

Arguments for Psychodiagnosis

Practitioners who favor the use of diagnostic procedures in therapy generally argue that such procedures enable the therapist to acquire sufficient knowledge about the client's past and present behavior to develop an appropriate plan of treatment. This approach stems from the medical model of mental health, according to which different underlying causal factors produce different types of disorders. Goldenberg (1977) cites six purposes of psychodiagnosis that are generally mentioned by those who support its use in therapy:

1. Each diagnostic label encompasses a wide range of behavioral characteristics, and this allows professionals to communicate common meanings effectively.
2. Diagnosis facilitates the selection of the most suitable form of therapy.
3. A diagnostic explanation of the causal factors involved in a client's problems can suggest measures that will alleviate the client's symptoms.
4. Diagnosis is useful in predicting the course and outcome of a person's disorder.
5. Diagnosis provides a framework for research into the effectiveness of various treatment approaches.
6. Diagnostic classifications facilitate such administrative tasks as the collection of statistical data regarding the incidence of particular disorders and the type of psychological services provided in the community.

Psychoanalytically oriented therapists favor psychodiagnosis, since this form of therapy was patterned after the medical model of mental health and stresses the understanding of past situations that have contributed to a dysfunction. Most psychological-assessment devices used in psychodiagnosis involve projective techniques that rest on psychoanalytic concepts.

For different reasons, practitioners with a behavioristic orientation also favor a diagnostic stance, inasmuch as they emphasize specific treatment programs. Although they may not follow the medical model, these practitioners value observation and other objective means of appraising both a client's specific symptoms and the factors that have led up to the client's malfunctioning. Such an appraisal, they would argue, enables them to use the techniques that are appropriate for a particular disorder and to evaluate the effectiveness of the treatment program.

Arguments against Diagnosis

Although many professionals see diagnosis as an essential component of psychotherapy, there are as many critics who view it as unnecessary or harmful. Generally, existential-humanistic or relationship-oriented therapists fall into this group. Their arguments against diagnosis include the following:

1. Diagnosis is typically done by an expert observing a person's behavior and experience from an external viewpoint, without reference to what they mean to the client.
2. Diagnostic labels can rob persons of their uniqueness.
3. Diagnosis can lead people to accept self-fulfilling prophecies or to despair over their conditions.
4. Diagnosis can narrow the therapist's vision by encouraging the therapist to look for behavior that fits a certain disease category.
5. The best vantage point for understanding another person is through his or her subjective world, not through a general system of classification.
6. There are many potential dangers implicit in the process of reducing human beings to diagnostic labels.

Many psychologists and some psychiatrists have objected to the use of diagnosis in therapy. Carl Rogers (1942, 1951, 1961) has consistently maintained that diagnosis is detrimental to counseling because it tends to pull clients away from an internal and subjective way of experiencing themselves and to foster an objective and external conception *about* them. The result may be to increase tendencies toward dependence and cause clients to act as if the responsibility for changing their behavior rested with the expert and not with themselves. Of course, client-centered therapy is grounded on the belief that clients are in the best position to understand and resolve their personal difficulties. Rogers (1951) states: "When the client perceives the locus of judgment and responsibility as clearly resting in the hands of the clinician, he is, in our judgment, further from therapeutic progress than when he came in" (p. 223).

Rogers (1951) is also concerned about psychological diagnosis because of the long-range implications of the "social control of the many by the few" (p. 224). A similar concern is expressed by Szasz (1974), who has labeled the whole concept of mental illness a "myth." According to Szasz' theory of human behavior, people are always responsible for their actions. What we call mental "diseases" aren't diseases at all, in the medical sense, but social/psychological phenomena. Szasz sees the classification of behavior as a control strategy. Like Rogers, he emphasizes the dangers of demeaning human beings by giving them psychiatric labels that miss the essence of the person.

Kempler (1973) argues that diagnostic categories provide therapists with pigeonholes in which they can put people, with the result that they fail to meet their clients creatively. Diagnoses, Kempler maintains, "confuse the patient, if he hears them, and they can astigmatize the vision of the therapist who sees the chart before he sees the patient. And worst of all, they impair the vision of the therapist who makes them" (p. 275)

R. D. Laing (1967), a psychiatrist who has criticized traditional types of diagnosis, expresses concern about the effects of diagnosis on those who are being labeled *and* on those who are doing the labeling. For the person being labeled, diagnosis can result in a self-fulfilling prophecy whereby the person acts as he or she is expected to act. Thus, a person who knows he or she is diagnosed as a schizophrenic may take great delight in telling ward attendants "After all, I'm crazy! What can you expect from me?" In turn, hospital or ward personnel may see people only through the stereotypes associated with various diagnoses. If they expect certain behaviors from the patients, there is a good chance that the patients will adopt these behaviors and live up to the staff's expectations.

In his provocative book *The Death of Psychiatry,* Torrey (1974), also a psychiatrist, develops the thesis that traditional psychiatry (including its emphasis on psychodiagnosis) is no longer functional. For Torrey, the medical model is based on a contract between a patient and society. This contract specifies that, although people may originally have been responsible for getting a disease, once the disease takes hold, they are no longer responsible (p. 79). Torrey contends that most people who are labeled "mentally ill" suffer from problems in living rather than from physical disabilities. Since they are not "sick," he believes that they are done an injustice when they are labeled and treated in the framework of the medical model. He expresses the crux of his argument concerning diagnosis as follows: "As a medical model approach to problems of human behavior, it produces confusions rather than solutions. If we are wise, we will allow it to die with dignity and not try to prop it up to do a job it is no longer able to do" (p. 5).

Our Own Position on Psychodiagnosis

We believe that diagnosis, broadly construed, is a legitimate part of the therapeutic process. The kind of diagnosis we have in mind is the result of a joint effort by the client and the therapist. We agree with Carkhuff and Berenson (1967) that "a meaningful diagnostic process flows out of an ongoing interactional process between therapist and client. There is no separate and distinct diagnostic process" (p. 235). Thus, both therapist and client should be involved in discovering the nature of the client's difficulty, a process that commences with the initial sessions and continues until therapy is terminated. Even practitioners who oppose conventional diagnostic procedures and terminology need to raise such questions as:

- What is going on in this client's life at this time?
- What are the client's resources for change?
- What does the client want from therapy, and how can it best be achieved?
- What should be the focus of the sessions?
- What are some factors that are contributing to the client's problems, and what can be done to alleviate them?
- What are the prospects for meaningful change?

The counselor and the client can discuss each of these questions as a part of the therapeutic process. Counselors will develop hypotheses about their clients, and they can talk about their conjectures with their clients in an ongoing way. The diagnosis performed by counselors does not have to be a matter of labeling their clients; rather, counselors can describe behavior and think about its meaning. In this way, instead of being done mechanically and technically by an expert, diagnosis becomes a process of thinking *about* the client *with* the client.

Current Issues in Diagnosis

Those who support the traditional forms of diagnosis agree that there are limitations to present classification systems and that some of the problems mentioned by the critics of diagnosis do exist. However, rather than abandoning diagnostic classifications altogether, they favor updating diagnostic manuals to reflect improvements in diagnosis and treatment procedures. The American Psychiatric Association is currently developing a revised manual that is intended to reflect recent research data, deemphasize orthodox psychoanalytic concepts, and offer definitions that a greater number of psychologists and psychiatrists can agree upon, regardless of their theoretical orientations.

Another important issue regarding diagnosis is whether or not clients should know their diagnosis and have access to all the information concerning themselves that their therapists have. Some practitioners contend that they should decide how much information to reveal to their clients. Others believe that it is unethical to keep pertinent information from their clients. Can you think of situations in which you would not be willing to share your hunches or information about a client with that client?

There is also a practical matter pertaining to diagnosis—the fact that many insurance companies who pay for psychological services require a diagnosis on the insurance form. Presumably, clients who consult a therapist regarding problems that don't fit a standard category are not to be reimbursed for their psychotherapy. These insurance carriers take the position that psychotherapy is for treatment of specific mental or emotional disorders; consequently, if a therapist doesn't write down a specific diagnosis, the client's insurance may not cover his or her expenses.

What is your position on this practical reality? If you were a therapist in private practice, how do you think you'd deal with it? Would you tell your client his or her diagnosis? What would you do if you believed that your client didn't fit any diagnostic classification? Would you have any reservations about who would have access to the diagnosis and how it might be used against your client? If so, how would you handle this matter with your client? Take a moment now to jot down your thoughts on these and other questions we've raised concerning the use of diagnosis in therapy.

_____

_____

_____

_____

_____

_____

THE ISSUE OF USING TESTS IN COUNSELING

At some point in your career you may need to decide on the place that testing will occupy in your counseling. This section focuses on when and how you would use tests in your work with clients.

As is true of diagnosis, the proper use of testing in counseling and therapy is the subject of some debate. Generally, those therapeutic approaches that emphasize an objective view of counseling are inclined to use testing procedures as tools to acquire information about clients or as resources clients themselves can use to help them in their decision making. The client-centered and existential approaches tend to view testing in much the same way that they view diagnosis—as an external frame of reference that is of little use in counseling situations. Writing from an existential-humanistic viewpoint, Arbuckle (1975) has this to say about the place of testing in counseling:

> Thus if one sees the other person, in the traditional scientific pattern, as being what one is measured to be by outside criteria, then testing—and diagnosis—should be an integral part of the counseling process. If, on the other hand, one sees the basic reality of the human being from within, then testing and diagnosis will tend to remove the person even further from the reality of who he is. [p 261].

We think that the core of the issue is not whether you will use tests as an adjunct to counseling but rather under what circumstances, and for what purposes, you may want to use tests. There are many different types of tests that can be used for counseling purposes, including measures of aptitude, ability, achievement, intelligence, values and attitudes, vocational interests, and personality characteristics. The following questions may help you to think about the circumstances in which you might want to use tests for counseling purposes.

1. What do you know about the tests you may use? It's important for counselors to be familiar with any tests they use and to have taken them themselves. They should know the purpose of each test and how well it measures what it purports to measure. You'll need to decide whether you're willing to invest the time necessary to become acquainted with the tests you might want to use. In many counseling centers, one person assumes the responsibility for administering and interpreting tests. If you or your clients want to use a test, you may want to refer them to a person who specializes in testing.

2. How much say do you think clients should have in the selection of tests? Some counselors assume the responsibility for deciding whether and when to use tests and prescribe specific tests for clients. Other counselors believe that clients should decide whether they want testing and, if so, what general type of testing they want (aptitude, interest, achievement, personality). These counselors claim that clients who are not actively involved in decisions about tests may become passive, relying too heavily on test results to determine what they should do instead of using the results to make informed decisions of their own. Brammer and Shostrom (1968) cite evidence that "client participation in test selection tends to facilitate the client's development of self-direction or self-actualization more than when the counselor alone prescribes tests" (p. 303).

3. Do you know *why* you want to use a particular test? Is it merely because a client asks for it? Is it because you don't know what to do next and hope that a test will point to a direction? Does your agency require that you administer certain tests?

Your reasons for using tests will depend on the particular circumstances. If you're doing vocational counseling, your client may want to take a vocational-interest inventory, and you may agree that such a test could be useful in helping the client to pinpoint some areas of interest. In another case, a client's behavior may concern you, and you may want to administer some projective tests or other personality-assessment devices to help you determine the severity of his or her difficulty. Whatever your reasons for testing are, you should be able to state a clear rationale for any test you use.

4. If a client requires testing, do you explore the reasons for the request with the client? Some clients may think that a test will give them answers and, in effect, make decisions *for* them. Clients need to be aware that tests are only tools that can provide useful information about themselves, which they can proceed to explore in their counseling sessions. They also need to know what the tests are designed for and what they expect from the testing. Are you willing to explore the values and limitations of tests with your clients, as well as their reasons for wanting to take them?

5. How do you integrate the test results into the counseling sessions? How might you use them for counseling purposes?

In general, it's best to give test *results*, not simply test *scores*. In other words, you should explore with your client the *meaning* the results have for him or her. However, just as clients need to be involved in the selection of tests, they also should be involved in the interpretation of the results. In this connection you'll need to evaluate your clients' readiness to receive and accept certain information, and you'll need to be sensitive to the ways in which they respond to the test results. Your clients may need an opportunity to express and explore discrepancies between what they think their abilities and interests are and what the test results indicate. Are you willing to allow your clients to talk about any possible disappointments? Do you use this opportunity to encourage them to ask whether some of their prior decisions were realistic?

6. Are you concerned about maintaining the confidentiality of test results? Test results may be handled in different ways, depending on the purpose and type of each test. Nevertheless, your clients need to feel that they can trust you and that test results will neither be used against them nor revealed to people who have no right to this information. The uses and confidentiality of test results are matters that you may want to discuss with your clients.

7. Are you critical in evaluating tests? Too often mistakes have been made because counselors have had blind faith in tests. If personality assessments have low reliability and validity, will giving a battery of these tests result in more accurate information? You should know the limitations of the tests you use, and you should keep in mind that a test can be useful and valid in one situation, yet inappropriate in another. Are you willing to acquire the knowledge you need to properly evaluate the tests you use?

CHAPTER SUMMARY

To a large degree, your therapeutic techniques and procedures flow from your theoretical assumptions; in this sense, counseling theory and practice are closely related. Whether or not you have a clearly articulated theory, you tend to operate on the basis of fundamental views of people and of the therapeutic process. Consequently, in this chapter we've asked you to consider your basic assumptions, some aspects of various theories that most appeal to you, the role of techniques in counseling, the issue of responsibility, your role as a counselor, therapeutic goals, and practical issues related to the use of diagnosis and testing.

Although it's unrealistic to expect that you'll operate from a clearly defined and unified theory at the outset of your practice, we do think that you can at least raise the issues that we've focused on in this chapter. We believe that counselors who give little thought to the theoretical issues that affect their professional practice will spend a lot of time floundering. Reflecting on why you make the interventions you do will enable you to have a more meaningful impact on your clients and to develop a framework for assessing the effects of your therapeutic work.

ACTIVITIES, EXERCISES, AND IDEAS FOR THOUGHT AND DISCUSSION

1. Do this exercise in dyads. Describe your theoretical bias, and tell your partner in simple language how you see counseling.
2. Of the theoretical approaches that were briefly reviewed in the self-inventory earlier in the chapter, which one appeals to you the most? Which one appeals to you the least? Why? Could you select at least one concept or assumption from *each* approach that you'd like to incorporate into your own approach to counseling?
3. Go back to the self-inventory on theoretical approaches to counseling, and, for each approach, circle the *one* item that you react to most strongly (either positively or negatively). In class, form small groups to discuss your reactions to the statements you've circled.
4. In what ways do you think your theoretical assumptions will determine the way you counsel?
5. How do you determine for yourself the proper division of responsibility in counseling? How might you avoid assuming responsibility that you think belongs to your client? How might you ensure that you will accept your own share of responsibility?
6. Suppose you're applying for a job as a counselor, and the following question appears on the application form: "Describe in not more than three lines how you see your role as a counselor." How would you respond to this question? In class, form small groups and discuss your responses.
7. Suppose the same application form asks "What are the *most important* goals you have for your clients?" How would you respond?
8. In class, debate the role of diagnosis in therapy. One person makes a case *for* diagnosis as a valuable part of the therapeutic process, and the other person argues against the use of diagnosis. Or have a class discussion on trends in diagnosis, its uses and abuses, and its purpose and value.
9. Suppose that a client comes to you and asks you to administer a battery of interest, ability, and vocational tests. How would you respond? What kinds of questions would you ask the client before agreeing to arrange for the testing?
10. What is your position on the use of techniques in counseling? When do you think they are appropriate? How can you determine for yourself whether you're using techniques as gimmicks to allay your anxiety or as extensions of your personal style as a counselor?

Values
and the
Therapeutic Process

5

For each statement, indicate the response that most closely identifies your beliefs and attitudes. Use the following code: A = I strongly agree; B = I slightly agree; C = I slightly disagree; D = I strongly disagree.

____ 1. It is both possible and desirable for counselors to remain neutral and keep their values from influencing clients.

____ 2. Counselors should influence clients to adopt values that seem to be in the clients' best interests.

____ 3. It is appropriate for counselors to express their values, as long as they don't try to impose them on clients.

____ 4. The search for meaningful values is a central part of psychotherapy.

____ 5. Counselors should challenge clients to make value judgments regarding their own behavior.

____ 6. I can work only with clients whose value systems are similar to my own.

____ 7. Before I can effectively counsel a person, I have to decide whether our life experiences are similar enough that I'll be able to understand that person.

____ 8. The clarification of values is a major part of the counseling process.

____ 9. I could work effectively with people who had certain values that I did not respect.

____ 10. I might be inclined to subtly influence my clients to consider my values.

____ 11. I consider it my job to challenge my clients' philosophies of life.

____ 12. I have a clear idea of what I value and where I acquired my values.

____ 13. I tend to continually question my own values.

____ 14. I see myself as open and receptive to people whose values are different from mine.

_____ 15. I tend to be intolerant of people who think very differently from the way I do.

INTRODUCTION

The question of values permeates the therapeutic process. This chapter is intended to stimulate your thinking about your values and life experiences and the influence they will have on your counseling. We ask you to consider the possible impact of your values on those of your clients, the effect your clients' values will have on you, and the conflicts that may arise when you and your client have different values.

Perhaps the most fundamental question we can raise about values in the therapeutic process is whether it is possible for counselors to keep their values out of their counseling sessions. In our view, it is neither possible nor desirable for counselors to be scrupulously neutral with respect to values in the counseling relationship. Although we don't see the counselor's function as persuading clients to accept a certain value system, we do think it's crucial for counselors to be clear about their own values and how they influence their work and the directions taken by their clients. Since we believe that counselors' values do inevitably affect the therapeutic process, we also think it's important for counselors to be willing to express their values openly when they are relevant to the questions that come up in their sessions with clients.

Not everyone who practices counseling or psychotherapy would agree with this position. At one extreme, some counselors who have definite, absolute value systems believe that their job is to exert influence on clients to adopt their values. These counselors tend to direct their clients toward the attitudes and behaviors that *they* judge to be in their clients' best interests. At the other extreme are the counselors who are so anxious to avoid influencing their clients that they immobilize themselves. They keep themselves and their values hidden so that they won't contaminate their clients' choices. We'd like to comment briefly on each of these extremes.

First, we don't view counseling as a form of indoctrination; nor do we believe that the therapist's function is to teach clients the right way to live. We think it's unfortunate that some well-intentioned counselors believe that their job is to help people conform to socially acceptable standards or to straighten out their clients. It seems arrogant to suppose that counselors know what's best for others. We question the implication that counselors have greater wisdom than their clients and can prescribe ways of being happier. No doubt, teaching is a part of counseling, and clients do learn in both direct and indirect ways from the input and example of their counselors; but this is not to say that counseling is synonymous with preaching or instruction.

On the other hand, we don't favor the opposite extreme of trying so hard to be "objective" that we keep our personal reactions and values hidden from our clients. Counselors who adopt this style are unlikely to do more than mechanical, routine counseling. Clients demand a lot more involvement from their therapists than mere reflection and clarification. They often want and need to know where their therapists stand in order to test their own thinking. We think that clients deserve this kind of honest involvement on the part of their therapists.

Krasner (1967), a behavior therapist, has formulated a provocative concept of the therapist as a "reinforcement machine." He argues that, regardless of their theoretical approach, therapists are bound to influence the behavior and values of their clients. However neutral therapists might think they are, they are continually giving positive and negative reinforcement by their words and behavior, and this reinforcement, whether intended or not, does affect the direction clients take in therapy: "For the therapist not to accept this situation and to be continually unaware of influencing effects of his behavior on his patients would itself be 'unethical'" (p. 204).

Krasner's view points to a central issue in this chapter—the nature and degree of influence exerted by the therapist's values in the therapeutic relationship. The following questions may help you to begin thinking about the role of your values in your work with clients.

- Is it possible for therapists to interact honestly with their clients without making value judgments? Is it desirable for therapists to avoid making such judgments?
- Do you have a need to see your clients adopt your beliefs and values?
- Can you remain true to yourself and at the same time allow your clients the freedom to select their own values, even if they differ sharply from yours?
- How do you determine whether a conflict between your values and those of your client necessitates a referral to another professional?
- How does honestly exposing your clients to your viewpoint differ from subtly "guiding" them to accept your values?
- To what degree do you need to have life experiences that are similar to those of your clients? Is it possible that too much similarity in values and life experiences might result in therapy that is not challenging for the client?

Now list other questions that you'd like to raise concerning the role of values in counseling.

_____

_____

_____

_____

_____

SOME VIEWPOINTS ON THE ROLE OF VALUES IN THE THERAPEUTIC PROCESS

Different theoretical orientations take various approaches to the question of values in therapy. In this section we review a number of theoretical viewpoints and ask you to draw your own conclusions on this issue.

Carl Rogers

According to Carl Rogers (1961, 1969), it is the attempt to win the love and approval of others that leads people to give up their internal orientation in deciding on what they value. We learn to distrust what we think, feel, want, and believe as we look outside ourselves and adopt standards that we *should* hold. These internalized values tend to be rigid rather than open to change. For Rogers, this is a basic problem of many clients in psychotherapy. They have lost contact with what they deeply think or feel because they have taken over the conceptions of others as their own. Consequently, a major task facing the therapist is to help clients regain contact with their own experience so that they can derive values from within themselves. For Rogers, therapy is largely a process by which clients learn to trust themselves and develop an internal locus of control.

Rogers describes the general direction taken by clients with respect to values as their therapy progresses. This description may give an idea of what people tend to value as they become psychologically healthier:

- They tend to drop their defenses and move away from facades. They become more real and more accepting of all of their feelings.
- They tend to move away from living by others' expectations and from being compulsively driven by "oughts" and "shoulds." They are increasingly interested in pleasing themselves rather than others.
- They value inner direction and feel increasingly confident that they can make their own choices. They move toward accepting their freedom and responsibility in directing their own lives.
- They become more willing to be processes instead of finished products. They realize that they are experiencing change and that they aren't always consistent.
- They are willing to be increasingly open to all of their inner and outer experience; they have less need to deny and distort their experiencing. They learn to value this openness instead of regarding it as something threatening or frightening.
- As they become more accepting of themselves, they show a greater willingness to accept others and increasingly value deep and meaningful relationships.

Abraham Maslow

In *Motivation and Personality*, Maslow (1970) described some of the personal characteristics of people who, in his view, are healthy and functioning at peak levels. His "self-actualizing" subjects demonstrated the following value orientations in their lives:

- They perceive and accept reality as it is.
- Their ethics are internally based; they avoid being pressured by others and living by others' standards.
- They value peak experiences in which they feel one with the universe.
- They value creativity, which is an expression of themselves in some natural and inventive way.
- They have a concern for humanity, they have some meaningful relationships, and they also value privacy and solitude.
- They exhibit faith in themselves and others; they are autonomous; they accept themselves as worthwhile people; and they find meaning in their lives. They may have a life mission in which their potentialities can be fulfilled.

Maslow (1968) sees therapy as the search for values: "I think it is possible that we may soon even *define* therapy as a search for values, because ultimately the search for identity, is, in essence, the search for one's own intrinsic, authentic values" (p. 177). If we use Maslow's portrait of self-actualizing people as a general framework for optimum human functioning, the values embraced by these people can provide directions that clients can consider in their search for meaningful ways to live.

Viktor Frankl

Viktor Frankl sees the search for values that give meaning to living as the essence of psychotherapy. In *Man's Search for Meaning,* Frankl (1963) develops the thesis that finding meaning is the primary motivational force in human life. He demonstrates how people are able to live and even die for the sake of their ideals and values.

For Frankl, then, the therapist's task is to help clients find meaning in their lives and to challenge them to live by values that will generate meaning. However, it is not for the therapist to decide *what* clients should value; each person must take responsibility for creating his or her own meaning. "In a word, each man is questioned by life; and he can only answer to life by *answering for* his own life; to life he can only respond by being responsible" (p. 172).

In contrast to the peak experiences of the self-actualizing people described by Maslow, a sense of meaninglessness and emptiness leads some people to seek therapy. In *The Will to Meaning,* Frankl (1969) describes this "existential vacuum" and argues that dealing with this "inner void" is a challenge for the psychotherapist. Because we are not determined by inner drives and in many respects have rejected traditions and values that tell us how we should live, we often don't know what we *want* to do. If we decide to do simply what others want or expect us to do, we find ourselves without clear, personal values that give meaning to life; we experience an inner void. In this way the search for meaningful values becomes the central problem in psychotherapy.

Behavior Modification

A common misconception regarding behavior therapists is that they choose specific goals and values for their clients. Although this might be partly true for therapy in institutional settings, it is not the trend in modern behavior therapy. If you were to consult a behavior therapist, you would be expected to choose which specific behaviors you wanted to modify. Your goals and values would thus be more important than those of the therapist.

It is true that some earlier proponents of the behavior-therapy approach seem to have emphasized the expertise of the therapist in the selection of therapeutic goals. More recent practitioners, however, attach importance to the client's active involvement and cooperation in the entire therapeutic process, including goal selection. They recognize that therapists cannot impose conditioning or relearning on clients if therapy is to have much chance for success. Thus, the task of the therapist is to reinforce the target behaviors chosen by clients. Whether clients want to lose weight, stop smoking, learn to be more assertive in social situations, or lose their fear of riding on airplanes, the modifications they want to make in their behavior are reflections of their own values.

In some institutional settings, the use of behavior-modification techniques does raise the issue of whether values are being imposed on the patients by their therapists. For instance, those in charge of an institution may decide that people should refrain from physically hurting themselves, or learn how to make contact with others, or acquire certain survival skills. They may therefore decide *for* the clients what behavior is desirable. Through behavior modification, they may impose socially accepted goals on their clients. This procedure raises the question of whose interests are being served by this application of behavior therapy. Some institutions have been criticized for misusing behavioral techniques to make patients more compliant and thus make life easier for the staff.

Reality Therapy

William Glasser's Reality Therapy rests on the concept that questions of morality and value are the essential core of psychotherapy. Glasser (1965) criticizes conventional psychiatry for failing to deal with issues of right and wrong in the course of therapy. His view is that people become clients because their behavior doesn't satisfy their need to be loved and to love others and because they don't really feel worthwhile as persons. Therapists cannot avoid getting involved in the realm of morals and values, for they must challenge clients to judge their own behavior and assess whether it is really meeting their basic needs. As Glasser puts it, "Our job is to face this question, confront them with their total behavior, and *get them to judge* the quality of what they are doing. We have found that unless they judge their own behavior, they will not change" (p. 56).

Glasser does not claim that Reality Therapists have found the key to a universal moral code, but he does assert that responsible therapists should assist clients to judge the moral quality of their behavior. How do we assess whether behavior is moral? "When a man acts in such a way that he gives and receives love, and feels worthwhile to himself and others, his behavior is right or moral" (p. 57).

Even though Glasser disavows any intention to make therapists into moralists, there is a fine line between merely challenging clients to assess their behavior and actively teaching them what they should value. Glasser concedes that therapists should not infringe on their clients' responsibility by making judgments and decisions for them, but he also expects therapists to offer praise when clients act in responsible ways and to show disapproval when they do not. Glasser maintains that clients *demand* this type of judgment and that therapists should teach clients that the key to finding happiness is to accept responsibility. This position raises some central ethical concerns, such as:

- As a therapist, what are your criteria for judging acceptable and realistic behavior?
- Who defines "reality"? Is the therapist's view of reality more valid than the client's?
- Does this approach encourage the view that conformity to the moral code of the majority is synonymous with responsible and realistic behavior?
- If therapists give praise when clients act "responsibly" and show disapproval when they do not, are they, in effect, encouraging clients to adopt their value systems? Does this type of value judgment encourage clients to develop inner direction, or does it tend to make them dependent on the approval of their therapists?

Rational-Emotive Therapy

Rational-emotive psychotherapy, which was developed by Albert Ellis, stresses values, beliefs, and a philosophy of life as central concerns in therapy. According to this approach, people become emotionally disturbed because they unquestioningly accept self-defeating values and beliefs. Events themselves do not cause people to become disturbed; rather, their beliefs about events produce their difficulties. For example, being rejected is not in itself the cause of an emotional problem. What makes this event a source of difficulty is the way it is evaluated: "Being rejected means that I'm worthless and unlovable."

Therapists who use the rational-emotive approach actively direct their clients to examine their belief systems and teach them that their illogical and irrational beliefs are the source of their problems. They see their function as helping clients substitute a rational philosophy of life for an irrational one. To this end they try to show clients how they developed their values and attitudes, demonstrate that they maintain their own emotional disturbances by continuing to indoctrinate themselves with illogical, self-defeating ideas, and get them to modify their thinking. Since merely working on specific symptoms or problems will not necessarily prevent other illogical ideas from emerging, these therapists attack the core of their clients' irrational thinking and teach them how to substitute rational beliefs and values for their irrational ones.

Ellis (1973) claims that people must be depropagandized and deindoctrinated if they are to succeed in changing their ways of life. To achieve this result, he will "persuade, cajole, and at times even command" the client to act differently as an integral part of the therapeutic process (p. 154). This approach raises several questions about the therapist's proper role in challenging the values and beliefs of the client. Some of these concerns are:

- Who decides what counts as an "irrational belief"?
- Is it appropriate for therapists to teach clients a philosophy of life? Is this a form of imposing a new set of values on the client?
- Does this approach give therapists an inordinate degree of power and influence over their clients? Is there a danger that clients will abandon a set of values they have never evaluated critically and be persuaded to accept the "rational" beliefs propounded by their therapists?

The rational-emotive approach to psychotherapy does bring to the forefront the issue of the power therapists have to influence their clients' values and behavior. As you reflect on this issue, consider the following example provided by Ellis (1973):

> On one occasion I very firmly gave a thirty-year-old male, who had never really dated any girls, an assignment to the effect that he make at least two dates a week, whether he wished to do so or not, and come back and report to me on what happened. He immediately started dating, within two weeks had lost his virginity, and quickly began to overcome some of his most deep-seated feelings of inadequacy [p. 154].

Summary

It appears from the foregoing survey that values play a role in every major theory of counseling. No such theory claims that values are *not* an integral part of the therapeutic process, but the various approaches differ with respect to the way in which therapists should deal with the problem of values.

For humanistic therapies, values and meaning are the core of therapy. Therapy focuses on clients' struggles to make their own choices, and these choices ultimately depend on what each client values. Existentially oriented therapists believe they should challenge their clients to derive their values from within instead of living by externally derived "oughts" and "shoulds." Within this framework, therapists may disclose their own values to their clients, but not with the purpose of telling clients what they should do or what values they should embrace. To make these specific decisions for clients would be to deprive them of responsibility for their own lives. The goal of therapy is not to teach clients what to value but to help them learn to trust their own choices.

At the other extreme are the highly didactic therapies, such as Ellis' rational-emotive therapy, in which therapists intervene forcefully to persuade clients to think differently. Between these two viewpoints lies behavior therapy, in which clients generally choose specific target behaviors and thus help to determine the goals of therapy in the light of their present values.

Pause a few moments now to consider the issue of values in therapy in terms of this survey of theoretical approaches.

1. What are some risks you see in actively prescribing for the client? Could this kind of approach be a reflection of the therapist's needs?

_____

_____

_____

_____

2. To what degree do you think it is ethical and appropriate to make decisions for your clients, even if you're convinced that you know what is best for them?

_____

_____

_____

3. Since any approach to therapy reflects, to some degree, a view of life, how can therapists avoid subtly imposing their values on their clients?

_____

_____

_____

4. Do you think an exploration of values is a legitimate part of therapy? If so, how would you counsel a client who resisted any exploration of his or her basic values?

_____

_____

_____

5. What are the values implicit in the views of therapy espoused by such theorists as Rogers, Maslow, and Frankl? Is it proper for therapists to encourage clients to adopt these values if they come into conflict with clients' previous styles of life? Why or why not?

_____

_____

_____

_____

CLARIFYING YOUR OWN VALUES AND THEIR EFFECTS ON YOUR WORK

If, as we have maintained, your values will significantly affect your work with clients, then it is incumbent upon you to clarify your values and the ways they enter the therapeutic process. For example, counselors who have "liberal" values may find themselves working with clients who have more traditional values. If these counselors privately scoff at conventional values, can they truly respect clients who don't think as they do? Or if counselors have a strong commitment to values that they rarely question, whether these values are conventional or radical, will they be inclined to promote these values at the expense of hindering their clients' free exploration of their own attitudes and beliefs? If counselors never reexamine their own values, can they expect to provide a climate in which clients can reexamine theirs?

Whatever your own values are, there may be many instances in which they present some difficulty for you in your work with clients. In this section we examine some sample cases and issues that may help you clarify what you value and how your values might influence your counseling. As you read through these brief examples, you might keep the following questions in mind:

- What is my position on this particular issue?
- Where did I develop my views?
- Are my values open to modification?
- Have I challenged my views, and am I open to being challenged by others?
- Do I insist that the world remain the same now as it was earlier in my life?
- Do I feel so deeply committed to any of my values that I'm likely to push my clients to accept them?

The Right to Die

How do you react to the following statement?

The choice of suicide is ours to make. It is our life we are giving up, and our death we are arranging. The choice does not infringe on the rights of others. We do not need to explain and excuse.[1]

In the article from which this quotation is taken, Doris Portwood (1978) makes a case for the right of elderly people to choose to end their own lives if they decide that each day there is less to live for or if they are in a state of physical and

[1]From "A Right to Die?" by D. Portwood, *Psychology Today*, January 1978, p. 68.

psychological deterioration. Pointing out that many old people are subjected to an undignified ending to life, particularly if they have certain terminal illnesses, she argues persuasively that they have the right to end their lives before they become utterly miserable and a drain on their families.

Apply this argument to yourself. Might there come a time in your life when there is nothing for you to live for? Imagine yourself in a rest home, growing more and more senile. You are unable to read, to carry on meaningful conversation, or to go places, and you are partially paralyzed by a series of strokes. Would you want to be kept alive at all costs, or might you want to end your life? Would you feel justified in doing so? What might stop you?

Now apply this line of thought to other situations in life. If you accept the premise that your life is yours to do with as you choose, do you believe it is permissible to commit suicide at *any* period in your life? In many ways, people who choose suicide are really saying that they want to put an end to the way they are living *now*. Suppose you felt this way even after trying various ways of making your life meaningful, including getting intensive psychotherapy. You feel as if nothing works, that you always wind up in a dead-end street. Would you continue to live until natural causes took you? Would you feel justified in ending your own life if your active search has failed to bring you peace?

Perhaps thinking about conditions that might lead you to consider suicide is so unpleasant that you have never really allowed yourself to imagine such situations. However, if you give some thought to how this issue applies to you, you may feel less threatened in entering into real dialogues with individuals who are contemplating the balance sheet of their lives. If you are closed to any personal consideration of this issue, you may tend to interrupt these dialogues or cut off your clients' exploration of their feelings.

In discussing suicidal impulses of clients, Burton (1972) points out that therapists need to avoid becoming unduly frightened by the possibility that a client will commit suicide. When suicide is explored in therapy, it is an indication that clients are being reached and that they need to be reached on a deeper level. The contemplation of suicide can be a way of refusing to live in old ways, and the therapist's task is to give protection and support as the client searches for new reasons to live. Burton sees this struggle with the issue of whether or not to live as a central dimension of psychotherapy:

> Long-term psychotherapy, if it is to be effective, must bring the client to question his life and its values. Since these are so often found wanting, suicidal impulses come as no great surprise. They have constructive as well as destructive aspects. A person who contemplates dying really wants to live—but in a different way [p. 66].

The ethical questions associated with suicide can come up in other ways as well. Consider the following example. Emily, who is in her early twenties, is dying painfully with cancer. She expresses her wish to forego any further treatment and to take an overdose of pills to end her suffering. Her parents cling to hope, however, and in any event they deeply believe that it is always wrong to take one's own life. If her parents were coming to you for counseling, what might you say to them? Do you feel that Emily has the right to end her life? What role should your opinion play in your counseling? How might your values affect the things you say to the family?

_____

_____

_____

_____

_____

_____

Learning

You may find yourself working with clients for whom schooling is a major issue. What are your values with respect to obtaining a formal education? What about other sources of learning about life? Have you ever allowed yourself a moratorium period in which you didn't feel any pressure to achieve anything beyond just sampling life? The point of these questions is that, if you've devoted your school years to producing and achieving, this personal value might affect the way you'd work with a client who wanted to take some time off. For example, suppose you have a client, Paul, who is tired of college and is thinking about quitting until he knows what he wants to do with his life. Rather than seek employment, he'd like to have some time in which he won't have to make any major decisions. Will you encourage Paul to stay in school until he gets his degree? Or will you be supportive of his plans to do nothing for a while? Do you think that he'd be wasting time and that he should be using these years to accomplish more tangible goals? How would your views on this issue affect your work with Paul?

_____

_____

_____

_____

_____

_____

Security

Many of your clients will experience a struggle between maintaining security and taking risks. One client might lean toward staying in a marriage that he feels is dead, because he is frightened by the prospect of living alone. Another may be trying to decide whether to stay with a job that she knows how to do well or accept promotion to a job that sounds exciting but that she's not sure she can do well. Imagine yourself in these situations. Would you want to settle for whatever security a marriage might offer if you were miserable in that marriage? Would you be deterred by the thought of divorcing and perhaps being alone? As a counselor, would you try to influence the man's decision, or would you support him regardless of whether his decision agrees with your personal values? In the case of the woman, how would you feel if you were in her position? Do you think you would lose a lot by remaining in a job you've mastered instead of accepting a promotion? Which do you value more for yourself, security or taking a risk? How would your personal bias affect your work with these clients?

_____

_____

_____

_____

_____

_____

Sexuality

What are your values with respect to sexual behavior? Do they tend to be liberal or conservative? What are your attitudes toward:

- the belief that sex should be reserved for marriage only?
- sex as an expression of love and commitment?
- casual sex?
- group sex?
- extramarital sex?
- premarital sex?
- homosexuality?

An important issue is whether you can counsel people who are experiencing conflict over their sexual choices if their values differ dramatically from your own. For example, if you have very liberal views about sexual behavior, will you be able to respect the conservative views of some of your clients? If you think their moral views are giving them difficulty, would you try to persuade them to become more liberal and adopt your views? How would you view the guilt they may experience? Would you treat it as an undesirable emotion that they need to free themselves of? Or, if you have fairly strict sexual standards that you use as guidelines for your own life, would you tend to see the more permissive attitudes of some of your clients as a problem? Could you be supportive of choices that conflict with your own values?

_____

_____

_____

_____

_____

The Family

Your views of family life may have a strong influence on how you counsel parents and children, marital partners, and people contemplating marriage or divorce. They may affect how you deal with family conflicts and what kinds of suggestions you make when you work with family-related matters. It's therefore important for you to be able to sort out your values with respect to family life and how they affect the interventions you decide to make.

Suppose you have a 15-year-old client, Sharon, who says "I'm never going to get married, because I think marriage is a drag! I don't want kids, and I don't want to stay with one person forever." What is your reaction to this statement? Perhaps your values clash with Sharon's desire to be free of responsibility. If so, you might tell her that a refusal to accept any responsibility in life is a sign of immaturity and that she will have a more complete life if she has a family of her own. Or perhaps you envy her independence and wish that you didn't have to be responsible for anyone except yourself. In what ways do you think that you might work with Sharon differently, depending on what your own attitude toward family life is? If you don't feel comfortable with a commitment to marriage and a family, do you think you could be objective enough to help her explore some of the possibilities she might be overlooking? Or might your doubts be useful in your work with Sharon?

_____

_____

_____

_____

_____

_____

Love

When we open ourselves to loving another person, we become vulnerable. Those we love might cease to love us; they might leave; they might be seriously hurt or die; in many ways they might hurt us. Perhaps you keep yourself insulated and choose not to develop intimate relationships because you don't want to be vulnerable. If so, do you think that you could encourage others to take the chance of opening themselves to loving others? Can you value something for another person, even if you don't value it for yourself? Or suppose you believe in the value of intimate relationships, not only for yourself but for everyone. Could you be supportive of a client who was trying to decide whether a more solitary life suited him or her? Or would you try to change your client's views about intimacy? You might reflect on your own experiences and conflicts with respect to love and determine how they might influence what you say and do when you work with people who are struggling to clarify their values in this area.

Suppose you have a client, Steve, whom you experience as a person who doesn't allow others to get close to him. Steve tells you that he trusted a person once and got burned and that, on the whole, he prefers to go his own way. If you value intimacy in your own life and think that love is worth the risk, would you encourage Steve to risk developing new relationships again? If you felt that he was keeping himself needlessly isolated, would you be willing to see him go on refusing the possibility of love? Or if you sympathized with his feelings, would you be inclined to support them without challenging him?

_____

_____

_____

_____

_____

_____

Religion

What role does religion play in your life? Does it provide you with a source of meaning? What are your views concerning established and organized religion? Has religion been a positive, negative, or neutral force in your own life? Even if religious issues are not the focus of a client's concern, religious values may enter into the sessions indirectly as the client explores moral conflicts or grapples with questions of meaning in life. Do you see yourself as being able to keep your religious values out of these sessions? How do you think they will influence the way you counsel? If you're hostile to organized religions, can you empathize with clients who feel committed to the teachings of a particular church?

Religious beliefs and practices affect many dimensions of human experience that are brought into counseling situations. How people handle guilt feelings, authority, and moral questions are just a few of these areas. The key issue here is whether you can understand your clients' religious beliefs and their meaning for your clients, even if these views differ from your own. For example, you may think that a client has accepted an unnecessarily strict and authoritarian moral code. Yet you need to be able to understand what these beliefs mean to your client, whatever your own evaluation of them for yourself might be.

Suppose you have a client, Janet, who seems to be suffering from a major conflict because her church would disapprove of the way she is living. Janet experiences a great deal of guilt over what she sees as her transgressions. If you sharply disagreed with the values she accepted from her church or thought they were unrealistic, how might your views affect your counseling? Do you think you might try to persuade Janet that her guilt is controlling her and that she would be better off freeing herself from her religious beliefs? Why or why not?

_____

_____

_____

_____

Now assume that you have a client, Tom, who complains that his life seems empty and meaningless. If you believe that your religion gives meaning to what you do and that without it your life would be void of meaning, would you think that Tom's lack of religious beliefs is the source of his complaint? How would your religious views help or hinder your work with Tom? Whether or not you consider yourself a religious person, would you encourage Tom to explore what a religion might have to offer?

_____

_____

_____

_____

THE ISSUE OF CONVERTING CLIENTS TO YOUR VALUES

Even if you think it's inappropriate or unethical to impose your values on clients, you may unintentionally influence your clients in subtle ways to embrace your values. What you pay attention to during counseling sessions will reinforce what your clients choose to talk about. Even your nonverbal clues and body messages give your clients indications of when you like or dislike what they do. Since your clients may feel a need to have your approval, they may respond to these clues by acting in ways that they imagine will meet with your favor instead of developing their own inner direction. Suppose, for example, that an unhappily married man knew or surmised that you really thought he was wasting good years of his life in the marriage. This client might be influenced to obtain a divorce simply because he thinks you would approve. So, even though you've made a clear decision not to push clients to believe and act in ways that agree with your own values, you still need to be sensitive to the subtle messages that can be powerful influences on their behavior.

Patterson (1959) develops the idea that counselors' philosophies of life are reflected in their techniques and in the way they work with clients. Even though therapists may not impose their values, their values are bound to have some influence on their clients:

> While the therapist does not teach or impose specific values or a philosophy of life, it should be clear that he does implement in his therapy a philosophy of counseling which in effect is his philosophy of life. His goals, his methods and techniques, and his ethics all express his basic philosophy. No therapist can avoid this [p. 74].

In addition to any indirect influence you have on your clients' values, can you think of times when you would feel justified in *imposing* your values on a client? Consider the following brief cases, and ask yourself whether you would attempt to change the behavior and values of these people in a definite direction.

Cathy is 17 years old. She tells you that she takes many different kinds of potentially dangerous drugs. Your attempts to explore her reasons for doing so don't get very far. Cathy seems very casual about taking large doses of drugs, even though she has had to be hospitalized several times for overdoses. She maintains that she knows what she's doing, that she feels excited when she's on her drug trips, and that she's unwilling to quit using drugs in spite of the risks.

How would you deal with this issue in your sessions with Cathy? Would you actively work on convincing her to live without drugs? Would you attempt to convince her that her behavior was actually self-destructive? Would you explore with her what she wants from you?

_____

_____

_____

_____

_____

Greg is 16 years old. He is in a juvenile prison for gang fighting. He steadfastly maintains that he "has to be" involved in gangs—"everyone else is"—and that he has to fight to prove his manhood.

Would you be able to accept Greg's standard of manhood? Would you attempt to change his views so that he wouldn't feel the need to fight any more? If you see his behavior as self-destructive, illegal, and harmful to others, would you try to persuade him to change in a direction you deemed socially responsible? Can you imagine yourself supporting his behavior on the grounds that he felt it was right for him?

_____

_____

_____

_____

_____

CONFLICTS OF VALUES IN COUNSELING

Being clear about your own values doesn't eliminate the possibility that a conflict of values between you and your client may interfere with effective therapy. Do you see yourself as being able to work effectively with anyone who seeks counseling from you? Some counselors believe that they can work with any kind of client or with any type of problem. They may be convinced that being professionals means being able to assist anyone. On the other hand, some counselors are so unsure of their abilities that they are quick to refer anyone they feel uncomfortable with to another counselor.

Somewhere between these extremes are the cases in which your values and those of your client clash to such an extent that you question your ability to function in a helping way. Obviously there are no easy ways to determine what to do when this happens. The burden must be on counselors to honestly assess whether their values are likely to interfere with the objectivity they need to be useful to their clients. To make such an assessment, counselors must be clear about their feelings concerning value-laden issues, they must be honest about their own limitations, and they must be honest with potential clients when they think value conflicts will interfere with the therapeutic relationship. At times counselors may need to tell clients that, because of their own views, they could not work effectively with them and that a referral to another professional would be in their best interests.

Consider the circumstances in which you would be inclined to refer a client to someone else because of a conflict of value systems. For each of the following, indicate the response that best fits you. Use the following code: A = I definitely could work with this type of person; B = I probably couldn't work with this type of person; C = I feel quite certain that I could not effectively work with this type of person.

_____ 1. a man with fundamentalist religious beliefs who refuses to explore his religious values

_____ 2. a woman who claims that she is seeking a way to put Christ in the center of her life and that, if she only could turn her life to Christ, she would find peace

_____ 3. a person who shows little conscience development, who is strictly interested in his or her own advancement and uses others to achieve personal aims

_____ 4. a homosexual couple who want to work on conflicts they are having in their relationship

_____ 5. a man who wants to leave his wife and children for the sake of sexual adventures with other women that might bring zest to his life

_____ 6. a woman who has decided to leave her husband and children in order to gain her independence, but who wants to explore her fears of doing so

_____ 7. a woman who wants an abortion but wants help in making her decision

_____ 8. a man who is disturbed because he periodically becomes violent with his wife and has beaten her severely a number of times

_____ 9. a person who chooses not to work

_____ 10. a man who lives by extremely rigid "macho" expectations of what a man should be

_____ 11. a person who lives by logic and is convinced that feelings are dangerous and should be avoided

_____ 12. a person whose physical attractiveness strikes you so strongly that you find it difficult to concentrate on what is said in the sessions

_____ 13. a man who strongly believes that the only way to bring up his children is by punishing them severely, if necessary by beating them

_____ 14. a person who sees very little value in therapy and doesn't believe that therapy can really help him or her make any real-life changes

_____ 15. a person who is convinced that his or her decisions are the right ones only if you approve of them or actually make them for the person

Now go back over the list and pay particular attention to the items you marked "C." Why do you think you'd have particular difficulty in working with these types of people? What other kinds of people do you envision you'd have trouble working with because of a clash of values?

_____

_____

_____

_____

_____

Case Studies of Possible Value Conflicts

In this section we present some case studies of possible value conflicts. Try to imagine yourself working with each of these clients. How do you think your values would affect your work with each one?

Candy. Candy is a 14-year-old client whom you are seeing because of family conflicts. Her parents have recently divorced, and Candy is having problems coping with the breakup. Eventually, she tells you that she is having sexual relations with her boyfriend. Moreover, she tells you that she's opposed to any birth-control devices because they seem so contrived. She assures you that she won't be one to get pregnant.

What are your feelings about Candy having sex? If you sense that her behavior is an attempt to overcome her feelings of isolation, how might you deal with it? How would you respond to her decision not to use birth-control measures?

_____

_____

_____

_____

_____

After you've been working with Candy for a few months, she discovers that she is pregnant. Her boyfriend is also 14 and is obviously in no position to support her and a baby. Candy tells you that she has decided to have an abortion but feels anxious about following through on her decision. How would you respond?

_____ I'd encourage Candy to do whatever she wants to do.
_____ I'd encourage her to consider other options besides abortion, such as adoption, keeping the child as a single parent, marrying, and so on.
_____ I'd reassure her about having an abortion, telling her that thousands of women make this choice.

_____ I'd refer Candy to another professional because of my opposition to abortion.

_____ I'd tell Candy that I am personally opposed to (or in favor of) abortion, but that I want to remain her counselor during this difficult time and will support whatever decision she makes for herself.

_____ I would reprimand Candy and tell her that I knew this was going to happen.

Other: _____

Candy's case illustrates several thorny problems. What do you do if you feel that you cannot be objective because of your views on abortion? Do you refer Candy to someone else? If you do, might she feel that you were rejecting her because she has committed some horrible offense? If you're firmly opposed to abortion, could you support Candy in her decision to go ahead with it? Would you try to persuade her to have the baby because of your views on abortion?

A possible course of action would be to tell Candy about your values and how you felt they would influence your work with her. If you felt that you couldn't work effectively with her, perhaps you should ask yourself why. Why is it crucial that her decision be compatible with your values? Do you necessarily have to approve of the decisions your clients make?

Consider the possible decisions Candy might make, and ask yourself what your goals in working with her would be. What are *your* values in a case such as Candy's?

_____

_____

_____

_____

_____

_____

Ronald. Ronald is a 22-year-old college junior. He tells you that he wants to get into counseling with you in order to sort out conflicts that he is experiencing between his sexual feelings and his religion. Ronald sees himself as a good Christian and a believer in the Bible. He has had very little experience in dating and hasn't had any sexual relationships. Ronald is troubled because he experiences far more intense feelings toward men than he does toward women. This is what he tells you:

I haven't yet acted on my sexual feelings for other men, because I feel that this would be morally wrong. My religious beliefs tell me that it's very wrong for me even to have sexual desires for other men, let alone *act* on these desires! If I did have homosexual experiences, I'd feel extremely guilty. But I just don't have much interest in women, and at the same time I'm intensely interested in having a close emotional and physical relationship with a man. I'm torn by what I feel I want to experience and what my religion tells me I *ought* to do. So, I was wondering whether you think you can help me, and I'd also like to know what your views are about religion and about homosexuality.

From what you know about Ronald, would you want to accept him as a client? Do you think you could help him clarify his feelings and achieve some resolution of his conflict? What kind of answer would you give Ronald concerning your view of homosexuality? What would you tell him about your religious values? How would your views either help or hinder Ronald in resolving his struggle?

Let's examine the responses that three different counselors might make to Ronald. As you read these responses, think about the degree to which they represent what you might say if you were counseling Ronald.

Counselor A: "Well, Ronald, the answer to whether or not I can help you really depends on several factors. First of all, you need to know that I'm a Christian counselor, and I share many of your beliefs about religion, morality, and the Bible. I think that I could be very supportive in helping you work through some of your religious doubts. I think you should know that I believe my clients will find real serenity when they make Christ the center of their lives and when they live by the example He gave us. Next, you need to know that I cannot condone homosexuality, because I do believe that it is immoral. I'm not implying that you're sinful for merely having homosexual wishes, but I think it would be morally wrong for you to act on these impulses."

Do you share any of Counselor A's views? Do you see Counselor A as *imposing* or merely *exposing* his or her beliefs? Do you think Counselor A can work effectively with Ronald? Why or why not?

_____

_____

_____

_____

_____

_____

Counselor B: "I'm not sure whether I'm the counselor for you or not. Ultimately, I think you'll need to decide whether you feel you want to work with me. Before you decide, you should know that I think that religion is a negative influence on most people. In your case, for example, you were taught to feel guilty over your impulses. I see guilt as a way of controlling people, so, if I worked with you, I'd probably challenge some of your religious values and the source of your guilt feelings. I'd have you look carefully at where you obtained your notions of right and wrong. As far as your homosexual feelings are concerned, I'd want to explore the relationship you had with your father and mother, and I'd challenge you to look at your motivations in not making more contact with women. Is it because you're afraid of them? Do you have enough experience with either sex to know whether you want to be homosexual or heterosexual?"

What do you agree or disagree with in Counselor B's thinking? Do you think this counselor would impose his or her views on Ronald? Or do you think that Counselor B's values will challenge Ronald to decide what *he* values?

_____

_____

_____

_____

_____

_____

Counselor C: "Ronald, your sexual preference really doesn't affect me one way or the other. I'd want you to decide to do what *you* think is right for you. For instance, if you decided on a homosexual life-style, I'd be supportive, and I'd want to help you work through any problems that might arise as a result of your choice. Your religious views also don't affect me one way or the other. I realize that your religion is a part of you, and we could work on how your teachings might cause you difficulty in living the way you want to. I really don't see why it's important that I tell you my personal values, because they won't be entering into our relationship that much, and I wouldn't want them to influence you. I want you to choose whatever way is right for you, and I'll support whatever that is."

Do you see Counselor C as being neutral, passive, or accepting and nonjudgmental? Do you think Counselor C can keep his or her values out of the therapeutic relationship? What do you agree or disagree with in Counselor C's approach?

_____

_____

_____

_____

_____

After thinking about the three different approaches we've considered, how do you think you would respond to Ronald? Would you have any reservations about accepting him as a client? Would you be able to accept his choice of homosexuality if that is what he wanted? Would you prefer that he not make this choice? Would you be more concerned about his religious struggles than about his choice of sexual orientation? Take a moment now to write down the essence of what you might want to say to Ronald about the direction your work with him would take.

_____

_____

_____

_____

_____

Molly. Molly is 28, married, and has returned to college to obtain a teaching credential. During the intake session, Molly tells you that she is going through a lot of turmoil and is contemplating some major changes in her life. A few years ago she and her husband began experimenting with an open marriage. He initiated taking her to several parties for swingers, and they tried group sex for a time. Molly never liked these activities, but her husband insisted that they were necessary to keep their marriage from becoming dull. Now Molly says that she doesn't want to stay in the marriage any longer and has found another man she wants to live with. She wants her husband to take custody of their three children, because she wants the freedom to pursue her own interests for a while without being responsible to anyone.

The following statements represent some possible responses that counselors might have to Molly, whether or not they actually voiced them to her. Which of these statements can you see yourself making to Molly? Which of them represent reactions you might have but would keep from her?

- "Maybe you should stay married and make the best of things, because that way you can finish school, and *then* you can decide what to do."
- "Don't you feel any responsibility to your children? After all, you did decide to bring them into this world, and giving them up seems rather impulsive and selfish."
- "I really think that what you are doing is terrific. You have a lot of courage, because many women in your place would continue to play the role of selfless mother and wife and fail to take care of themselves. I think you're entitled to make these changes, and I hope you won't let anyone pressure you to do otherwise."
- "It seems that, with all the turmoil you've been going through, it would be best not to make any big decisions right now. Instead, maybe you could persuade your husband to give up his affairs and put more into your marriage."
- "I'd hate to see you divorce without having some marriage counseling first to determine whether that's what you both want."
- "Maybe you ought to look at the prospects of living alone for a while. The idea of moving out of a relationship with your husband and right into a new relationship with another man concerns me."
- "Frankly, I don't know why you put up with your husband as long as you did. It seems like he's keeping you around for his convenience. I think you'll be able to respect yourself more when you do separate."

If Molly were your client, which of your own values might influence your counseling with her? For example, what do you think of divorce? Would you want her to use divorce only as a last resort? How much do you value keeping her family intact? What are your feelings about Molly leaving the children with her husband?

_____

_____

_____

_____

_____

_____

DIFFERENCES IN LIFE EXPERIENCES AND PHILOSOPHIES OF LIFE

Many people would claim that the life experiences and value systems of counselors must be similar to those of their clients. The idea is that counselors can understand and empathize with their clients' conflicts only if they have had the same kinds of subjective experiences. Thus, an elderly person may feel that a counselor who hasn't reached this stage of life cannot hope to understand what it means to cope with loss, physical decline, loneliness, and anxiety about the future. Many people who belong to racial or ethnic minorities think it is extremely important to seek counselors of their own ethnic group, in the belief that counselors who haven't had to contend with discrimination and prejudice could not really understand how they see the world. Similarly, many women are convinced that men cannot effectively counsel women, because their life experiences and biases prevent them from being able to understand women's needs. People who are committed to a homosexual life-style may seek gay therapists, because they are convinced that heterosexual counselors lack the experience and understanding to work with them on their conflicts. Many drug addicts and alcoholics reveal failure after failure in their psychotherapy experiences with professionals who haven't experienced drug and alcohol problems.

The growth of self-help groups reflects the idea that people who have encountered and resolved certain difficulties possess unique resources for helping others like themselves. Thus, overweight people share their problems in Overeater's Anonymous. Alcoholics who have chosen to live one day at a time without alcohol provide support for fellow alcoholics who are trying to quit drinking. Many drug addicts who have entered Synanon have found that they cannot deceive former addicts with their games and that being confronted by people who once played the same games forces them to look at how they are living. Members of Recovery Incorporated find support in facing the world once they have left state mental hospitals.

To what degree do you share the view that you must have similar life experiences to those of your clients? Do you think you need to have the same philosophy of life that your clients have in order to work effectively with them? Do you think that you can be helpful to people whose experiences, values, and problems are different from yours by tuning into their feelings and relating them to your own? Consider for a moment whether you could communicate effectively with:

- an elderly person
- a person with a strict religious background
- a person of a different race or ethnic group
- a physically handicapped person
- a delinquent or a criminal
- an alcoholic
- a psychotic person
- a person with a different sexual orientation
- an obese person

To facilitate your reflection on the issue of whether you need to have life experiences or value systems that are similar to those of your clients, we'll present a number of situations that you might be faced with as a counselor. In each case, assess what factors in your life would either help or hinder you in establishing a good working relationship with the client we describe.

Frances is a 60-year-old teacher who is thinking about going to law school just because it's something she has wanted to do for a long time. For 30 years she has taught government and history in community colleges, and now she wants to retire early in order to take up a new profession. Frances wonders whether she has the stamina to endure long hours of study, and she is asking herself whether leaving teaching at this stage in life would be a wise move.

1. What experiences have you had that could help you understand Frances' desires and conflict?

2. How do you feel about women becoming lawyers?

3. How do you feel about a person going into law at the age of 60?

4. Would you be inclined to encourage Frances to take a risk, or would you favor staying with a secure job in her situation?

5. How might your answers to the preceding questions affect the way you would counsel Frances?

Terry is a Black college student majoring in psychology who comes to you about the difficulty he is having staying in school. He failed statistics and is convinced that his statistics instructor "had it in for me because I'm Black." He also has particular trouble writing essays, and some remedial English courses haven't alleviated the difficulty he has in communicating his thoughts in writing. Terry's ambition is to get a doctorate in psychology and teach at the college level.

1. Have you ever had to really struggle with your own course work in college?

   _____

   _____

2. Would you challenge Terry for blaming his failure in the statistics course on a prejudiced instructor? Why or why not?

   _____

   _____

   _____

3. Would you challenge Terry on the realism of his educational plans and career choice? Why or why not?

   _____

   _____

   _____

4. Would the fact that Terry is Black influence the way you would counsel him? If so, in what way?

   _____

   _____

   _____

At a community clinic, Sylvia, who is 38, tells you that she is an alcoholic. During the intake interview, she says "I feel so much remorse, because I've tried to stop my drinking, and I haven't succeeded. I'm fine for a while, and then I begin to think that I have to be a 'perfect' wife and mother. I see all the ways in which I don't measure up, how I let my kids down, the many mistakes I've made with them, the embarrassment I've caused my husband, and then I get so down I feel compelled to take that next drink to stop my shaking and to blur my depression. I see that what I'm doing is self-destructive, but I haven't been able to stop, in spite of going to A.A."

1. What experiences have you had that would help you understand what it's like for Sylvia to feel compelled to drink?

   _____

   _____

   _____

2. How do you see Sylvia? As having a disease? As suffering from a lack of willpower? As an irresponsible, indulgent person?

   _____

   _____

   _____

3. How does the fact that Sylvia is a woman affect your view of her problem?

_____

_____

_____

You are the probation counselor for Ramon, a Mexican-American youth who has a history of being expelled from school. He has spent most of his life in the barrio, and the customs of the gang he belongs to dictate how he lives. He's very silent during most of your first session, but he does let you know that he doesn't really trust you, that he's only here because the court sent him, and that you can't possibly understand what his life is about.

1. Have you had any life experiences that would qualify you to counsel Ramon?

_____

_____

_____

2. Would you want to convert Ramon to any of your values? For example, would you want to see him finish school? Stop being involved in gang fights? Take counseling seriously?

_____

_____

_____

3. If you haven't had the kinds of experiences growing up that Ramon has had, could you still communicate effectively with him and understand his view of the world?

_____

_____

_____

Frank is a middle-aged businessman who says that he's not seeking personal counseling but rather wants advice on how to manage his teenage daughter. According to Frank, his daughter is immature and unruly. She isn't learning self-discipline, she socializes too much and works too little, she doesn't respect her parents, and in other ways she is a disappointment and a worry to him. Frank seems to be oppressive rather than loving, and to him the full responsibility for the conflict in his family rests with his daughter. You surmise that he doesn't see any need to examine his own behavior or his role in contributing to the family's difficulties.

1. How do you imagine you might relate to a person like Frank who seems very rigid and closed to looking at himself?

_____

_____

_____

2. Would your own values get in the way of understanding Frank's values?

_____

_____

_____

3. Do you think you might want to get Frank to look at his own part in the family disturbances? Would you want to challenge his values as they pertain to his daughter's behavior?

_____

_____

_____

4. Would you accept Frank as a client, even if he wanted to focus on how he could change his daughter?

_____

_____

You can add your own examples of clients whom you might have difficulty in counseling because of a divergence in values or life experiences. How would you deal with such clients? You could decide to refer most of them to other counselors, but you might also look at how to broaden yourself so that you can work with a wider range of personalities. If you have difficulty relating to people who think differently from the way you do, you can work on being more open to diverse viewpoints. This openness doesn't entail accepting other people's values as your own. Instead, it implies being secure enough in your own values that you aren't threatened by really listening to, and deeply understanding, people who think about life differently. It implies listening to your clients with the intent of understanding what their values are, how they arrived at them, and the meaning these values have for them. This kind of accepting attitude requires a willingness to let your clients be who they are without trying to convince them that they should see life the way you do. Achieving this acceptance of your clients can significantly broaden you as a person and as a professional.

CHAPTER SUMMARY

In this chapter we've looked at a variety of practical, value-laden counseling situations and issues. Of course, you'll encounter many other kinds of value questions in your work. Our intent has been to focus your attention on the ways in which your values and those of your clients will affect your counseling relationships.

The central theme of this chapter has been the importance of being clear about what _you_ value. We've suggested that counselors cannot be neutral in the area of values and should frankly acknowledge those values that are related to questions clients are struggling with. It takes honesty and courage to recognize how your values affect the way you counsel, and it takes wisdom to determine when you cannot work with a client because of a clash of values. These questions have no ready-made or universally appropriate answers. They demand ongoing introspection and discussions with supervisors or colleagues to determine how to make the optimal use of your values.

ACTIVITIES, EXERCISES, AND IDEAS FOR THOUGHT AND DISCUSSION

1. Have a panel discussion on the topic: "Is it possible for counselors to remain neutral with respect to their clients' values?" The panel can also discuss different ways in which counselors' values may affect the counseling process.
2. Invite several practicing counselors to talk to your class on the role of values in counseling. Each of these counselors can have a different theoretical orientation. For example, you might ask a behavior therapist and an existential-humanistic therapist to talk to your class at the same time on the role of values.
3. Various students can do a more in-depth study of different theoretical viewpoints on the role of values in the therapeutic process and present these results to the class in the form of a symposium. The students can take the roles of theorists such as Carl Rogers, Abraham Maslow, Viktor Frankl, a behavioristic writer, William Glasser, and Albert Ellis.
4. For a week or so, keep a record of your principal activities. Then look over your record and, on the basis of what you do and how you use your time, list your values as reflected in your record in order of their priority. How do you think these values might influence the way you counsel others?
5. In class, do the following exercise in pairs. First, discuss areas that each of you might have trouble with in counseling situations because of a conflict of values. For example, one student might anticipate difficulty in working with clients who have fundamentalist religious beliefs. Then, choose one of these situations to role-play, with one student playing the part of a client and the other playing the part of the counselor. The client brings up some problem that involves the troublesome value area. It is important for you and your partner to really get into the particular frame of reference being role-played and to feel the part as much as possible.
6. As a variation of the preceding exercise, you can assume the role of a client whose values you have difficulty identifying with. For instance, if you think you'd have trouble counseling a woman who wanted an abortion, become this client and bring her problem to another student, who plays the part of a counselor. This type of role-reversal exercise can help you understand people whose value systems are different from your own.
7. For this exercise, work in small groups. Discuss the kinds of life experiences you've had that you think will enable you to effectively counsel others. You might also talk about the *limitations* of your life experiences so far as they might hinder your understanding of certain clients.
8. Interview some practicing counselors about their experiences with values in the counseling process. You could ask such questions as: What are some kinds of clients that you've had difficulty working with because of your value system? How do you think your values influence the way you counsel? How are your clients affected by your values? What are some of the main value issues that clients bring into the counseling process?

9. Do this exercise in pairs. One student plays a counselor; the other plays a client. The counselor actively tries to convert the client to some value or point of view that the counselor holds. The student who assumes the role of the client can actually bring in a personal issue that involves a value issue. For instance, the client can be a college student trying to decide whether to go on to graduate school or get a job and start earning money immediately after graduation. The job of the counselor is to try to persuade the client to do what the counselor thinks would be best for the client. This exercise can give you a feel for what it's like to persuade a person to adopt your point of view and what it's like to be subjected to persuasion.

10. This exercise can also be done in pairs. Each person interviews the other on the following issue: What are some of your central values and beliefs, and how do you think they will inhibit or facilitate the work you will do as a counselor?

Ethical Issues I: Therapist Responsibilities, Therapist Competence, and Confidentiality

6

For each statement, indicate the response that most closely identifies your beliefs and attitudes. Use the following code: A = I strongly agree; B = I slightly agree; C = I slightly disagree; D = I strongly disagree.

_____ 1. A therapeutic relationship should be maintained only as long as it is clear that the client is benefiting.

_____ 2. Much of therapy is really the "purchase of friendship."

_____ 3. Counselors are ethically bound to refer clients to other therapists when working with them is beyond their professional training or when personal factors would interfere with the therapeutic relationship.

_____ 4. Possession of a license or certificate from a state board of examiners shows that a person has therapeutic skills and is competent to practice psychotherapy.

_____ 5. There are no situations in which I would disclose what a client told me without the client's permission.

_____ 6. Clients should be informed of the limits of confidentiality prior to the initial counseling session.

_____ 7. What is ethical can sometimes conflict with what is legal.

_____ 8. Continuing education should be a requirement for renewal of a license to practice psychotherapy.

_____ 9. A therapist's only real responsibility is to the client.

_____ 10. Ultimately, every practitioner must create his or her own ethical standards.

INTRODUCTION

Various professional organizations have established codes of ethics that provide broad guidelines for practitioners of psychological services. Some of these organizations are: The American Psychological Association, the American Personnel and Guidance Association, the American Psychiatric Association, the American Academy of Psychotherapists, the American Association of Marriage and Family Counselors, the National Association of Social Workers, and the Association of Humanistic Psychology. Although you should be familiar with the ethical standards of your specialization, you will still be challenged to develop your own personal code of ethics to govern your practice. The general guidelines offered by most professions do not make specific choices for the practitioner, and they usually represent minimal standards of ethical conduct. Your own ethical awareness and your reflection on issues that aren't clear-cut will determine how you interpret and translate general guidelines into your day-to-day choices as a professional.

In this chapter and the next, we provide an opportunity for you to reflect on the personal ethical system you will draw upon in making sound judgments in your professional practice. We present general ethical principles from various organizations, as well as open-ended cases and examples dealing with therapist responsibilities and competence, confidentiality, and privileged communication. We encourage you to take a position on the situations presented in light of the principles of professional ethics discussed in the chapter.

We believe that the opportunity for an in-depth exploration of ethical and professional issues should be an integral part of training programs in every helping field. Unfortunately, some students in mental-health programs graduate with very little formal exposure to professional ethics. Jorgensen and Weigel (1973) found that the majority of training programs in clinical and counseling psychology do provide some exploration of professional and ethical issues in some part of the curriculum. They reported that a formal course in professional problems was offered by 33% of the training programs responding, with 48% covering the topic in related courses. Ethics courses were reported by 14% of the programs responding, and an additional 79% thought that ethical issues were adequately covered in other courses. However, Jorgensen and Weigel were disconcerted to find that formal exposure to ethical and professional issues was *not required* in over 20% of the training programs. They recommended that programs that do not offer such courses should assess their students' familiarity with ethical and professional principles.

ETHICAL RESPONSIBILITIES OF THERAPISTS

Most professional organizations affirm that a therapist's *primary* responsibility is to the client. However, therapists also have responsibilities to members of the client's family, to the agency they work for, to a referring agency, to society, to the profession, and to themselves. In this section, we explore some of these responsibilities and some situations in which conflicts arise.

Client Welfare

One of the therapist's central responsibilities is to be genuinely concerned about the welfare of the client. This means that the needs of the client, not the therapist, assume primary importance in the therapeutic relationship. It also implies that a therapeutic relationship should be maintained only as long as the client is benefiting from counseling. The American Psychological Association

(1977a) states: "The psychologist attempts to terminate a clinical or consulting relationship when it is reasonably clear that the consumer is not benefiting from it" (p. 23). This principle raises several questions we'd like you to consider:

- What criteria can you use to determine whether your client is benefiting from the therapeutic relationship?
- What do you do if your client feels he or she is benefiting from therapy but you don't see any signs of progress?
- What do you do if you're convinced that your client is coming to you to "purchase friendship," as Schofield (1964) calls it, and not really for the purpose of changing?

Put yourself, as a therapist, in each of the following two situations. Ask yourself what you would do, and why, if you were confronted with the problem described.

After five sessions with you, your client, George, asks "Do you think that I'm making any headway toward solving my problems? Do I seem any different to you now than I did five weeks ago?" Before you give him your impressions, you ask him to answer his own question. He replies "Well, I'm not sure whether coming here is doing that much good or not. I suppose I expected resolutions to my problems before now, but I still feel anxious and depressed much of the time. It feels good to come here, and I usually continue thinking after our sessions about what we discussed, but I'm not coming any closer to decisions. Sometimes I feel certain this is helping me, and at other times I wonder whether I'm just fooling myself."

1. What criteria can you employ to help you and your client assess the value of counseling for him?

   _____

   _____

   _____

2. Does the fact that George continues to think about his session during the rest of the week show that he is most likely getting something from counseling? Why or why not?

   _____

   _____

   _____

3. Does it sound as if George has unrealistic expectations about finding neat solutions and making important decisions too quickly? Is he merely impatient with the process?

   _____

   _____

Joanne has been coming regularly to counseling for some time. When you ask her what she thinks she is getting from the counseling, she answers "This is really helping. I like to talk and have somebody listen to me. I often feel like you're the only friend I have and the only one who really cares about me. I suppose I really don't do that much outside, and I know I'm not changing that much, but I feel good when I'm here."

1. If it became clear to you that Joanne wasn't willing to do much to change her life and wanted to continue counseling only because she liked having you listen to her, do you think you'd be willing to continue working with her? Why or why not? Would you say that she is benefiting from the relationship with you? If so, how?

   _____

   _____

   _____

   _____

2. Is it ethical to continue the counseling if Joanne's main goal is the "purchase of friendship"? Why or why not?

   _____

   _____

3. If you thought that Joanne was using her relationship with you to remain secure and dependent, but she believed that she was benefiting from the relationship, what might you do? How do you imagine you'd feel if you continued to see Joanne even though you were convinced that she wasn't changing?

   _____

   _____

4. Do you think it's necessary for you to see change in your clients? Is it enough if clients feel they are benefiting from counseling, even if you don't agree? Why or why not?

   _____

   _____

   _____

Making Referrals

Therapists also have a responsibility to know *when* and *how* to refer clients to appropriate resources. It is crucial for professionals to know the boundaries of their own competence and to refer clients to other professionals when working with them is beyond their professional training or when personal factors would interfere with a fruitful working relationship. For example, after counseling with a client for a few sessions, you might determine that he or she needs more intensive therapy than you're qualified to offer. Even if you have the skills to undertake long-term psychotherapy, the agency you work for may, as a matter of policy, permit only short-term counseling. Or you and a client may decide that, for whatever reason, your relationship isn't productive. The client may want to continue working with another person rather than discontinue counseling. As we discussed in Chapter 5, there may be times when the discrepancy or conflict between your values and those of a client necessitates a referral. For these and other reasons, you will need to develop a framework for evaluating *when* to refer a client, and you'll need to learn *how* to make this referral in such a manner that your client will be open to accepting your suggestion.

To make the art of referral more concrete, consider the following exchange between a client and her counselor. Helen is 45 years old and has seen a counselor at a community mental-health center for six sessions. Helen suffers from periods of deep depression and frequently talks about how hard it is to wake up to a new day. In other respects it is very difficult for her to express what she feels. Most of the time she sits silently during the session.

The counselor decides that Helen's problems warrant long-term therapy that he doesn't feel competent to provide. In addition, the center has a policy of referring clients who need long-term treatment to therapists in private practice. The counselor therefore approaches Helen with the suggestion of a referral:

Counselor: Helen, during your intake session I let you know that we're generally expected to limit the number of our sessions to six visits. Since today is our sixth session, I'd like to discuss the matter of referring you to another therapist.

Helen: Well, you said the agency *generally* limits the number of visits to six, but what about exceptions? I mean, after all, I feel like I've just started with you, and I really don't want to begin all over again with someone I don't know or trust.

C: I can understand that, but you may not have to begin all over again. I could meet with the therapist you'd be continuing with to talk about what we've done these past weeks.

H: I still don't like the idea at all. I don't know whether I'll see another person if you won't continue with me. Why won't you let me stay with you?

C: Well, there are a couple of reasons. I really think you need more intensive therapy than I feel I'm trained to offer you, and, as I've explained, I'm expected to do only short-term counseling.

H: Intensive therapy! Do you think I'm *that* sick?

C: It's not a question of being sick, but I *am* concerned about your prolonged depressions, and we've talked before about my concerns over your suicidal fantasies. I'd just feel much better if you were to see someone who's trained to work with depression.

H: *You'd* feel better, but *I* sure wouldn't! The more you talk, the more I feel crazy—like you don't want to touch me with a ten-foot pole. You make me feel like I'm ready for a mental hospital.

C: I wish I could make you understand that it isn't a matter of thinking you're crazy; it's a matter of being concerned about many of the things you've talked about with me. I want you to be able to work with someone who has more training and experience than I do, so that you can get the help you need.

H: I think you've worked with me just fine, and I don't want to be shoved around from shrink to shrink! If you won't let me come back, then I'll just forget counseling.

This exchange reflects a common problem. Even though the counselor explains why he wants to refer Helen to another therapist, Helen seems determined to reject the idea. She doesn't want to open herself up to anyone else right now. She clings to her feeling that she is being helped by her counselor, and she interprets the suggestion to see someone else as a sign that her counselor won't work with her because she's too sick.

What do you think of the way Helen's counselor approached his client? Can you see anything that you would have done differently? If you were Helen's counselor, would you agree to continue seeing her if she refused to be referred to someone else?

If you didn't want Helen to discontinue counseling, there would be a number of alternatives open to you. You could agree to see her for another six sessions, provided that your director or supervisor approved. You could let her know that you would feel a need for consultation and close supervision if you were to continue seeing her. Also, you could say that, although this might not be the appropriate time for a referral, you would want to work toward a referral eventually. Perhaps you could obtain Helen's consent to have another therapist sit in on one of your sessions so that you could consult with him or her. There may be a chance that Helen would eventually agree to begin therapy with this person. What other possibilities can you envision? What would be the consequences if you refused to see Helen or could not obtain approval to see her?

_____

_____

_____

_____

_____

ETHICAL ASPECTS OF THERAPIST COMPETENCE

What is competence, and how can you determine whether or not you're competent to carry out certain therapeutic functions? Professional codes of ethics provide only the most general guidelines with respect to competence. In the "Ethical Standards for Marriage and Family Counselors," the California Association of Marriage and Family Counselors states:

> The marriage and family counselor recognizes the boundaries of his competence and the limitations of his techniques. The marriage and family counselor assists his client in obtaining appropriate professional help for aspects of his problem that fall outside of his own competence.

A similar statement is made in the American Psychological Association's *Ethical Standards of Psychologists* (1977a):

> Psychologists recognize the boundaries of their competence and the limitations of their techniques and only provide services, use techniques, or offer opinions as professionals that meet recognized standards [p. 22].

These statements leave several questions unanswered. What are the boundaries of one's competence, and how do professionals know when they have exceeded them? How can they determine whether or not they should accept a client when they lack the experience or training they would like to have?

This problem becomes more complicated when we consider the question of what criteria to use in evaluating competence. Is completing a professional degree a necessary or sufficient condition of competence? There are many people who complete doctoral programs and yet lack the skills or knowledge needed to carry out certain therapeutic tasks. Obviously, degrees alone don't confer competence to perform any and all psychological services.

Licenses and certification aren't necessarily any more useful as criteria of competence than degrees. We've met licensed psychiatrists, psychologists, social workers, and marriage and family counselors who don't possess the competencies specified by their licenses. Conversely, we've met some unlicensed people who are far more competent than are some licensed therapists. Licenses mainly assure the public that the licensees have completed *minimum* educational programs, have had a certain number of hours of supervised training, and have gone through some type of evaluation and screening. Licenses imply that their holders have had a certain level of professional training, but they don't assure the public that practitioners can effectively and competently *do* what their licenses permit them to do.

A further consideration is that most licenses are generic in nature; that is, they usually don't specify the types of clients or problems the licensee is competent to work with, nor do they specify the techniques that a practitioner is competent to use. A licensed psychologist may possess the expertise needed to work with adults yet lack the competencies for working with children. The same person might be qualified to do individual psychotherapy yet have neither the experience nor the skills required for family counseling or group therapy. Most licensing regulations do specify that licensees are to engage only in those therapeutic tasks for which they have adequate training, but it is up to the licensee to put this rule into practice. A license permits the professional to provide a wide range of services, and it is the professional's responsibility to determine which services he or she is actually competent to provide. Counselors therefore have a responsibility to consult other professionals, take additional workshops, or in other ways acquire the competencies they see a need to acquire.

You can clarify the issue of competence for yourself by determining what kinds of therapeutic services you're qualified to offer for what kinds of clients. You can begin by asking yourself honestly what techniques you are skilled in by virtue of your training and experience. Consider the following list of techniques, and check those you feel competent to use:

_____ interpretation of dreams
_____ assertion training
_____ systematic desensitization
_____ administration of projective tests
_____ hypnosis
_____ play therapy
_____ group therapy with psychotics
_____ family therapy
_____ relaxation training
_____ working on blocks and tension areas in the body

You also need to assess how far you can safely go with clients and when you should refer them to other specialists. Similarly, it's important to learn when to consult another professional if you haven't had extensive experience in working with a certain problem. If you were to refer all the clients you encountered difficulties with, you'd probably have few clients. Keep in mind that many beginning counselors experience a great deal of self-doubt about their general level of competence; in fact, it's not at all unusual for even experienced therapists to wonder seriously at times whether they have the personal and professional abilities needed to work with some of their clients. Thus, difficulty in working with some clients doesn't by itself imply incompetence.

One way to develop or upgrade your skills is to work with colleagues or professionals who have more experience in certain areas than you do. You can also learn new skills by going to conferences and conventions, by taking additional courses in areas you don't know well, and by participating in workshops that combine didactic work with supervised practice. The feedback you receive can give you an additional resource for evaluating your readiness to undertake certain therapeutic tasks.

The Issue of Continuing Education

Most professional organizations are currently supporting efforts to make continuing education a mandatory condition of relicensure. In the past people could obtain licenses to practice professionally and then act as though there were no need to obtain any further education. We question how ethical it is to neglect taking substantive steps to keep current with new developments. In any event, the trend now is to encourage professionals to engage in ongoing education and training in areas related to their specializations. For instance, some professionals advocate making training in sex therapy a stipulation for renewal of one's license as a psychologist. We can think of many areas in which practitioners could profit by opening themselves to new learning.

We are in basic agreement with the view of continuing education for psychologists described by Lewinsohn and Pearlman (1972):

> It is generally acknowledged that predoctoral training is not sufficient to guarantee a high level of competence in professional areas of functioning. There can be little doubt that even the best present education and training will become obsolete within a relatively short period of time, unless the psychologist makes a very determined effort to refurbish and to expand his professional base of knowledge and technique [p. 48].

Lewinsohn and Pearlman report a survey in which 29% of the psychologists responding fully supported the proposal that continuing education be required for renewal of licenses and certification. An additional 27% responded positively, but with reservations; 43% did not favor mandatory continuing education. Lewinsohn and Pearlman concluded that: (1) there is both interest in and support for continuing education among practitioners, provided that there is no coercion, and (2) continuing education will become an increasingly important issue for psychologists. In this connection, they raise some critical questions: Should evidence of continuing education be required for recertification or relicensure? Who will determine what the nature of this continuing education must be? What standards should be used in making this judgment?

Take a few moments now to reflect on the issue of continuing education as it applies to you. What are some kinds of continuing education you want for yourself? Through what means do you think you can best acquire new skills and keep current with advances in your field?

_____

_____

_____

_____

Before concluding this discussion of competence, we want to mention the danger of rarely allowing yourself to experience any self-doubt and being convinced that you can handle any therapeutic situation. There are therapists who feel this way; they tell themselves they have it made and attend conventions to show off how much they know and impress their colleagues with their competence. Sidney Jourard (1968) has warned about this delusion that one has nothing new to learn. Jourard maintains that contact at exciting workshops or with challenging colleagues can keep therapists growing. He urges professionals to find colleagues they can trust, so that they can avoid becoming "smug, pompous, fat-bottomed and convinced that they have *the word*." Such colleagues can "prod one out of such smug pomposity, and invite one back to the task" (p. 69).

With Jourard, we see the development of competence as an *ongoing process, not* a goal that counselors ever attain once and for all. This process involves a willingness to continually question whether you're doing your work as well as you might and to search for ways of becoming a more effective person and therapist.

CONFIDENTIALITY, PRIVILEGED COMMUNICATION, AND PRIVACY

An important obligation of practitioners in the various mental-health specialties is to maintain the confidentiality of their relationships with their clients. This obligation is not absolute, however, and practitioners need to develop a sense of professional ethics that they can draw upon in determining when the confidentiality of the helping relationship should be broken. It also behooves them to be familiar with the legal protection afforded the privileged communication of their clients, as well as the limits of this protection.

Confidentiality, privileged communication, and privacy are related concepts, but there are important distinctions between them. Shah (1969) defines *confidentiality* as follows: "Confidentiality relates to matters of professional ethics. Confidentiality protects the client from unauthorized disclosures of any sort by the professional without informed consent of the client" (57). In another article, Shah (1970a) notes that the purpose of confidentiality is to safeguard the client's rights and that there are sanctions for violations of confidentiality. Clients must be able to assume that their private communications with the professional will be kept private. Shah comments that psychologists have a moral, ethical, and professional obligation not to divulge information without the client's knowledge and authorization, unless it is in the client's interest to do so (for example, in consulting with other professionals).

Shah (1969) defines *privileged communication* as "the legal right which exists by statute and which protects the client from having his confidences revealed publicly from the witness stand during legal proceedings without his permission" (57). Privileged communication, then, is a *legal* concept and refers to the right of clients not to have their privileged communications used in courts of law without their consent. If a client waives this privilege, the professional has no grounds for withholding the information. Some other relationships that are protected in various jurisdictions in the United States include those between attorneys and clients, marital partners, physicians and patients, psychiatrists and clients, priests and penitents, accountants and clients, and nurses and patients.

Shah (1969) also discusses the concept of *privacy,* whose legal boundaries are still being developed. Shah sees the concept of privacy as the freedom people have to choose for themselves when to share or withhold from others information about their attitudes, beliefs, opinions, and behavior.

Ethical and Legal Ramifications of Confidentiality

The ethics of confidentiality rest on the premise that clients in counseling are involved in a deeply personal relationship and have a right to expect that what they discuss will be kept private. Surely no genuine therapy can occur unless clients trust that what they say will be kept confidential. Professionals therefore have an obligation to discuss with clients the circumstances that might affect the confidentiality of their relationship.

Shah (1970a) raises the question, "Whose agent is the psychologist?" He notes that in some governmental agencies and in some institutions the psychologist is *not* primarily the client's agent. In such cases psychologists might be faced with conflicts between their obligations to the agency or institution and their obligations to their clients. For this reason, Shah maintains that any possible conflict should be clarified before a psychologist enters into a diagnostic or therapeutic relationship with a client. In short, clients should be informed about the limits of confidentiality.

Most professional organizations specify that it is the therapist's responsibility to safeguard information about a client and also to inform the client of the limits of confidentiality (see, for example, American Psychological Association, 1977a, p. 22). The Ethical Standards of the American Personnel and Guidance Association (1961) make the provision that "the counseling relationship and information therefrom must be kept confidential consistent with the obligations of the member as a professional person."

Since confidentiality is not absolute, it becomes necessary to determine under what circumstances it cannot be maintained. These circumstances are not clearly defined by accepted ethical standards, and each therapist must exercise his or her professional judgment. When assuring their clients that what they reveal will ordinarily be kept confidential, therapists should point out that they have obligations to others besides their clients. For instance, they are bound to act in such a way as to protect others from harm. Sometimes this can be done in a way that protects the identity of the client. Thus, the American Personnel and Guidance Association (1961) guidelines state that, if the counselor learns from a client of some condition that is likely to have a negative effect on others, the counselor is "expected to report *the condition* to the appropriate responsible authority, but in such a manner as not to reveal the identity" of the client.

The American Psychological Association's ethical standards give the following guidelines for breaking confidentiality: "Information received in confidence is revealed only after most careful deliberation and when there is clear and imminent danger to an individual or to society, and then only to appropriate professional workers or public authorities" (American Psychological Association, 1977a, p. 22).

A similar rule can affect the client's legal right of privileged communication. The California state legislature has created this specific exception to the right of privileged communication:

> There is no privilege if the psychotherapist has reasonable cause to believe that the patient is in such mental or emotional condition as to be dangerous to himself or to the person or property of another and that disclosure of the communication is necessary to prevent the threatened danger.

Currently there is a real concern on the part of directors of college counseling centers because a court case appears to have set the precedent that therapists are required to warn other persons who are in *potential* danger, even when this knowledge is acquired in the course of a therapeutic relationship. In *Tarasoff v. the Regents of the University of California*, the California Supreme Court determined that "privilege ends where the public peril begins." In this case a client told his therapist, who worked in a University of California hospital, that he intended to kill his girlfriend. The therapist told the campus police of this threat and requested that the client be held. The campus police released the client after talking with him. Later, he did kill his girlfriend. The victim's parents sued the therapist, the university regents, and the campus police for failing to notify the intended victim of her grave danger. The Supreme Court ruled in favor of the parents and charged that a failure to warn the intended victim was irresponsible.

Stimulated mainly by this ruling, most college counseling centers have developed guidelines regarding the limits of confidentiality when the welfare of others is at stake. These guidelines generally specify how to deal with emotionally disturbed students, violent behavior, threats, suicidal possibilities, and other circumstances in which counselors may be legally and ethically required to break confidentiality.

The question raised by these documents is: What are the responsibilities of counselors to their clients or to others when, in the professional judgment of the counselor, there is a high degree of probability that a client will commit suicide, seriously harm another person, or destroy property? Many counselors find it difficult to predict when clients pose a serious threat to themselves or to others. Clients are encouraged to engage in open dialogue in therapeutic relationships; believing that what they say is confidential, they may express feelings or thoughts about ending their own lives or doing physical harm to others. Generally, these are expressions of feelings, and relatively few of these threats are actually carried out. Counselors should therefore *not* be expected to routinely reveal all threats, for such a policy of disclosure could seriously disrupt clients' relationships with their therapists or with the persons who are "threatened." Counselors have the obligation *not* to disclose confidential material unless such disclosures are necessary to prevent harm to clients or to others.

What is expected of counselors is that they exercise reasonable professional judgment and apply practices that are commonly accepted by professionals in their specialty. If they determine that clients pose a serious danger of violence to others, they are obliged to exercise reasonable care to protect the would-be victims. Some guidance may be obtained from the following procedures, developed for use in the counseling center at California State University, Fullerton:[1]

1. When clients make threats against others, everything that goes on in the session should be recorded and documented. Counselors may be legally expected to prove that they used "sound professional judgment."
2. Counselors should inform the director of the center in writing of any serious threat.
3. Counselors should consult with professional colleagues for other opinions and suggestions concerning how to proceed. This consultation should also be documented.
4. The police and other proper authorities should be alerted.
5. The intended victim must be notified; in the case of a minor, the parents should also be notified.
6. Counselors need to inform their clients of the possible actions they must take to protect a third party.

Imagine now various situations in which clients might be dangerous to themselves or to others. What would be your own guidelines for dealing with such situations and possible disclosures of information you received in confidence from a client?

_____

_____

_____

_____

_____

At a recent conference on ethical and legal issues in counseling, there was a great deal of interest and anxiety expressed about the issue of dealing with potentially violent clients. Most of the counselors expressed fears of lawsuits and were very concerned about what "exercising sound professional judgment" really means. In discussing the tone of this conference, the three of us became concerned that some counselors are primarily worried about protecting themselves and not about their clients' welfare. Although counselors will surely want to protect themselves legally, we hope that they don't allow this problem to paralyze them and render them useless. While minimizing unnecessary risks, professionals do need to realize that counseling is a risky venture. Although they should be familiar with the laws that govern privileged communications and should know what they can and cannot do legally, we hope that counselors do not become so involved in legalism that they cease being sensitive to the *ethical* implications of what they do in their practice.

To assist you in considering the practical issues involved in confidentiality,

[1]Adapted from "Counselor's Duty: Emotionally Disturbed or Potentially Violent Students" and "Procedures for Handling Potentially Violent Counselees." Used by permission of California State University, Fullerton.

we'll present two case studies, one involving drug use and the other involving a suicide threat. We'll describe the actions of the counselor in each case and ask you to evaluate the counselor's handling of the situation.

An adolescent who uses drugs. Larry was 14 years old when he was sent to a family-guidance clinic by his parents. He was seen by a counselor who had nine years of counseling experience. At the first session, the counselor saw Larry and his parents together. She told the parents in Larry's presence that what she and Larry discussed would be confidential and that she would not feel free to disclose information acquired through the sessions without Larry's permission. The parents seemed to understand that confidentiality was necessary in order for trust to develop between their son and his counselor.

Larry was reluctant at first to come in for counseling, but eventually he began to open up. As the sessions went on, he told the counselor that he was "heavily into drugs." Larry's parents knew that he had been using drugs at one time, but he had told them that he no longer used drugs. The counselor listened to anecdote after anecdote about Larry's experimentation with dangerous drugs, about how he "got loaded" at school every day, and about a few brushes with death when he was under the influence of drugs. Finally, she told the client that she did not want the responsibility of knowing he was experimenting with dangerous drugs and that she would not agree to continue the counseling relationship unless he stopped using them. At this stage, she agreed not to inform his parents, on condition that he quit using drugs, but she did tell him that she would be talking with one of her colleagues about the situation.

Larry apparently stopped using drugs for several weeks. However, one night while he was under the influence of LSD, he tried to fly by jumping off a building. He broke his back and became paralyzed for life. Larry's parents angrily asserted that they should have been informed that he was unstable to the point of committing such an act, and they filed suit against both the counselor and the agency.

1. What is your general impression of the way Larry's counselor handled the case?

   _____

   _____

   _____

   _____

2. Do you think the counselor acted in a responsible way toward (a) herself? (b) the client? (c) the parents? (d) the agency?

   _____

   _____

   _____

   _____

3. Suppose you had been Larry's counselor and had been convinced that he was likely to hurt himself or others because of his drug use and his

emotionally unstable condition. Would you have informed his parents, even though doing so would probably have ended your counseling relationship with him? Why or why not?

_____

_____

_____

4. Which of the following courses of action might you have taken if you had been Larry's counselor? Check as many as you think are appropriate.

___ Consulted with the director of the agency.
___ Referred Larry for psychological testing to determine the degree of his emotional disturbance.
___ Referred Larry to a psychiatrist for treatment.
___ Continued to see Larry without any stipulations.
___ Insisted upon a session with Larry's parents as a condition of continuing counseling.
___ Informed the police or other authorities.
___ Requested supervision and consultation from the agency.

5. List other specific courses of action you might have pursued:

_____

_____

_____

_____

A client who threatens suicide. Emmanuel was a middle-aged man who complained of emptiness in life, loneliness, depression, and a lack of will to live any longer. He was in individual therapy for seven months with a clinical psychologist in private practice. Using psychodiagnostic procedures, both objective tests and projective techniques, she determined that Emmanuel had serious depressive tendencies and was potentially self-destructive. Emmanuel had come to her for therapy as a final attempt to find some meaning that would show him that his life had significance. In their sessions he explored in depth the history of his failures, the isolation he felt, the meaninglessness of his life, and his bouts with feelings of worthlessness and depression. With her encouragement, he experimented with new ways of behaving in the hope that he could find reasons to go on living. Finally, after seven months of searching, he decided that he wanted to take his own life. He told his therapist that he was convinced he had been deluding himself in thinking that anything in his life would change for the better and that he felt good about finally summoning the courage to end his life. He informed her that he would not be seeing her again.

The therapist expressed her concern that Emmanuel was very capable of taking his life at this time because so far he had not been able to see any light at the end of the tunnel. She acknowledged that the decision to commit suicide was not a sudden one, for they had discussed this wish for several sessions, but she let him know that she wanted him to give therapy more of a chance. Emmanuel replied that he was truly grateful to her for helping him to find his answer within himself and that at least he could end his life with dignity in his own eyes. He stated firmly that he didn't want her to attempt to obstruct his plans in any way. She asked that he postpone his decision for at least a week and return to discuss the matter more fully. Emmanuel told her he wasn't certain whether he would keep this appointment, but he agreed to consider it.

The therapist did nothing further. During the following week she read in the newspaper that Emmanuel had committed suicide by taking an overdose of sleeping pills.

1. What do you think of the way the therapist dealt with her client?

    _____

    _____

    _____

2. What is your view of suicide?

    _____

    _____

    _____

3. What might you have done differently if you had been Emmanuel's therapist?

    _____

    _____

    _____

4. How do you think that your viewpoint regarding suicide influenced your answer to the preceding question?

    _____

    _____

    _____

5. Which of the following courses of action might you have pursued if you had been Emmanuel's counselor?

    ____ Committed Emmanuel to a state hospital for observation, even against his will, for a period of 48 hours.
    ____ Consulted with another professional as soon as I determined that he was acutely depressed or as soon as he began to discuss suicide as an option.
    ____ If suicide was his choice after seven months of therapy, I would have respected that choice, even if I didn't agree with it.
    ____ Informed the police and reported the seriousness of his threat.

____ Informed members of his family of his intentions, even though he didn't want me to.

____ Bargained with him in every way possible in an effort to persuade him to keep on trying to find some meaning in life.

6. List any other steps you might have taken in this case:

_____

_____

_____

_____

Open-Ended Situations Involving Confidentiality

The following are some brief cases that deal with ethical and legal aspects of confidentiality. What do you think you would do in each of these situations?

You're seeing a married couple together and also individually. The wife has told you about a current love affair that she has kept from her husband. In your sessions with the husband, you frequently feel that he is trying to get you to reveal what his wife tells you. He seeks continual reassurance that she loves him and won't leave him. Which of the following courses of action might you take?

____ Tell the husband about the wife's affair.

____ Firmly tell the husband that it would be unethical to reveal anything his wife says in her sessions.

____ Confront the husband during a joint session with his attempt to get you to reveal information.

____ Encourage the wife to tell her husband about her affair.

Other:

_____

_____

_____

_____

You're working with a young man, Kevin, whom you think is potentially violent. During his sessions with you, Kevin talks about his impulses to hurt others and himself, and he describes times when he has seriously beaten his girlfriend. He tells you that she is afraid to leave him because she thinks he'll beat her even more savagely. He later tells you that sometimes he gets so angry that he comes very close to killing her. You believe that he is very likely to seriously harm and possibly even kill the girl. Which of the following might you do?

____ Notify Kevin's girlfriend that she may be in grave danger.

____ Notify the police or other authorities.

_____ Keep Kevin's threats to myself because I couldn't be sure that he would act on them.
_____ Seek a second opinion from a colleague.
_____ Inform my director or supervisor.
_____ Refer Kevin to another therapist.
_____ Arrange to have Kevin hospitalized.

Other:

_____

_____

_____

_____

You're counseling a client, Tony, who is on probation. Tony knows that his probation officer contacts you regularly to learn of his progress. In the course of your counseling sessions, he reveals to you that he has stolen some very expensive lab equipment from the chemistry department of the community college that he attends. He tells you that the only reason he has revealed the theft to you is that he feels he can trust you not to tell anyone else. Although Tony has no intention of returning the equipment, he assures you that he won't steal again in the future. What would you do in this situation?

_____ Persuade Tony to find a way of returning the equipment without disclosing his identity.
_____ Report the matter to the campus police after informing Tony of my intended action.
_____ Consult several colleagues or a supervisor and ask what action they would take.
_____ Let Tony know that I would tell the chemistry department about his action.
_____ Let Tony's probation officer know what I had found out.
_____ Continue counseling Tony only if he reported the theft to his probation officer.

Other:

_____

_____

_____

_____

You're a student counselor. For your internship you're working with college students on campus. Your intern group meets with a supervisor each week to discuss your cases. One day, while you're having lunch in the campus cafeteria with three other interns, they begin to discuss their cases in detail, even mentioning names of clients. They joke about some of the clients they're seeing, while nearby are other students who may be able to overhear this conversation. What would you do if you were in this situation?

____ Tell the other interns to stop talking about their clients where other students could overhear them, and tell them that I think they're behaving unprofessionally.

____ Bring the matter up in our next practicum meeting with the supervisor.

____ I wouldn't do anything, since the students who could overhear the conversation would most likely not be that interested in what was being said.

____ I wouldn't do anything, because it's natural to discuss cases and make jokes to relieve one's own tensions.

____ Encourage them to stop talking and to continue their discussion in a private place.

Other:

_____

_____

_____

_____

You're leading a counseling group on a high school campus. The members have voluntarily joined the group. In one of the sessions, several of the students discuss the drug traffic on their campus, and two of them reveal that they sell marijuana and various pills to their friends. You discuss this matter with them, and they claim that there is nothing wrong about using these drugs. They argue that most of the students on campus use drugs, that no one has been harmed, and that there isn't any difference between using drugs (which they know is illegal) and relying on alcohol (which many of them see their parents doing). What would you do in this situation?

____ Since their actions are illegal, I'd report them to the police.

____ I'd do nothing, because their drug use doesn't seem to be a problem for them and I wouldn't want to jeopardize their trust in me.

____ Report the *condition* to the school authorities, while keeping the identities of the students confidential.

____ Let the students know that I would inform the school authorities of their actions and their names.

____ I wouldn't take the matter seriously, because the laws relating to drugs are unfair.

____ Explore with the students their reasons for making this disclosure.

Other:

_____

_____

_____

_____

You're counseling children in an elementary school. Barbara was referred to you by her teacher because she was becoming increasingly withdrawn. After several sessions Barbara tells you that she is afraid that her father might kill her and that he frequently beats her as a punishment. Until now she has lied about obvious bruises on her body, claiming that she fell off her bicycle and hurt herself. She shows you welts on her arms and back but tells you not to say anything to anyone because her father threatened a worse beating if she told anyone. What would you do in this situation?

_____ Respect Barbara's wishes and not tell anyone what I knew.

_____ Report the situation to the principal and the school nurse.

_____ Immediately go home with Barbara and talk to her parents.

_____ Take Barbara home with me for a time.

_____ Report the matter to the police.

_____ Ask Barbara why she was telling me about the beatings if she didn't want me to reveal them to anyone else.

_____ Tell Barbara that I had a legal obligation to make this situation known to the authorities but that I would work with her and not leave her alone in her fears.

Other:

_____

_____

_____

_____

CHAPTER SUMMARY

This chapter has focused on the therapist's ethical responsibilities, particularly with respect to client welfare, referrals, competence, and confidentiality. One of the most important ethical responsibilities of therapists is to safeguard the confidential nature of the therapeutic relationship. However, therapists also have responsibilities to their agencies, to the profession, to the community, to the members of their clients' families, and to themselves.

Ethical dilemmas arise when there are conflicts of responsibilities—for instance, when the agency's expectations conflict with the concerns or wishes of clients, or when the obligation of confidentiality conflicts with the rights of others to be protected from harm. Members of the helping professions need to know and observe the ethical codes of their professional organizations and the standards of ethics that have been generally agreed upon by members of the profession. However, many times they are called upon to exercise judgment by applying and interpreting these guidelines to specific instances. In this chapter we've encouraged you to think about specific ethical issues and to develop a sense of professional ethics so that your judgment will be based on more than what "feels right."

ACTIVITIES, EXERCISES, AND IDEAS FOR THOUGHT AND DISCUSSION

1. Invite several practicing counselors to talk to your class on the topic of ethical issues they encounter in their work. You might have a panel of practitioners who work in several different settings and with different kinds of clients. For

example, you could invite a therapist in private practice, a counselor who works in a college counseling center, and a counselor who works in a community mental-health center.

2. Choose one or more of the open-ended cases presented in the chapter to role-play with a fellow student. One of you can choose a client you feel you can identify with, and the other can become the counselor. Conduct a counseling interview. Afterwards, talk about how each of you felt during the interview, and discuss alternative courses of action that could have been taken. If time permits, you can reverse roles; this will give you a chance to experience both sides of the encounter and to see a different way of dealing with the same situation.

3. In small groups, explore the topic of when and how you might make a referral. If there is time, role-play a referral, with one student playing the client and another the counselor. After a few minutes, the "client" and the other students can give the counselor feedback on how he or she handled the situation. As a variation, one student can play the role of a client who simply does not want to accept a referral. Each person in the group can have a few minutes to work with the client. When everyone has had a chance to work with the client, the client can talk about how he or she felt with each person. This role-play can lead into a discussion about ways of making referrals without alienating a client.

4. In small groups, explore what you think the criteria should be for determining whether or not a therapist is competent. Make up a list of specific criteria, and share it with the rest of the class. Are you able as a class to come up with some common criteria for determining when a therapist is competent?

5. In small groups, discuss specific circumstances in which you would break confidentiality, and see whether you can agree on some general guidelines concerning this issue. When your class convenes for a general meeting, the results of all the small groups can be shared and discussed.

Ethical Issues II: The Client/Therapist Relationship

7

For each statement, indicate the response that most closely identifies your beliefs and attitudes. Use the following code: A = I strongly agree; B = I slightly agree; C = I slightly disagree; D = I strongly disagree.

_____ 1. Unethical behavior is best defined as anything that is in violation of a professional code of ethics.

_____ 2. Unethical behavior is anything that results in harm to the client.

_____ 3. Clients should be made aware of their rights at the outset of a diagnostic or therapeutic relationship.

_____ 4. Involuntary commitment is *not* a violation of the human rights of people when they are unable to be responsible for themselves or their actions.

_____ 5. Mental patients in institutions should be consulted with respect to the type of treatment they might receive.

_____ 6. Dependence on the part of the client should be avoided, since it is generally counterproductive in therapy.

_____ 7. There are ethical problems involved in treating only one member of a couple in sex therapy.

_____ 8. It is ethical and often wise to use a sex surrogate for a client who doesn't have a partner, provided that the surrogate is not the sex therapist of the client.

_____ 9. Touching, whether erotic or not, is best avoided in counseling, because it can easily be misunderstood by the client.

_____ 10. Although it may be unwise to form social relationships with clients during the time they are in counseling, there are no ethical or professional limits concerning social relationships with clients *after* the termination of counseling.

INTRODUCTION

In this chapter we discuss unethical practice relating to the client/therapist relationship. In this context we raise specific issues about the rights of clients and explore several examples of unethical or questionable practice. Although some of these issues and cases may seem clear-cut to you, in the sense that you might judge certain behavior to be clearly unethical, others may not be so clear-cut. In these cases it becomes a personal challenge to make an honest appraisal of your behavior and its impact on clients. To us, unethical behavior is behavior that reflects a lack of awareness or concern about the impact of the behavior on clients. For some counselors, it may take the form of placing their personal needs above the needs of their clients, at the expense of their clients' welfare. Since this abuse of clients is often done in a subtle way, you might think about specific ways of recognizing when and how you might be meeting your needs at the expense of your clients. We hope you will develop your own guidelines for determining when you're exploiting your clients.

Consider the following list of behaviors, and ask yourself whether you think these practices are ethical, clearly unethical, or merely unwise. Use the following code: A = ethical; B = unethical; C = unwise.

_____ 1. tape-recording a counseling session without the client's knowledge or consent

_____ 2. discussing the details revealed to you by a 15-year old girl with her parents, without the girl's permission

_____ 3. reporting one of your clients to the authorities after you find out that he is peddling drugs on campus

_____ 4. developing a social relationship with a client

_____ 5. kissing and embracing a client

_____ 6. having sexual intercourse with a client

_____ 7. having sexual intercourse with a former client

_____ 8. consistently putting the focus on yourself in a session by talking about your present or past problems

_____ 9. encouraging your client to come more frequently to sessions mainly because you need money

_____ 10. not referring a client, even when you doubt whether you can be useful to the person, because you don't want to admit that you can't work with everyone

_____ 11. deceiving a client, under the guise of being helpful

_____ 12. accepting close friends or relatives as clients

_____ 13. imposing your values on clients by subtly steering them toward goals you think are worthwhile

Now decide which of these behaviors you consider to be the most serious breaches of professional ethics. What are your reasons for considering them unethical? Are there any conditions under which you think they might be ethical?

_____

_____

_____

_____

_____

_____

THE RIGHTS OF CLIENTS

Part of ethical practice is talking with clients about their rights. Depending on the setting and the situation, this discussion can involve such questions as the possibility of involuntary hospitalization, the possibility of being forced to submit to certain types of medical and psychological treatment, matters of privacy and confidentiality, the possible outcomes and limitations of therapy, the circumstances that may affect the client's decision to enter the therapeutic relationship, and the responsibilities of the therapist toward the client.

Frequently, clients don't realize that they have any rights. Because they are vulnerable and sometimes desperate for help, they may unquestioningly accept whatever their therapists say or do. They may put up with therapists who are consistently late, or who frequently cancel appointments, or who keep the therapy process mysterious by not discussing what is going on. A client who feels dissatisfied with a particular therapist may not think of asking about the possibility of seeing another therapist in the same center. We contend that therapists have an obligation to discuss clients' rights with them. What are some specific rights that you would want to talk about with your clients?

_____

_____

_____

_____

One right of prospective clients is to be informed of important aspects of the potential relationship that might affect their decision to undertake therapy. Let's consider some of the factors that may have an impact on the client's experience of counseling.

1. *An agency policy of limiting the number of sessions.* If the counselor's agency has such a policy, clients need to be clear at the outset that they cannot receive long-term psychotherapy; they should not be informed at the sixth session that they cannot return.

2. *Tape-recording or videotaping of sessions.* Many agencies require recording of interviews for training or supervision purposes. Clients have a right to be informed about this procedure at the initial session, and it is important that they understand why the recordings are made, how they will be used, and who will have access to them. Often therapists make recordings because they can benefit from listening to them or perhaps having colleagues listen to their interactions with clients and give

them feedback. Again, if this is to be done, clients should be informed and their consent obtained. Frequently, clients are very willing to give their consent if they are approached in an honest way. Clients, too, may want to listen to a taped session during the week to help them remember what went on or to evaluate what is happening in their sessions.

3. *Counseling by someone other than the person doing the intake.* If clients will be seen by someone other than the person doing the intake, this needs to be clearly stated.

4. *Counseling by interns, paraprofessionals, and the like.* In many agencies and counseling centers, peer counselors, paraprofessionals, and student interns render personal counseling. Clients have a right to know who their counselors are.

5. *Consultation with colleagues.* Student counselors generally meet regularly with their supervisors and fellow students to discuss their progress and any problems they encounter in their work. It is good policy for counselors to inform their clients that they are meeting with others and may be talking with them about some of the sessions. Clients can be assured that their identities will not necessarily be disclosed, and they can be informed of the reasons for these meetings with supervisors and others. Even though it is ethical for counselors to discuss their cases with other counselors, it's wise to routinely let clients know about this possibility. Clients will then have less reason to feel that the trust they are putting in their counselors is being violated. Counselors can explain that these discussions may well focus on what *they* are doing and feeling as counselors, rather than on their clients as "cases."

6. *The limits of confidentiality.* Any limitations on the confidentiality of the counseling relationship should be explained to clients at the outset of counseling. These limitations may be greater in some settings and agencies than in others. If clients are informed about the conditions under which confidentiality may be broken, they are in a better position to decide whether to enter counseling; if they're required to "get counseling," they can decide what personal material they will or will not disclose in their sessions.

7. *Personal relationships.* Before therapists accept supervisees, students, employees, colleagues, close friends, or relatives as clients, it's essential that they discuss with their prospective clients the problems that may be associated with a dual relationship. Both the therapist and the prospective client should assess the merits and demerits of the relationship to determine whether it would be wise to attempt it.

8. *The therapeutic process.* Although it may be difficult to give clients a detailed description of what occurs in therapy, some general ideas can be explored. We support the practice of letting clients know that counseling might open up levels of awareness that could cause pain and anxiety. Clients who want ongoing counseling need to know that they may experience changes that could produce disruptions and turmoil in their lives. Some clients may choose to settle for a limited knowledge of themselves rather than risk this kind of disruption. We believe that a frank discussion of the chances for change and its personal and financial costs is an appropriate way to spend some of the initial sessions.

At this point we ask you to think of additional issues that you would want to discuss with your clients during the first few sessions. What factors might influence the relationship between you and your client?

_____

_____

_____

_____

_____

INVOLUNTARY COMMITMENT AND HUMAN RIGHTS

The practice of involuntary commitment of people to mental institutions raises difficult professional, ethical, and legal issues. Jorgensen and Lyons (1972) indicate that 250,000 people are committed to mental institutions in the United States each year. They contend that the rights of people convicted of crimes are generally better protected than are the rights of people who undergo civil commitment to mental hospitals. They argue that "the person facing involuntary commitment is entitled to all the due process protections available for defendants in criminal trials" (p. 149).

In discussing the moral, legal, and ethical aspects of the civil rights of mental patients, Tolchin, Steinfeld, and Suchotliff (1970) claim that the laws protecting the rights of the mentally ill have lagged behind those that protect criminals. They further allege that psychologists have remained silent while the moral and legal rights of mental patients have been consistently violated. This silence, they argue, is both irresponsible and unethical. Their summary of some of the abuses of the human rights of those who are involuntarily hospitalized includes the following:

1. Patients may be held involuntarily and given no choice with respect to treatment or incarceration.
2. Patients are deprived of their freedom and autonomy within the institution on the grounds that the psychiatrist knows what is best for them or under the guise of helping them or protecting them from themselves and others.
3. Generally, mental patients are the last persons to be consulted about the treatment they receive. They may not be informed of the nature of their treatment program or given the option of refusing treatment once a treatment plan has been formulated.
4. Patients are rarely given the results of psychological tests.
5. Patients may not be told the name or quantity of medication they receive.

Imagine yourself in the following situation. You're employed as a counselor at a state mental hospital. The ward on which you work is overcrowded, and there aren't nearly enough professionals on the staff to provide for much more than custodial services. You observe patients who seem to be psychologically deteriorating, and the unattractive surroundings reinforce the attitude of hopelessness that is so prevalent among the patients. You become aware that the rights of patients are often ignored, and you see many of the hospital's practices as destructive. For instance, when patients are given medication, there is rarely an ongoing evaluation of the effects of the drug treatment and whether it should be continued. Moreover, you recognize that some of the people who have been hospitalized against their wills really don't belong there, yet institutional procedures and policies make it very difficult for them to be released or placed in a more appropriate agency. Finally, although some members of the staff are both competent and dedicated, others who hold positions of power are incompetent.

What do you think you might do if you were involved in this situation? What do you see as your responsibility, and what actions might you take? Check as many of the following statements as you think appropriate:

_____ Since I couldn't change the people in power, I'd merely do what I could to treat the patients with care and dignity.

_____ I'd bring the matter to public attention by writing to newspapers and talking with television newspeople.

_____ I'd attempt to rectify the situation by talking to the top administrators and telling them what I had observed.

_____ I'd form a support group of my peers and see what we could do collectively.

_____ I'd keep my views to myself because the problem is too vast and complex for me to do anything about it.

_____ I'd encourage the patients to revolt and demand their rights.

_____ I'd directly confront the people I thought were incompetent or who were violating the rights of patients and attempt to change them.

Other:

_____

_____

_____

_____

_____

HANDLING CLIENT DEPENDENCE AS AN ETHICAL ISSUE

Clients frequently experience a period of dependence on therapy or on their therapists. This temporary dependence isn't necessarily a bad thing. Some clients are people who have exaggerated the importance of being independent. They see the need to consult a professional as a sign of weakness. When these people do allow themselves to need others, their dependence doesn't necessarily present an ethical issue.

An ethical issue does arise, however, when counselors *encourage* dependence on the part of their clients. They may do so for any number of reasons. Counselor interns need clients, and sometimes they may keep clients coming to counseling longer than is necessary because they will look bad if they "lose" a client. Some therapists in private practice might fail to challenge clients who show up and pay regularly, even though they appear to be getting nowhere. Some therapists foster dependence in their clients in subtle ways out of a need to feel important. When clients play a helpless role and ask for answers, these counselors may readily tell them what to do. Dependent clients can begin to view their therapists as all-knowing and all-wise; therapists who have a need to be perceived in this way might act in ways that will keep their clients immature and dependent, thus feeding off the dependency needs of clients in order to gain a sense of significance.

Like many of the other ethical issues discussed in this chapter, the issue of encouraging dependence in clients is often not a clear-cut one in practice. Since our main purpose here is to stimulate you to think of possible ways that you might foster dependence or independence in your clients, we'll present a couple of illustrative cases and ask you to respond to them.

Marcia is single and almost ready to graduate from college. Marcia tells you that she has ambivalent feelings about graduating, because she feels that now she's expected to get a job and live on her own. This prospect frightens her, and she doesn't want to leave the security she has found as a college student. As she puts it, she doubts that she can "make it in the real world." Marcia doesn't trust her own decisions, because when she does make choices the result, in her eyes, is disastrous. Her style is to plead with you to advise her whether or not she should date, apply for a job, leave home, go on to graduate school, and so forth. Typically, Marcia gets angry with you because you aren't being directive enough. She feels that you have more knowledge than she does and should therefore give her more guidance. She says "Why am I coming here if you won't tell me what to do to straighten out my life? If I could make decent decisions on my own, I wouldn't need to come here in the first place!"

1. How do you imagine you'd feel if Marcia were your client?

   _____

   _____

2. How might you respond to her continual prodding for answers?

   _____

   _____

3. How do you imagine you'd feel about Marcia's statement that you aren't doing your job and that you aren't being directive enough?

   _____

   _____

4. What steps would you take to challenge Marcia?

   _____

   _____

   _____

5. In what ways do you think it would be possible for you to tie into her dependency needs and foster her dependence upon you for direction, instead of freeing her from you?

   _____

   _____

   _____

6. How would you deal with Marcia if you eventually believed that you should terminate the relationship, and she didn't feel ready to leave?

_____

_____

_____

Ron, a young counselor, encourages his clients to call him at home at any time and as often as they feel like it. He frequently lets sessions run overtime, lends money to clients when they're "down and out," devotes many more hours to his job than he is expected to, and overtaxes himself by taking on an unrealistically large case load. Ron says that he lives for his work and that it gives him a sense of being a valuable person. The more he can do for people, the better he feels.

1. In what ways could Ron's style keep his clients dependent on him?

_____

_____

_____

2. What could Ron be getting from being so "helpful"? What do you imagine Ron's life would be like if there were no clients who needed him?

_____

_____

_____

3. If you were Ron's colleague and he came to you to talk about how "burnt out" he felt because he was "giving so much," what would you say to him?

_____

_____

_____

4. Can you identify with Ron in any ways? Do you see yourself as potentially needing your clients more than they need you?

_____

_____

_____

MANIPULATION AS UNETHICAL BEHAVIOR

If psychotherapy is basically a process that teaches people how to be honest with themselves, then it is of the utmost importance for therapists to be honest with their clients. Unfortunately, there are many ways for therapists to deceive or manipulate clients, often under the guise of being helpful and concerned. Therapists who have plans for what they want their clients to do or to be and who keep these plans hidden are examples of manipulative therapists. Other therapists may attempt to control their relationships with their clients by keeping therapy a mysterious process and maintaining a rigid "professional stance" that excludes the client as a partner in the relationship. Therapy thus becomes a matter of the therapist *doing* therapy on an unquestioning client.

To offset the danger of manipulating clients toward ends they have not chosen, some therapeutic approaches emphasize strategies designed to ensure that clients will have an active role in deciding what happens to them in the therapeutic relationship. As we saw in Chapter 4, many therapists use a contract as a basic prerequisite for continuing therapy. The contract contains a specific statement of goals and criteria for evaluating when these goals are effectively met. The nature of the therapeutic relationship is thus defined by the contract, which is agreed upon by both the client and the therapist. Its proponents claim that this procedure emphasizes the partnership of client and therapist, demystifies the therapeutic process, and minimizes the chance that clients will be manipulated toward ends that well-intentioned therapists have for them.

Sidney Jourard contrasts manipulation with dialogue in counseling. He sees psychotherapy as "an invitation to authenticity" in which the therapist's role is to be an exemplar. Therapists can foster their clients' honesty and invite them to drop their pretenses only by dropping their own and meeting their clients in an honest manner. Jourard (1968) says "I believe that the psychotherapist is the teacher in the therapeutic dance, and the patient follows the leader" (pp. 64–65). One of the best ways for therapists to demonstrate their goodwill is by avoiding manipulation and being open, trusting, and thus vulnerable to their clients. If counselors manipulate their clients, they can expect manipulation in return; if they are open, however, their clients may be open as well. Jourard (1968) expresses this concept descriptively as follows:

> If I want him to be maximally open, but I keep myself fully closed off, peeking at him through chinks in my own armor, trying to manipulate him from a distance, then in due time he will discover that I am not in that same mode; and he will then put his armor back on and peer at me through chinks in it, and he will try to manipulate me" [p. 64].

THE ISSUE OF SOCIAL AND PERSONAL RELATIONSHIPS WITH CLIENTS

Do social relationships with clients necessarily interfere with therapeutic relationships? Some would say no—that counselors and clients are able to handle a social relationship in conjunction with a therapeutic one, so long as it is clear where the priorities lie. They see this as being particularly true with clients who aren't deeply disturbed and who are seeking personal growth. Some peer counselors, for example, claim that the friendships they have had with people prior to or during counseling were actually positive factors in establishing trust and good, productive therapeutic relationships.

Other counselors take the position that counseling and friendship should not be mixed. They argue that attempting to manage a social and professional relationship simultaneously can negatively affect the therapy process, the friendship, or both. Some of the reasons they offer for discouraging the practice of accepting friends as clients or becoming socially involved with clients include: (1) counselors might not be as confrontive with clients they know socially; (2) counselors' own need to be liked and accepted may lead them to be less challenging, lest the friendship or social relationship be jeopardized; (3) counselors' own needs may interlock with those of their clients to the point that objectivity is lost; (4) by the very nature of the counseling relationship, counselors are in a more powerful position than clients, and the danger of exploiting clients becomes more likely when the relationship becomes other than a professional one.

The American Psychological Association (1977a) says the following about "dual relationships" with clients:

> Psychologists are continually cognizant of their own needs and of their inherently powerful position *vis à vis* clients, in order to avoid exploiting their trust and dependency. Psychologists make every effort to avoid dual relationships with clients and/or relationships which might impair their professional judgment or increase the risk of client exploitation [p. 23].

Burton (1972) raises the question "Is it possible to meet clients socially and still carry interpersonal psychotherapy forward to completion?" Burton acknowledges the fact that some therapists have become life-long friends with, or even married, former clients. In general, however, he contends that therapists should avoid social relationships with clients on the grounds that therapy does not usually leave the participants free to be friends.

Obviously, this is not a closed issue that can be resolved with a dogmatic answer. Counselors need to be aware of their own motivations, as well as the motivations of their prospective clients, and they must honestly assess the impact a social relationship might have on the client/therapist relationship. This issue can take several forms. To illustrate, we'll ask you to respond to a specific case.

You are an intern in a college counseling center, and one of your clients says to you "I really like working with you, but I hate coming over here to this cold and impersonal office. I always feel weird waiting in the lobby as if I were a 'case' or something. Why can't we meet outside on the lawn? Better yet, we could get away from campus and meet in the park nearby. I'd feel more natural and uninhibited in a more informal setting."

1. Would you agree to meet your client outside of the office? Why or why not?

   _____

   _____

   _____

2. Would your decision depend on how much you liked or were attracted to your client? Would your client's age and sex have much to do with your decision?

   _____

   _____

   _____

Later, your client invites you to a party that he or she is having and lets you know that it would mean a lot if you were to come. Your client says "I'd really like to get to know you on a personal basis, because I'm being so deeply personal in here. I really like you, and I'd like more time with you than the hour we have each week."

1. What are your immediate reactions? Assuming that you like your client and would like to go to the party, do you think it would be wise to attend? What would your decision be, and what would you say to your client?

_____

_____

_____

_____

2. What effect do you think meeting your client on a social basis would have on the therapeutic process?

_____

_____

_____

Each of the three of us has wrestled with the issue of social relationships with clients for a long time. We work as a team doing week-long, residential growth groups several times a year. Our clients are college students, and the setting and the way we work are informal, although intense. We often develop personal feelings toward some of the people we work with and continue to have some contact with them outside of the group. For instance, we often meet them on the campus, and we've been invited to social functions group members have held. One problem that each of us has had to face is the impossibility of maintaining ties with as many people as attend our workshops. We have at times felt burdened with the feeling that we should see some of these people more often and that we have to make time for keeping these relationships going. We're learning that we can have intense, meaningful encounters with people for a week and that the value of this contact is not diminished if we don't see them regularly after the workshop ends.

THE ISSUE OF EROTIC AND SEXUAL CONTACT WITH CLIENTS

The issue of sexual relations with clients is a very controversial one that is frequently the subject of symposia or panels at professional conventions. Holroyd and Brodsky (1977) reported the results of a nationwide survey of 500 male and 500 female licensed psychologists, all Ph.D.s, which was conducted to assess their attitudes and practices with respect to erotic and nonerotic contact with clients. Holroyd and Brodsky reported a 70% return rate. Some of their findings included the following:

1. Erotic contact and intercourse are almost always between male therapists and female clients.

2. Therapists who crossed the sexual boundary once were likely to repeat this practice. Of those therapists who reported intercourse with patients, 80% repeated it.

3. Of the male therapists, 5.5% reported having had sexual intercourse with clients; for female therapists the figure was .6%.

4. On the issue of *nonerotic* contact with clients, approximately half of the therapists thought hugging, kissing, or affectionate touching might be beneficial on occasion.

5. On the issue of *erotic* contact, only 4% of the respondents thought that such contact might be beneficial. Seventy percent of male therapists and 88% of female therapists took the position that erotic contact is *never* beneficial to clients.

Most of the psychologists responding strongly disapproved of erotic contact in therapy and stated that it should never occur in a professional relationship. They took the position that such contact is totally inappropriate and is an exploitation of the relationship by the therapist. Erotic contact with clients was thus viewed as unprofessional, unethical, and antitherapeutic. One therapist made the comment "I feel without qualification that erotic patient-therapist contact is unethical at best and devastating at worst—it reflects pathological needs on the part of the therapist" (Holroyd & Brodsky, 1977, p. 848).

Professional opinion on this issue is not unanimous, however. Some therapists argue that erotic contact can help their clients feel validated as sexual persons, learn to free themselves of inhibitions and guilt feelings that keep them from enjoying their sexuality, and talk about other sexually taboo areas. Those who make this argument are generally male therapists who are speaking of the values of erotic contact for female clients. Such therapists might be asked "Would you be quite so willing to be helpful if your client were unattractive to you?" In writing on this issue, Lowry and Lowry (1975) make this comment: "If a therapist finds that attractive patients need his 'reassurance' more, he should question his motives to make sure that he provides sexual services to the elderly, ugly, to the crippled, to the incontinent, to the same sex, and to all races, creeds, and religions. We are not aware of a direct intervention sex therapist who meets these criteria" (p. 233).

Even though having sexual intercourse with clients may appear to be an example of clearly unethical behavior, most codes of ethics, at least until recently, have not explicitly prohibited therapists from having sex with their clients. However, Koch and Koch (1976) note that the American Psychiatric Association ethical standards specifically state that a therapist is not to have sex with a client, even though the client may initiate or encourage such activities; and the 1977 American Psychological Association's Ethical Standards state: *"Sexual intimacies with clients are unethical"* (p. 23). Also, the January, 1978 *Newsletter* of the California Association of Marriage and Family Counselors reported that the Ethical Standards/Peer Review Committee adopted the following ethical standard: "It is considered unethical to have sexual relations with one's clients and/or clients' spouse-partner. In a clinical setting for research, competent MFCC authorities in sexual therapy may observe sexual intercourse during treatment procedures for clients" (p. 2).

Those therapists who are convinced that sexual intimacy between a therapist and client is both unethical and professionally inappropriate behavior state a number of grounds. The general argument typically involves the abuse of the power that therapists have by virtue of their function and role. Clients reveal deeply personal material about their hopes, sexual desires and struggles, and intimate relationships, and in many ways they become vulnerable to their therapists. It's easy to take advantage of this trust and exploit it for personal motives. Although it may be true that some clients provoke and tease their therapists, those who consider sexual intimacies to be unethical professional behavior contend that therapists should refuse to collaborate in such sexual game playing and instead confront their clients with what is occurring. Steinzor (1967) puts the point this way:

> To use the patient for my own persistent need for physical contact and sexual embrace would be an exploitation. As a therapist I have been sought out because I promise more and mean more to her than a transient affair. The possible moments of pleasure would soon give way to embarrassment and hurt [p. 63].

Another reason given by those who oppose erotic contact in therapeutic relationships is that it fosters dependence. Clients can easily come to think of their therapists as ideal persons when they see them only in the limited context of the office. Instead of forming meaningful relationships with others, clients may begin to live for the affection and attention they receive from their therapists once a week. Further, many would argue that, when sexual activity becomes a part of therapy, the objectivity of the therapist is lost. Therapists are likely to become more concerned about the feelings their clients have toward them than about challenging their clients to take an honest look at their own lives. Corlis and Rabe (1969) take a very clear stand that, when clients become sexual partners of therapists, they cease to be clients, and their therapists cease to be therapists: "The consuming concentration of the sexual encounter obviates any considerations but those which serve that particular partnership, with its physical power, and with its own personal merging. Sex may be therapeutic, but it is not therapy" (p. 99).

A final argument against sexual involvement with clients is that often they eventually feel taken advantage of and may discount the value of any part of their therapy. They may become embittered and angry, and they may terminate therapy with psychological scars. The problem is compounded if they are closed to the idea of initiating therapy with anyone else because of the traumatic experience and thus feel stuck with their unresolved feelings.

We've heard feminist therapists report many anecdotes relating to abuses of power by male therapists and the results some female clients have experienced. Accounts such as these have prompted some feminist therapists to seriously question whether men are capable of working objectively and honestly with women. Indeed, some therapists—male and female—have cautioned women to beware of selecting male therapists. In their controversial book, *Repression or Revolution,* Glenn and Kunnes (1973) present a critical and even cynical view of the value of therapy as it is usually practiced, and they warn: "Women must be wary of male therapists. Any woman in therapy should be in a women's liberation or consciousness-raising group at the same time; perhaps she should only be in a C-R group, and not in therapy at all" (p. 84).

One of the authors of this statement openly describes how he has oppressed women and encouraged them to engage in sexual game playing during counseling sessions. He writes: "I've thus encouraged women to placate and please me with their bodies, and have gotten my jollies off them in therapy sessions when I was supposed to be helping them with their problems" (p. 85). He describes how he encouraged clients to talk about the depth of their feelings for him and in other ways manipulated them for his own ends.

At this point we ask you to reflect on the following brief case and decide how you would respond to the situation.

For several months you've been working with a client whom you find attractive and exciting. You're aware that your client has loving feelings toward you and would be willing to become sexually involved with you. Your own feelings are growing in intensity, and you often have difficulty in paying attention during sessions because of your own fantasies.

There are a number of different things you might do in this situation.

1. You could attempt to ignore your feelings for your client and your client's feelings toward you and focus on other aspects of the relationship. Do you think that you'd be able to avoid dealing with these feelings? If you did, what effect might this have on your ability to pay attention to your client?

_____

_____

_____

2. You could tell your client that your feelings of attraction are strong enough that you don't want to continue the therapeutic relationship and that you think a referral to another therapist is in order. How ethical do you think this option is? Might your client feel abandoned? If you did make the referral, would you then be willing to enter into a sexual relationship with your former client? Why or why not?

_____

_____

_____

_____

_____

3. You could openly express your feelings toward your client and acknowledge his or her feelings toward you. For example, you might say "I'm glad you find me an attractive person, and I'm strongly attracted to you as well. But I don't want to act on my sexual feelings, because I value our therapeutic relationship, and I feel pretty sure that such an involvement would get in the way of therapy. If you weren't my client, I could see myself being involved with you in this way." Can you imagine yourself saying this to a client? Why or why not? Might you also consult a colleague to discuss what you're feeling and to get feedback on your actions?

_____

_____

4. You could act on your feelings by getting sexually involved with your client, or you could terminate therapy and then begin another type of relationship. Is either of these alternatives acceptable to you? Why or why not?

We agree with those therapists who contend that it is both unwise and unethical to become sexually involved with clients. This is not to say, that counselors aren't human beings or will never have strong feelings of attraction toward certain clients. Counselors impose an unnecessary burden on themselves when they believe that they shouldn't have such feelings for clients or when they try to convince themselves that they should not have more feeling toward one client than toward another. What is important is how counselors decide to deal with these feelings as they affect the therapeutic relationship. Referral to another therapist isn't necessarily the best solution, unless it becomes clear that one can no longer be effective with a certain client. Instead, counselors may recognize a need for consultation or, at the very least, for an honest dialogue with themselves. It may also be appropriate to have a frank discussion with the client, explaining that the decision not to act on one's sexual feelings is based on a commitment to the primacy of the therapeutic relationship.

When we've discussed with students the issue of sexual involvement with clients, we've found that they almost universally see it as an unethical practice. However, we want to point out that the issue of erotic contact in therapy is not simply a matter of whether to have sexual intercourse with a client. Even if you decide intellectually that you wouldn't engage in sexual intimacies with a client, it's important to realize that the relationship between therapist and client can involve varying degrees of sexuality. Therapists may have sexual fantasies; they may behave seductively with their clients; they may influence clients to focus on romantic or sexual feelings toward them; or they may engage in physical contact that is primarily intended to arouse or satisfy their sexual desires. Although these therapists may not reach the point of having sexual intercourse with clients, their behavior is clearly sexual in nature and can have much the same effect as direct sexual involvement would have. Romantic overtones can easily distort the therapeutic relationship as the seductive play of the client and therapist becomes the real focus of the sessions. This is clearly an area in which counselors need to be able to recognize what they're doing. It's also crucial that they learn how to accept their sexual feelings and that they consciously decide how to deal with them in therapy.

THE THERAPEUTIC VALUE OF TOUCHING

Although we've contended that erotic contact with clients is unethical, we do think that nonerotic contact is often appropriate and can have significant therapeutic value. It's important to stress this point, because there is a taboo against touching clients. Sometimes therapists hold back when they feel like touching their clients affectionately or compassionately. They may feel that touching can be misinterpreted as exploitative; they may be afraid of their impulses or feelings toward clients; they may be afraid of intimacy; or they may believe that to physically express closeness is unprofessional.

In Holroyd and Brodsky's (1977) study, 27% of the therapists who responded occasionally engaged in nonerotic hugging, kissing, or affectionate touching with opposite-sex clients; 7% did so frequently or always. The percentages varied with different kinds of therapists; 25% of humanistic therapists engaged in nonerotic contact frequently or always, but less than 10% of eclectic therapists and less than 5% of psychodynamic, behavior-modification, or rational-cognitive therapists did so. Approximately half of the therapists took the position that nonerotic physical contact would be beneficial for clients at least occasionally. Most of the suggestions for appropriate nonerotic contact fell into four categories: (a) with socially or emotionally immature clients, such as those with histories of maternal deprivation; (b) with people who were experiencing acute distress, such as grief, depression, or trauma; (c) for providing general emotional support; and (d) for greeting or at termination.

Contending that the unexploitative touch is a "good discovery," Corlis and Rabe (1969) discuss touching as a potential therapeutic tool: "physical touch can open the road so often obscured by our thick growth of intellectual constructs, the road toward living with feeling again" (p. 102). We agree that touching can have therapeutic power, but we're convinced that touching should *not* be done as a technique or as something that therapists feel they're expected to do. Inauthentic physical contact is quickly detected and is likely to put distance between the client and the therapist. A client who senses that the touching isn't genuine is likely to distrust other things that the therapist says or does. Steinzor (1967) put it well when he wrote "I will never embrace a patient for a technical reason or to assure him that I am not afraid of sensual contact. The fraudulence of such a meeting will be laid bare very soon by the patient's skin and muscles as they sense the manipulative turns of my arms" (p. 63).

In summary, we think that touching should be a spontaneous and honest expression of the therapist's feelings. Again, in this area therapists need to be aware of their own motives and to be honest with themselves about the meaning of the physical contact. They also need to be sensitive to each client's readiness for physical closeness and to the impact such contact may have on the client.

ETHICAL AND PROFESSIONAL ISSUES IN SEX THERAPY

A relatively new issue in professional practice concerns the ethical and professional dimensions of sex therapy. There is some confusion regarding this issue, since clear standards have not been developed and practitioners are frequently left to exercise their own judgment.

Recent legislation in the state of California mandates training in human sexuality as a condition of licensure, both for those being licensed for the first time and for those seeking renewal of their licenses. This legislation applies to the following licensed practitioners: marriage, family, and child counselors, social workers, and psychologists. The content and length of the required training is very unclear, but the new law does illustrate the growing importance attached to sex therapy as a part of counseling and psychotherapy. In this section we briefly explore some of the central questions that need to be raised regarding ethical conduct in this specialized area of counseling.

Qualifications of Sex Therapists

One of the most basic issues that needs to be raised in this area is the question of who is qualified to do sex therapy. Ask yourself these questions:

- What personal and professional qualifications do I have that might eventually prepare me to do sex therapy?
- Is a single course in human sexuality enough course preparation to do this type of counseling?
- What preparation am I receiving in my training program to do this kind of therapy?
- What kind of practicum, specialized training, and supervision, do I think is essential if I am to become involved in sex therapy?

In many programs students are exposed to no more than a single general course in human sexuality; yet, when they begin practicing, many of their clients will bring in sexual difficulties that demand attention. At the very least, counselors who lack the knowledge and skills needed to work in depth with sexual problems can be aware of their limitations and refuse to attempt counseling they're not competent to perform, even if their licenses allow them to counsel people with sexual dysfunctions. They can recognize the importance of referring clients who are in need of this specialized treatment. To do so, they must be able to recognize when sex therapy is indicated, and they must be aware of good referral sources.

The Scope of Sex Therapy

Some people criticize the sex-therapy movement on the grounds that too much attention is paid to "fixing plumbing," and not enough to the emotional aspects of sexuality. They argue that sex therapists focus too much on symptoms and physical functioning, whereas effective treatment must include a consideration of the individual's psychodynamics, the factors that led to the problem to begin with, and the nature of the relationship between the client and his or her sexual partner.

Therapy for sexual difficulties doesn't have to be mechanistic, however, or focused only on removal of symptoms. Some sex therapists are aware of the need for a more comprehensive approach. For example, they may stress the acquisition of more effective social skills at the same time as they work on sexual dysfunctions. Also, even though they may *begin* by working with obvious symptoms, they are fully aware that in-depth and meaningful treatment must go beyond symptoms and concern itself with the total life of the client.

Conjoint Therapy as the Preferred Approach

Typically, the sex-therapy model prescribes working with both partners in a sexual relationship. The assumption is that one partner's sexual dysfunction is related in some way to the relationship with the other person. According to Kaplan (1974), the primary objective of sex therapy is to modify the couple's relationship and sexual life so that both persons are satisfied. Conjoint treatment, as opposed to separate treatment for each partner or for one partner alone, is also viewed as valuable because the shared sexual experiences of the couple become the central aspects of the treatment.

Of course, conjoint therapy depends on the willingness of both partners. What are the issues involved when one partner desires sex therapy, while the other refuses to cooperate in any type of counseling? Suppose a woman wants sex therapy and her husband refuses treatment. Would it really help to work with her alone? Would any change occur? If she did become free of her sexual dysfunction, what kinds of problems might this pose for her if her husband has not been involved in the therapy? Would you refuse treatment for her until her husband agreed to participate in the program? Would you encourage her to change, even if her husband was rigid and would fight any of her changes? Would you consider employing a sex surrogate in this case? These are just some of the difficult questions that arise when conjoint therapy is not possible.

The Use of Sex Surrogates

In some sex-therapy clinics, surrogates are used for clients who present themselves for treatment and are without partners. Kaplan (1974) indicates that a real dilemma is posed for sex therapists and clinics when these clients are told that a partner is necessary for successful treatment, especially when they say that they are too embarrassed by their problem to seek a partner. One answer to this dilemma is to use sex surrogates for working with clients without partners.

We think that there are a number of questions that need to be raised concerning the ethical and professional aspects of the use of surrogates as a standard practice. What are the motivations one might have in becoming a sex surrogate? Since it is crucial that surrogates serve the best interests of the client rather than their own needs, the issue of motivation assumes real importance. What are the standards of training for a surrogate? Who should be selected as a surrogate? Should a surrogate be used for a married person when the spouse refuses to be a part of the treatment? Finally, a question we think is extremely important is: Are the ethical and moral values of the client taken into consideration? The use of a surrogate may be contrary to the religious or moral beliefs of the client. These values need to be taken into account if the client is to be treated with respect.

Issues Related to the Therapeutic Relationship

In Chapter 3, we discussed transference and countertransference as problems that most counselors and therapists would eventually need to confront. In sex therapy these issues become even more vital. Because of the focus on the intimate details of the client's sexual behavior, feelings, and fantasies, there is a greater danger that the client will develop an erotic transference toward the therapist (Kaplan, 1974). This raises the ethical issue of therapists' encouragement of this erotic transference, which may be done seductively out of a need to be perceived as sexually attractive and desirable persons. Kaplan warns that, if therapists' clients fall in love with them with regularity, it can be inferred that the therapists' countertransference feelings are producing the situation.

Clearly, therapists' unawareness of their needs and their distorted vision because of their unresolved conflicts in regard to sex can greatly interfere with the therapy process. In order to achieve competence in the practice of sex therapy, Kaplan believes, therapists should be relatively free from their own sexual conflicts, guilt, and competitiveness, or at least be aware of how this personal material can influence the way they work with their clients in sex therapy. Therapists must be aware and responsive persons, not simply technicians:

> In sum, the therapist is not a treatment machine. His emotional responses are the indispensable instruments of superb therapy, and as such should be nurtured. On the other hand, he needs to guard against the emergence of neurotic countertransferential reactions, for these can lead to ineffective therapy or, even worse, to the destructive exploitation of his patients [Kaplan, 1974, p. 245].

CHAPTER SUMMARY

The underlying theme of this chapter has been the honesty and self-confrontation of therapists in determining the impact of their behavior on clients. Although certain behaviors are clearly unethical, most of the issues raised in this chapter are not cut-and-dried. Resolving them requires personal and professional maturity and a willingness to continue to question one's own motivations. A key question is: Whose needs are being met, the therapist's or the client's? Perhaps a sign of good faith on the part of therapists is their willingness to openly share their questions and struggles with colleagues. Such consultation may help to clear up many foggy issues or at least suggest a different perspective.

Becoming a therapist doesn't make you perfect or superhuman. You'll make some mistakes. What we want to stress is the importance of reflecting on what you're doing and on whose needs are primary. A willingness to be honest with yourself in your self-examination is your greatest asset in becoming an ethical practitioner.

We suggest that you review your responses to the open-ended questions and cases presented in the last two chapters and make a list of the ethical issues that are most significant to you at this time. Bringing these issues up for discussion with fellow students can be an excellent way of beginning to clarify them for yourself.

ACTIVITIES, EXERCISES, AND IDEAS FOR THOUGHT AND DISCUSSION

1. As a practitioner, how would you determine what was ethical and what was unethical? Think about how you would go about developing your guidelines for ethical practice, and make up a list of behaviors that you judge to be unethical. After you've thought through this issue by yourself, you might want to explore your approach with fellow students.

2. Develop a panel in your class to explore the question of what unethical behavior in counseling is and what forms it can take. Try to select the issues that have the most significance to you and that you think will lead to a thought-provoking class discussion.

3. Working in small groups in class, explore the topic of the rights clients have in counseling and therapy. One person in each group can serve as a recorder. When the groups reconvene for a general class meeting, the recorders for the various groups can share their lists of clients' rights with the rest of the class. Then the class can rate each of these rights on a scale from "extremely important" to "very unimportant." What are the rights that your class agrees are the *most* important?

4. Review the cases and situations presented in this chapter, and role-play some of them in dyads. By actually experiencing these situations, you may be able to clarify some of your thoughts. If you do the role-play in your small group, the group members can give you valuable feedback concerning how they experienced you as a client or as a counselor.

5. Interview a practicing counselor about some of the most pressing ethical concerns he or she encounters as a counselor and how he or she has dealt with these concerns.

6. What are your views about forming social relationships with clients during the time they're in counseling with you? About touching clients in nonerotic ways out of affection or for support?

7. What guidelines do you think are important for those who claim to be qualified to offer sex therapy? What are some of the major professional and ethical issues involved in sex therapy?

8. In small groups in your class, examine some of the questions we raised in this chapter concerning sex therapy. For example, you might discuss the following: (a) When does a person know that he or she is adequately trained to do sex therapy? (b) What are some of the special problems that therapists must be alert to in regard to the therapist/client relationship in sex therapy? What are the potential problems that can surface if transference and countertransference feelings are dealt with poorly? (c) What is your position on the use of sex surrogates for clients without partners? (d) How can the danger of treating only the symptoms of sexual problems be averted?

Ethical and Professional Issues Special to Group Work

8

For each statement, indicate the response that most closely identifies your beliefs and attitudes. Use the following code: A = I strongly agree; B = I slightly agree; C = I slightly disagree; D = I strongly disagree.

_____ 1. A group leader's actual behavior in a group is more important than his or her theoretical approach.

_____ 2. Ethical practice requires that prospective group members be carefully screened and selected.

_____ 3. It's important to systematically prepare group members so that they can derive the maximum benefit from the group.

_____ 4. There are times when requiring people to participate in a therapy group is an ethical practice.

_____ 5. It is unethical to allow a group to exert pressure on one of its members.

_____ 6. Confidentiality is less important in groups than it is in individual therapy.

_____ 7. Socializing among group members is almost always undesirable, since it inevitably interferes with the functioning of the group.

_____ 8. Ethical practice requires making some provision for evaluating the outcomes of a group.

_____ 9. A group leader has a responsibility to devise ways of minimizing any psychological risks associated with participation in the group.

_____ 10. People are not competent to be group leaders until they have completed a structured program of education and training approved by one of the major mental-health professions.

_____ 11. Trained group leaders should not have to follow formal guidelines for ethical practice; they should be free to practice in any way they see fit.

____ 12. Confrontation in groups is almost always destructive and generally inhibits the formation of trust and cohesion in the group.

____ 13. A group leader has a responsibility to teach group members how to translate what they've learned in the group setting to their lives outside the group.

____ 14. A group leader has a responsibility to ask potential group members who are being counseled by other therapists to consult with their therapists before joining the group.

____ 15. One way of minimizing the psychological risks of group participation is to negotiate contracts with group members.

INTRODUCTION

Most of the issues we've been exploring in this book have particular relevance for individual approaches to counseling and psychotherapy. In the remaining chapters we address ourselves to issues that go beyond individual approaches. Thus, in this chapter our focus is on ethical and professional issues special to group work. In the next chapter we look at the professional's involvement in the community and at issues related to the community mental-health movement. Finally, in the last chapter we examine ways of learning how to work within the system.

Groups seem to be increasing in popularity, and our hunch is that they will be a major approach in the future. In this chapter we discuss some of the professional and ethical problems that are unique to group work, from the selection of group members to the termination of the group experience. Our illustrations are drawn from a broad spectrum of groups, including therapy groups, encounter groups, personal-growth groups, sensitivity groups, and human-relations training groups. Obviously, these groups differ with respect to their member populations, purpose, focus, and procedures, as well as in the level of training required for their leaders. Although these distinctions among groups are important, the issues we discuss are common to most types of groups. For a more detailed description of the various kinds of groups and the differences among them, you may wish to consult *Groups: Process and Practice* (Corey & Corey, 1977).

THEORETICAL ASSUMPTIONS AND GROUP WORK

Theoretical assumptions are no less important in group work than they are in individual counseling and psychotherapy. A basic theoretical question is: Why use a group approach? Group leaders need a rationale for putting people into groups, and they need to be aware of the advantages and limitations of group counseling. Some of the questions group leaders should be able to answer are:

- When is a group approach preferred over individual counseling?
- Are groups merely more convenient, financially and practically, than individual approaches are?
- What effect does the leader's ideological approach have on the group process?
- How do the differences between the educational, growth-oriented model and the medical model of group therapy affect group goals and processes?

In regard to the last of these questions, we want to note that the model a group leader operates from has definite implications for practice. Typically, those practitioners who adhere to a personal-growth model are concerned with expanding awareness and helping participants learn skills to enhance their living, rather than with the treatment of disorders. Personal-growth models of group work are based on the assumption that people have within themselves the potential for growing as persons; recognizing blocks to personal growth is considered to be more important than merely solving problems. These models emphasize awareness, feelings, risk-taking behavior, experimentation with new behavior, here-and-now experiencing, and mutual feedback on the part of group members. The group leader's role is not to treat serious psychological disturbances but to act as a catalyst of meaningful group interaction.

In contrast, the medical-model approach to group work stresses treatment and the correction of problems. Group leaders may be less self-disclosing than those who follow a growth model, and comparatively more attention is given to understanding, conceptualizing, and becoming aware of how past history is manifested in present conflicts. Thus, there is a focus on defenses, resistances, and interpretation.

Although these basic orientations do influence the group process and the goals of a group, they are not incompatible. Many encounter-group leaders are coming to realize that the emphasis on here-and-now experiencing and open sharing of immediate feelings does have its limitations. They may therefore integrate the experiencing of intense emotions with some conceptualization. Participants can be encouraged to think about the meaning of their experiences, they can explore how their pasts are related to their present struggles, and they can work through conflicts and make new decisions. Cognitive awareness, which is so often neglected in encounter groups, can be integrated with feeling and doing to make the members' group experience more meaningful. Similarly, group therapists who are primarily concerned with treating deep personality problems can integrate many methods and techniques from the personal-growth model into their work.

Although we think it's important for group leaders to operate within a theoretical framework, we're not advocating rigid adherence to a single preexisting theory. We think it's valuable for group leaders to become familiar with a variety of theoretical models and then discover their own ways of blending concepts and techniques from several approaches. We see too many beginning group leaders who view theory as something abstract and impractical and who are excessively technique oriented. By studying various theories, group leaders may be stimulated to examine some of the following questions:

- What are the primary goals of each group, and how might they be met most effectively?
- Who should determine the group's goals? How should they be determined?
- What is the main role of the leader? How much responsibility does the leader have to structure and direct the group?
- What are the functions of the group members?
- Should the leader focus on individuals or on group interaction?
- Which techniques are most useful? Why use a particular technique? When should it be used?

We believe that, ultimately, a group leader's theory cannot be divorced from himself or herself as a person. The most meaningful theoretical perspective is one that is an extension of the leader's values and personality. However, it's unrealistic to expect that beginning group counselors will have developed and integrated well-defined personal theories to guide them in their practice. Rather, the development of a theoretical perspective is an ongoing task in which one's model undergoes continual revision. With new experience, new issues and questions are raised. Experiments can be tried to test out hunches, and ways of modifying old practices to fit new knowledge can be developed. Our main point is that group leaders need to constantly question how they practice and be open to changes in their theories and styles.

Yalom (1975) contends that, although the behavior of group leaders is not predictable from their particular ideological schools, their behaviors and leadership styles seem to be the critical variables in determining the effectiveness of a group. Yalom cites research demonstrating that four leadership functions have a direct relationship to the outcomes of group work. First, *caring* is essential; the greater the amount of caring, the greater the chance of positive outcomes. Second, *meaning attribution* (explaining, clarifying, providing a cognitive framework for change) is also directly related to positive outcome. Third, *emotional stimulation* (challenging, risk-taking, self-disclosure, activity) is important to give vitality to a group; however, too much of this stimulation tends to result in more emotional interaction than members can integrate. Fourth, the leader's *executive function*, which includes structuring, developing norms, and suggesting procedures, is valuable in providing the group with enough direction that the members do not flounder needlessly. However, excessive direction deprives members of their autonomy and restricts the free-flowing nature of a group.

At this point in your professional development, how do you see your style as a leader? Are you timid? aloof? shy? aggressive? verbal? controlling? confrontive? demanding? gentle? supportive? questioning? caring? solution oriented?

How might the outcomes of a group be affected by the style you've described?

THE TRAINING OF GROUP LEADERS

Since there are so many varieties of groups and so many different practitioners claiming to be competent, the training of group leaders becomes an important professional issue. What kind of training would you like to see group leaders receive? Consider the following list of experiences and requirements, and decide the degree to which you think each is important for a group leader. Rate each item on a scale from 1 to 5, with 1 representing "of very little value" and 5 representing "of great value."

Qualified group leaders should:

—— 1. be licensed psychiatrists, psychologists, or social workers.
—— 2. have led a number of groups under close supervision.
—— 3. have been *members* of several groups themselves.
—— 4. be required to demonstrate their competence to a certifying board.
—— 5. have had their own individual psychotherapy.
—— 6. have observed competent group leaders in action.

Now describe the kind of experience and training you would like to receive as a potential group leader.

_____

_____

_____

_____

Lakin (1972) addresses the ethical problem of poorly trained *sensitivity/ laboratory-group* facilitators and proposes guidelines that he claims will diminish poor practices. He contends that leaders should have at least the equivalent of master's degrees in one of a number of fields. They should also have some background in personality theory, psychopathology, and group dynamics, and they should have extensive supervised practice. In addition, Lakin proposes a three-year sequence of preparation that includes the following experiences:

- participating as members in two groups;
- co-leading five groups with experienced trainers;
- leading five groups alone, with observation and supervision;
- undergoing personal psychotherapy;
- being evaluated by local, experienced, well qualified trainers who will judge fitness of character and adequacy of preparation; and
- being given continuing education and periodic supervision, with emphasis upon the ethics of the group leader's function.

In discussing the training of group therapists, Yalom (1975), like Lakin, proposes a systematic approach. Yalom suggests four major components of a comprehensive training program:

1. *Observation of experienced group therapists at work, with an opportunity for post-session meetings with the therapists to ask questions and discuss what occurred in the group.*
2. *Supervised clinical group experience.* Yalom stresses that mere experience is not enough; without ongoing evaluation and feedback, mistakes may be reinforced.
3. *Personal group experience.* Yalom contends that such experience enables trainees to learn at the affective level as well as at the cognitive level.
4. *Personal therapy.* Yalom contends that an extensive self-exploratory experience is necessary if trainees are to be able to perceive countertransference feelings, recognize blind spots and biases, and use their personal attributes in a way that will contribute to the effectiveness of their groups.

As you consider issues related to the competence of group leaders, we ask you to answer these questions for yourself:

- Who is qualified to lead groups? What are the criteria for determining the competence of group leaders?
- Does ethical practice demand that group leaders receive some form of continuing education?
- Is it ethical for people to lead groups if they have never been participants in groups themselves?

Now list what you consider to be the central ethical issues involved in the training of group leaders.

_____

_____

_____

_____

CO-LEADERS

If you should decide to get involved in groups, it's likely that you'll work with a co-leader at some time or other. We think there are many advantages to the co-leader model. The group can benefit from the insights and feedback of two leaders. The leaders can complement and balance each other. They can grow by discussing what goes on in the group and by observing each other's style, and together they can evaluate what has gone on in the group and plan for future sessions. Also, with co-leaders the total burden does not rest with one person. While one leader is working with a particular member, the other can be paying attention to others in the group.

The choice of a co-leader is crucial. A group can suffer if its leaders are not working together harmoniously toward a common goal. If much of the leaders' energy is directed at competing with each other or at some other power struggle or hidden agenda, there is little chance that the group will be effective.

We think that the selection of a co-leader should involve more than attraction and liking. Each of the leaders should be secure enough that the group won't have to suffer as one or both of them try to "prove" themselves. We surely don't think it's essential that co-leaders always agree or share the same perceptions or interpretations; in fact, a group can be given vitality if co-leaders feel trusting enough to express their differences of opinion. Mutual respect and the ability to establish a relationship based upon trust, cooperation, and support are most important. Also, each person should be autonomous and have his or her own style yet be able to work with the other leader as a team.

In our view, it's essential for co-leaders to spend some time together immediately following a group to assess what happened. Similarly, we believe that they should meet at least briefly before each group session to talk about anything that might affect their functioning in the group.

The three of us have worked as a team leading groups for six years.

Philosophically we share a set of common values that have an impact on our view of group work. We're fortunate in this regard; if we had divergent philosophical and theoretical orientations, it would be difficult, if not impossible, to work together as an effective team. Our styles are very different, and the ways in which we each work and participate in our groups reflect our particular personalities. However, we have a high degree of respect and liking for one another, and our differences in style and personality actually seem to enhance our functioning in our groups. Before a group session, we do spend time together to prepare ourselves psychologically for the group. We meet again after each session to share our perceptions, discuss what is occurring in the group, talk about what we're feeling, challenge one another, and plan for future sessions. Working together in this way has been most rewarding for us and has enhanced the quality of our leadership abilities.

At this point, we ask you to draw up your own guidelines for selecting a co-leader.

1. What are the qualities you'd look for in a co-leader?

2. What kind of person would you *not* want to lead with?

3. If you disagreed with your co-leader, would you want to explore your disagreement in the group? What effect do you think your decision would have on the group?

4. If you found that you and your co-leader clashed on many issues and approached groups very differently, what do you think you'd do?

5. What ethical implications are involved when most of the group leaders' energy is directed toward power struggles and other conflicts and little energy is left for doing productive work within the group?

_____

_____

_____

_____

RECRUITMENT OF GROUP MEMBERS

Professional issues are involved in publicizing a group and recruiting members. How can group leaders make potential members aware of the services available? What information do clients have a right to expect before they decide to attend a group?

The American Psychological Association's *Guidelines for Psychologists Conducting Growth Groups* (1973b) states that prospective members should have access to the following information in writing:

- a statement of the purpose of the group and group goals;
- the types of techniques that may be used;
- the education, training, and qualification of the group leader;
- the fees and any other related expenses;
- a statement of whether or not follow-up service is included in the fee; and
- statements regarding the division of responsibility of the leader and the participants.

To this list Gazda (1977) adds the following stipulations:

- Announcements should include a statement of the length and duration of group sessions, as well as the number of participants.
- Group members should not be coerced to join a group.
- Claims that cannot be substantiated scientifically should not be made.

Of course, prospective clients need to be made aware of available group experiences, but consumers are entitled to an honest statement of the nature of a group. It is not uncommon to find many unprofessional types of advertisements whose promises of successful experiences are not substantiated.

If you were a beginning professional and wanted to start a group, what steps might you take to make your group known and to recruit members? How would you contact people? What would you say about your group?

_____

_____

_____

_____

_____

SCREENING AND SELECTION OF GROUP MEMBERS

Group leaders are faced with the difficult task of determining who should be included in a group and who should not. Are groups appropriate for all people? To put the question in another way, is it appropriate for *this* person to become a participant in *this* type of group, with *this* leader, at *this* time?

There are many groups whose leaders do not screen prospective participants. This is particularly true of weekend workshops that are essentially experiential groups and of marathon groups where strangers meet for one intensive weekend. Assuming that not everyone will benefit from a group experience—and that some people will be psychologically harmed by certain group experiences—is it unethical to fail to screen prospective group candidates? Some writers argue that truly effective screening is impossible. Others take the position that ethical practice demands the careful screening and preparation of all candidates.

Eric Berne (1961) views the selection of patients as a sign of professional inadequacy. His bias is toward a group approach to treatment. He contends that Transactional Analysis has been adequately tested with groups of neurotics, psychotics, sexual psychopaths, people with character disorders, and borderline cases and that groups can be formed of any of these types of people with some confidence. Berne's position on screening is well summed up in the following words:

> In general, the behavior of a patient in a group cannot be reliably predicted from his behavior in daily life or in individual interviews. A retarded depressive will not necessarily remain retarded in a group, nor will a deluded paranoid necessarily bring his delusions into the group as an unmanageable, disturbing factor. The only way to settle this in a given case is to try it [pp. 169–170].

In discussing the issue of screening people for an *encounter group*, Schutz (1971) frankly admits that he is not sure what kind of participant he would include or exclude if he did screen. He says: "I think it would be marvelous if people were screened so that those who would profit most would be admitted to encounter groups and those who would not profit, or who would be damaged, would be excluded. But I have very little idea of how to do this" (p. 313).

Others maintain that group leaders have a clear responsibility to determine what types of people should be excluded from a group. In its guidelines for psychologists conducting *growth groups*, the American Psychological Association (1973b) takes the position that screening interviews should be conducted by group leaders prior to the acceptance of any participant. Further, the APA statement says that group leaders are responsible for screening out those individuals they judge to be inappropriate for a given group.

Gazda (1977) agrees with the APA position and adds that screening procedures should be designed to ensure that prospective participants understand what is expected of them and that only those members will be selected who are likely to benefit from the group experience. Prospective group members should be told of the limits of confidentiality, and, if the group will be used for research purposes, the members should be informed. In addition, Gazda believes, members should be told:

- that membership is voluntary;

- that members have the "freedom of exit" from the group;
- that participants may need to be removed from the group if the leader determines that they are being harmed by the experience; and
- that any member who is in treatment with another professional should obtain clearance from that person to participate in the group.

In the context of *group psychotherapy*, Yalom (1975) argues that, unless careful selection criteria are employed, clients may terminate the group discouraged and unhelped. Yalom maintains that it is easier to identify the kinds of people who should be excluded from therapy groups than it is to identify those who should be included. Citing clinical studies, Yalom lists the following as poor candidates for out-patient, intensive group therapy: schizoid, paranoid, or sociopathic personalities; brain-damaged persons; monopolists (incessant talkers); depressives; people addicted to drugs or alcohol; people who are suicidal; and extremely narcissistic people.

In describing the kinds of people she would exclude from a *marathon therapy group*, Mintz (1971) lists people who have poor reality testing, people who are currently showing overt psychotic symptoms, and people who are extremely withdrawn. Mintz believes that therapists are ethically obliged to tactfully explain reasons for excluding a person and to make specific suggestions concerning where the person can obtain individual psychotherapy. She adds that people who are currently in individual therapy should not be accepted for a marathon without the knowledge and consent of their therapists.

Lakin (1972) contends that three types of people should be screened from *sensitivity training groups:* (1) people who will become too defensive under stress to listen to what others say to them, (2) people who tend to project their feelings onto others and to feel victimized by them, and (3) people whose self-esteem is so low that they need constant reassurance. Lakin points to the danger of accepting dominant people who would deal with their anxiety by monopolizing the group's time and draining its energy.

We want to make the point that screening ought to be a two-way process. While prospective group members are being screened, they should be deciding whether they want to work with a particular leader and whether the group in question is suitable for them. Hopefully, group candidates will involve themselves in a process of self-screening and not passively allow the matter to be decided for them by an expert. In addition, we believe that prospective group members have a right to know what they may be committing themselves to should they decide to enter a group. They have a right to know about the leader's philosophy, the approach and techniques used, and the expectations held for them as members. Group leaders should welcome the opportunity to respond to any questions or concerns prospective members have, and they should actively encourage prospective participants to raise questions about matters that will affect their participation.

In our own approach to screening, we've often found it difficult to predict who will benefit from a group experience. We realize that pre-group screening interviews are like any interviews in that people may tend to say what they think the interviewer expects. Often people who are interviewed for a group feel they must sell themselves or that they are being evaluated and judged. Perhaps these feelings can be lessened somewhat if leaders take the initiative to emphasize that these interviews are really designed as a two-way process in which leaders and prospective members can decide together whether a particular group, with a particular leader, at a particular time, is in the best interests of all concerned. Although we do have difficulty in predicting who will benefit from a group, we have found screening interviews most helpful in excluding some people who we believed would probably have left the group with negative feelings or who would have drained and sapped the group of the energy necessary for productive work.

It often happens that both the prospective member and the group leader are unsure whether a particular group is indicated for that person. For this reason, in a group that will be meeting several times, the first few sessions can be considered exploratory in nature. Members can be encouraged to come to the first session or two and then consider whether the group is what they're looking for. In this way, leaders encourage a process of self-selection that gives members the responsibility of deciding what is right for them. Actually experiencing the group for a time enables them to make an informed decision about participation. If, after a few sessions, either the leader or a particular member has any reservations, they can arrange a private meeting to explore these concerns and come to some agreement.

Pause a moment now to reflect on this issue of screening candidates for group participation.

1. If you were to organize a specific type of group and you decided to screen potential members, what are some characteristics or attitudes that you would *most* look for in accepting a person?

   _____

   _____

   _____

   _____

2. What kinds of persons might you exclude from your group? Why? How would you handle the matter of informing them that you would not accept them into your group?

   _____

   _____

   _____

   _____

   _____

   _____

3. If you were looking for a group for yourself, what are some of the characteristics of a *leader* that you would want to avoid? Check any of the following that apply.

   ____ rigid orientation
   ____ defensiveness
   ____ dogmatic attitude
   ____ lack of clarity about group goals
   ____ technique-oriented approach

_____ aloofness
_____ charismatic personality
_____ warmth and possessiveness
_____ lack of caring
_____ aggressiveness

Others:

_____

_____

THE PREPARATION OF GROUP PARTICIPANTS

To what extent are group leaders responsible for preparing participants to get the maximum benefit from their group experience? Many group practitioners do very little to systematically prepare members for a group. In fact, some therapists and group leaders are opposed to systematic preparation on the grounds that it will bias the members' experience. Many encounter-group leaders assume that part of the task of group members is to flounder and struggle and eventually define their own goals and give their group direction without much intervention by the leader. These leaders think that preparation and structuring on the part of the leader inhibits a group's spontaneity and autonomy.

Others take the position that members must be given some preparation in order to derive the maximum gains from a group experience. Goldberg (1977) has come to believe that both *encounter groups* and *therapy groups* are more profitable when clients are educated about therapeutic work. He makes the point that much of what practitioners frequently regard as resistance is really a result of clients' ignorance concerning the nature of therapy and a reaction to nondirective approaches.

Yalom (1975) is another advocate of systematic preparation for people in group therapy. His preparation includes exploring misconceptions and expectations, predicting early problems, and providing a conceptual framework that includes guidelines for effective group behavior. His preparatory interviews contain some of the following elements.

1. A brief explanation of the interpersonal theory of psychiatry is given.
2. Members are given guidelines for how they can best help themselves. This step includes talking about trust, self-disclosure, members' rights to privacy, risk taking, and experimentation with new behavior.
3. Stumbling blocks are predicted.
4. Members are told that the goal of the therapy group is to change behavior and attitudes, that treatment will take at least a year, and that significant changes should not be expected for months.
5. Members are told about the history of group therapy.
6. Confidentiality and extra-group socializing are discussed.

Yalom views this preparatory process as more than the dissemination of information. He claims that it reinforces the therapist's respect for the client, demonstrates that therapy is a collaborative venture, and shows that the therapist is willing to share his or her knowledge with the client.

In his skills/contract approach to *human-relations training groups*, Egan (1976) endorses the idea of systematic preparation of group members. Egan tells his readers: "The more clearly you understand the experience before you embark upon it, the more intelligently you will be able to give yourself to it and the more valuable it will be to you" (p. 3). Research cited by Egan suggests that a lack of structure during initial group sessions tends to intensify participants' fears and leads to unrealistic expectations. The research also indicates that groups are more effective if participants clearly understand group goals and processes, as well as what is expected of them.

In Egan's approach to groups, members begin by learning the elements of human-relations training. They learn that the group is a laboratory, that it is a place that encourages experimentation, that the focus is on the here-and-now, that self-disclosure is expected, that they will be giving and receiving feedback, that "cultural permission" is given to learn how to interact with others in new ways, and that interpersonal skills will be practiced and learned in the group.

It is our practice to systematically prepare the participants in our groups, whether these groups are weekly therapy groups, ongoing growth groups, or residential weekend or week-long therapeutic groups. At both the screening interview and the initial group session, we explore the members' expectations, clarify goals and objectives, discuss procedural details, describe group process, and talk about guidelines that we think will help members get the most from a group experience (see Corey & Corey, 1977, pp. 34–39). As part of member preparation, we like to include a discussion of the values and limitations of groups, the psychological risks involved in group participation, and ways of minimizing these risks. We also allow time for dealing with misconceptions that people have of groups and for exploring any fears or resistances the members may have. In most of our groups members do have certain fears about what they will experience, and, until we acknowledge these fears and talk about them, very little other productive work can occur. Further, we ask members to spend time before they come to the group defining for themselves what they most want to get from the group experience. To make their goals more concrete, we usually ask them to develop a contract that entails areas of concern that they're willing to work on in the group. We also ask them to do some reading and to write about their goals and about the significant turning points in their lives.

At this point, we ask you to write down a few things you might want to do to prepare people for a group.

_____

_____

_____

_____

_____

What is your position on the ethical aspects of failing to prepare group members for their experience in the group? What do you think would occur if you did little in the way of preparing group members?

_____

_____

_____

_____

_____

We have taken the position that group members can get the most from a group only if they are adequately prepared for it. However, there is a fine line between preparing people for an experience and setting them up to behave in predictable ways. For example, in our preparation we talk about potential risks, fears, misconceptions, and resistances. We realize that care must be taken so that we do not engender some of these very reactions. Thus, practitioners need to avoid fostering self-fulfilling prophecies while making their preparation explicit enough that the group does not flounder because of inadequate preparation.

INVOLUNTARY PARTICIPATION IN GROUPS

Should group membership always be voluntary? Are there situations in which it is ethical to require or coerce people to participate in a group? What are the problems involved in mandatory group participation? Before tackling these issues, we ask you to think about your own position by responding to the following situations. On the blank line following each statement, write "yes" if you tend to agree with the statement and "no" if you tend to disagree. You can also use this line to write any qualifications you may wish to add to your responses.

1. Encounter or growth-group experiences should always be voluntary.

   _____

2. Any form of coercion to get people to participate in a group experience is unethical.

   _____

3. It is ethical to require an experiential group for graduate students who are preparing to be counselors.

   _____

4. A school district has the right to expect an entire staff to participate in sensitivity-training sessions.

   _____

5. It is ethical to require patients who have been committed to a state mental hospital to attend group-therapy sessions.

   _____

6. It is ethical to require students to attend an experiential group as part of a required college course.

_____

7. It is ethical to require group participation of adolescents who have been sent to a youth facility by a court.

_____

Now state your views on the following issues as clearly and directly as you can.

1. What is your position on involuntary group participation?

_____

_____

_____

2. Suppose you worked for an agency in which most of the clients were not there by choice, and you were asked to conduct an ongoing group. How would you deal with this situation?

_____

_____

_____

3. What do you think about requiring students who are majoring in one of the mental-health fields to participate in a personal-growth and awareness group?

_____

_____

_____

Most writers on the subject of groups agree that group participation should be voluntary. For example, the American Psychological Association (1973b) guidelines state: "Entering into a growth group experience should be on a voluntary basis; any form of coercion to participate is to be avoided" (p. 933). Schutz (1971) has decided not to accept anyone in a group who is not there voluntarily. He has found that involuntary group members often block the group process, for they are unwilling to participate. Moreover, Schutz contends that participants should have the freedom to leave when they wish. Thus, for Schutz, members must take the responsibility for coming to the group and for either remaining or leaving once they're in the group. Lakin (1972) maintains that uncoerced participation is essential in sensitivity-training and encounter groups. He argues that, if people are to enter into the interactional aspects of a group, they must be there by choice and feel free from negative evaluation should they choose not to participate.

Although we surely think it is desirable for groups to be composed of willing members, we're aware that, particularly in an agency or institution, you may be expected to lead groups whose members have not chosen to be part of the group. If so, you'll have to determine for yourself how you'll deal with the ethical dilemma that arises if you're opposed to mandatory group participation. You may be able to find a way of creating a climate in which the group members will be receptive to using group time for their benefit, particularly if you respect their privacy and give them the freedom to explore only those matters they are willing to make known to others.

PSYCHOLOGICAL RISKS IN GROUPS

The fact that groups can be powerful catalysts of personal change means that they are also risky. We don't think groups should be free of risk, because learning how to grow entails taking risks. However, in our view, ethical practice demands that group leaders should at least inform prospective participants of the potential risks involved in the group experience. We also believe that group leaders have an ethical responsibility to take precautionary measures to reduce unnecessary psychological risks. We cannot agree with what we consider to be the abdication of responsibility represented in the positions of Schutz (1971) and Perls (1969), who tell group members "If you want to go crazy, that's your responsibility." Our view is that merely informing participants of the possible risks does not absolve leaders of all responsibility. Certain safeguards can be taken during the course of a group to avoid disastrous outcomes. In this section we discuss some of the risks that we believe participants should know about.

1. One risk of group participation is that members may experience major disruptions in their lives as a result of their work in the group. Of course, this risk is present in any type of therapy, not simply in groups. Members should be aware, however, that others in their lives may not appreciate their changes. This situation could lead to decisions that will change their life-styles.

2. Often group participants are encouraged to "let it all hang out." In this quest for complete self-revelation, privacy is sometimes invaded. Participants must learn the difference between appropriate and facilitative self-disclosure and disclosure that leaves nothing private. Group leaders need to be alert to attempts to force people to disclose more than they are ready to share. Otherwise participants may withdraw, feeling a sense of shame for having said more than they were ready and willing to say.

3. The risk of invasion of privacy brings up the related risk of group pressure. In most groups there are pressures to be open, to be honest, to take risks, to talk about personal matters, and to try new behavior. These behaviors are then positively reinforced. At times group pressure to get people to join in certain activities or to change their ideas and behavior can be very strong. More often it appears as a subtle pressure to conform unquestioningly to group norms and expectations. Can you imagine the reactions members would receive who did not conform to any of the group norms?

We think it's important to recognize that group pressure is inevitable and that it can even be useful in encouraging participants to take an honest look at themselves. However, even though not all group pressure is bad, it can be misused. In our view, participants' right to choose not to explore certain issues, or to say they wish to stop at a certain point, should be respected. Also, members should not be coerced into participating in an exercise if they're unwilling to do so. We agree with Goldberg (1977) that leaders need to respect the rights of participants to go at their own pace and remain as they are if they make that choice.

4. Scapegoating is another potential hazard in groups. We question the ethical sensitivity of leaders who fail to intervene actively when they see participants "ganging up" on a certain group member. Unchallenged projection and dumping can have dire effects on the person who is under attack.

5. Confrontation can be used or misused in groups. At times participants may view confrontation in a negative way, seeing it as a destructive tearing down of defenses that leaves a person in a highly vulnerable place. To be sure, confrontation can be done in a way that results in a devastating attack. Leaders and participants alike need to learn how to recognize this destructive type of behavior and prevent it from going on in a group. On the other hand, confrontation can be an act of caring, and it can be done in such a way that a member is *challenged*, without the hit-and-run effect of destructive confrontation. As Egan (1976) puts it, confrontation can be an *invitation* for people to examine their behavior and its consequences more carefully. When confrontation is positive, it occurs in such a way that confronters share their reactions to the person being confronted. Harmful attacks on others should not be permitted under the guise of "sharing."

6. Another risk involved in groups is that what members disclose may not always be kept confidential. Even though a leader may continue to stress the necessity of not discussing what goes on in the group with outsiders, there is no guarantee that all members will respect the confidential nature of what occurs in their group.

7. There have been occasions when people have been physically injured in groups as a result of such activities as wrestling, pushing, holding down, fighting with bataccas (soft, felt-covered clubs), and other forms of releasing aggression. We have seen irresponsible leaders goad participants to "let out your anger" and then watch helplessly, clearly unprepared for the ensuing violent outbursts of rage. In short, we think that it's unethical for leaders to work toward eliciting strong aggressive feelings unless they are competent to deal with the likely results. One safeguard is to tell members not to strike one another but to beat a pillow to release aggressive feelings in a symbolic way.

One way of minimizing psychological risks in groups is to use a contract approach, whereby leaders specify what their responsibilities are and members specify what their commitment to the group is by declaring what they're willing to explore and what they're willing to do. Goldberg (1977), who makes a strong case for contract negotiation as the basis for a group, believes that this device can reduce psychological risks. He adds the important point that leaders need to *respect* their contracts with the participants in terms of what they have agreed to do and what they have agreed not to do.

Egan (1976) uses the contract approach to ensure that participants know what they are agreeing to when they become members of a skills-training group. The contract states that participants will use group time to explore their own interpersonal styles and to alter these styles in ways *they* deem appropriate. Other aspects of the contract include:

- working with others to achieve the goals of the group,

- learning how to listen to others,
- responding to others concretely,
- letting others in your "world,"
- letting others know what you like about them or what keeps you at a distance from them,
- sharing what you learn about yourself in the group, and
- giving and asking for feedback.

If such a contract approach is used, many of the risks we've mentioned can be reduced. If members and leaders operate under a contract that clarifies expectations, we believe there is less chance for members to be exploited or to leave a group feeling they've had a bad experience.

Of course, a contract approach is not the only way to reduce potential risks; nor is it sufficient, by itself, to do so. Probably one of the most important safeguards against unnecessary risks in a group is the leader's training in group processes. Group leaders have the major responsibility for preventing needless harm to members, and to fulfill this role they need to have a clear grasp of the boundaries of their competence. This implies that leaders conduct only those types of groups for which they have been sufficiently prepared. A group leader may be trained to lead a group of peers in a personal-growth or consciousness-raising group yet be ill prepared to embark on a marathon or therapy group. Sometimes people who have attended a few marathon groups become excited about doing this type of group as leaders, even though they have little or no training and no opportunity for supervision. They soon find that they are in over their heads and are unable to cope with what emerges in the group. Working with an experienced co-leader is one good way to learn and also a way of reducing some potential risks.

Now write down a few things you would do as a group leader to minimize the risks to the members.

_____

_____

_____

_____

CONFIDENTIALITY IN GROUPS

In Chapter 6 we discussed the ethical, legal, and professional aspects of confidentiality in the practice of counseling and psychotherapy. We come back to this issue again because there are special implications of confidentiality in group situations. Some key questions that need to be raised are:

- Is confidentiality a prerequisite for the development of the trust needed for productive work to occur in a group?
- Are confidences that are divulged in group therapy protected under the laws of privileged communication?
- What are the ethical responsibilities of group leaders with respect to safeguarding the confidentiality of the disclosures made in groups?

Does the legal concept of privileged communication apply to group work? Meyer and Smith (1977) indicate that in almost *no* jurisdiction in the United States may psychotherapists guarantee their group-therapy clients that their communications are privileged. Even in jurisdictions that grant a client/therapist privilege, there is no certainty that this privilege applies to *group* therapy. Meyer and Smith suggest that new or remedial legislation at the state and national levels is needed. They also make the point that the silence of the therapist is not adequate, since the silence of the group members must also be assured. A possible approach mentioned is allowing civil suits by group members against other members who disclose information about group-therapy discussions.

Paul Bindrim (1977) describes a $50,000 judgment awarded in his favor by a California Superior Court. A member of one of his groups wrote a book about the experience, and, even though the names of the therapist and all the participants had been changed, the jury determined that the main character was identifiable as Bindrim and that the writer had presented a distorted picture of what occurred in the therapy session.

Bindrim also describes the procedures he uses to safeguard confidentiality. He asks all the participants in his groups to sign a contract in which they agree not to discuss or write about what transpired in the sessions or to talk about who was present. In addition, with the knowledge of the participants, he keeps tape-recordings of all the group sessions. Like Meyer and Smith, Bindrim believes that further legislation is obviously needed. It is his position that participants in therapy groups conducted by licensed professionals should have the right to civil action whether the statements made about them are libelous or not. Further, they should not have to prove that they are identifiable by other persons or that they have suffered actual financial damage. According to Bindrim, legislation is sorely needed that will extend to therapy groups the same right of privileged communication that now exists for individual therapy.

In his article *Confidentiality in Group Counseling,* Plotkin (1978) raises these critical questions: Are the members of a group under the same ethical and legal obligation as the group leader not to disclose the identities of other members or the content of what was shared in the group? If there is any obligation, how can it be enforced? Plotkin contends that most texts in group counseling are silent on these issues and that the professional and legal literature is unclear and unhelpful. He states that the maintenance of confidentiality by group members has not been recognized as an ethical problem either for the members or the group leader. Plotkin also observes that there are no judicial decisions, and little legal commentary, concerning breaches of confidentiality or invasion of privacy as a result of group experiences. For legal reasons alone, then, it's important for therapists to raise the issue of confidentiality in their groups. As Plotkin indicates, it is possible that therapists who fail to advise their groups about confidentiality obligations may eventually be sued for professional negligence.

With regard to the ethics of confidentiality in group work, we agree with Plotkin that confidentiality is the "ethical cornerstone" of the client/therapist relationship and that the same assurance of confidentiality must be extended to all the participants in a group situation. Plotkin believes that a persuasive argument can be made that, since group members are a "necessary and customary" part of the therapist's procedures and treatment approach, they have the same obligation as the therapist to maintain the confidential character of their group. In any event, as Plotkin maintains, these problems should be given serious professional attention before clients are injured or the integrity of group therapy is compromised. We like Plotkin's suggestions to group leaders:

. . . group leaders are well advised to rethink the contracts they enter into with their clients. These contracts should specify in writing, at a minimum, the therapist's duty to maintain the confidentiality of the relationship and should include those situations in which the law or ethics may require the therapist to reveal certain confidences. They should also spell out the client's obligation to maintain the confidentiality of any group sessions in which he or she participates [p. 14].

It is our position that leaders need to periodically reaffirm to group members the importance of not discussing with others what occurs in the group. In our own groups we talk with each prospective member about the necessity of confidentiality in establishing the trust and cohesion required if participants are to risk revealing themselves in significant ways. We discuss this point during the screening interviews, again during the pre-group or initial group meetings, at times during the course of a group when it seems appropriate, and again at the termination of the group. Since the three of us have done many intensive residential groups in which as many as 15 participants live together for an entire week, we have been concerned about maintaining the confidential character of the group. It has been our experience that most people in our groups do not maliciously attempt to hurt others by talking with people outside the group about specific members. However, it's tempting for members to share the nature of their experience with other people, and in so doing they sometimes make inappropriate disclosures. This is particularly true of participants in intensive, time-extended ("marathon") groups, who are likely to be asked many questions about what it was like when they return home. Because of this tendency to want to share with outsiders, we repeatedly caution participants in any type of group about how easily and unintentionally the confidentiality of the group can be broken.

If you were to lead any type of group, which of the following measures might you take to ensure confidentiality? Check any of the following statements that apply:

_____ I'd repeatedly mention the importance of confidentiality.

_____ I'd require group members to sign a statement saying that they would maintain the confidential character of the group.

_____ I'd let members know that they would be asked to leave the group if they violated confidentiality.

_____ I'd have a written document on hand describing the dimensions of confidentiality that all the members could refer to.

_____ With the permission and knowledge of the members, I'd tape-record all the sessions.

_____ I'd say very little about confidentiality and leave it up to the group to decide how they would deal with the issue.

Other:

_____

_____

_____

_____

USES AND ABUSES OF GROUP TECHNIQUES

Group techniques can be used to facilitate the movement of a group and as catalysts to deepen and intensify certain feelings. We think it's important for leaders to use only those techniques that they have experienced personally and to have a clear rationale for using each technique. This is an area in which theory can be a useful guide for practice.

Techniques can also be abused or used in unethical ways. Some of the ways in which leaders can use techniques unprofessionally are:

- springing any and all kinds of techniques on groups without knowing their potential impact,
- using techniques merely as gimmicks,
- using techniques to serve their own hidden agendas or to enhance their power,
- using techniques whose sole purpose is to create an explosive atmosphere, and
- using techniques to pressure members or in other ways rob them of dignity or the respect of others.

There are various views on the values and limitations of techniques and exercises in group work. In our own work, we have gradually come to agree in part with the position of Carl Rogers (1970). Rogers avoids using planned procedures, because he believes that group members have the resources within themselves to eventually find their own direction without structured exercises imposed on them by the group leader. Rogers writes that, on those occasions when he *has* resorted to using techniques to get groups moving, they have rarely worked. He admits that the reason planned techniques fail for him is because of his lack of faith in their usefulness. On the other hand, according to Rogers, nothing is a gimmick if it occurs with real spontaneity. Thus, he sees a wide range of exercises such as role-playing, psychodrama, and body contact as being useful when they are appropriate—that is, when they grow out of natural occurrences within the group and when they are expressions of what people are feeling at the time.

Like Rogers, we value techniques when they are appropriate ways of intensifying the experience of group participants. When we began leading groups together, we experimented with a variety of planned exercises that were designed to stimulate interactions and to elicit certain intense feelings. In fact, we were tempted to judge the effectiveness of these groups by the intensity of the feelings that were stirred up and expressed. We discovered, however, that significant learning and change occurred among people who did not have cathartic experiences. We also discovered that cathartic experiences *in and of themselves* did not seem sufficient to produce long-term changes. We therefore began to resist initiating many planned exercises designed to bring out certain feelings or to make things happen in the group. Still, we remain willing to invent techniques or to draw upon techniques we've borrowed from others when these procedures seem appropriate to what a participant is experiencing and when we think they will help a person work through some conflict. This kind of appropriateness has become our guideline for using techniques effectively. Of course, each group leader will need to develop his or her own guidelines for determining whether and when to use techniques.

To focus yourself on the issue of the uses and abuses of group techniques, respond briefly to the following questions.

1. What are the possible uses, values, and advantages of using techniques or exercises in groups?

_____

_____

_____

_____

2. What do you consider to be abuses of group techniques?

_____

_____

_____

_____

3. What ethical or professional concerns do you have about the uses and abuses of group techniques?

_____

_____

_____

_____

ISSUES CONCERNING TERMINATION AND REENTRY

The final phase of a group and the departure to the outside world are among the most important stages of the group experience. This is true for therapy groups as well as for encounter groups, and it is true for groups that meet on an ongoing basis as well as for concentrated group experiences such as marathon or residential groups. The final stage of a group provides an opportunity for members to clarify the meaning of their experience, to consolidate the gains they've made, and to make decisions about the kinds of new behavior they want to carry away from the group and apply to their everyday lives. We see the following professional issues involved in the termination of a group:

- What responsibilities do group leaders have for assisting participants to develop a conceptual framework that will make sense of, integrate and consolidate what they've learned in their group?
- To what degree is it the leader's responsibility to ensure that members aren't stuck with unnecessary psychological turmoil at the end of the group?
- How can group leaders help participants translate what they've learned as a result of the group into their daily lives? Should leaders assume this translation will occur automatically, or must they prepare members for maximizing their learning?
- What are some ways of minimizing post-group depression?

We agree with Goldberg (1977) that it is neither responsible nor useful to leave pending any serious concerns that arise from an encounter or therapy group. Goldberg contends that the problem of reentry can be eased by concluding a group with an application period. For example, at the end of his weekend encounter groups, Goldberg explores with the participants how the process of the weekend can be applied to their daily roles and functions. We are in strong agreement with Goldberg when he states:

> I view one of the major values of the encounter experience to be the inculcation of interpersonal knowledge that participants acquire, both on an affective and on a cognitive level, and with which they can affect conditions in their daily membership groups. Unless the encounter practitioner helps to bridge the encounter experience with the participants' daily lives, the value of an experiential group as a learning experience that can be generalized is lost [p. 194].

A common criticism of groups is that people are often stuck with feelings of depression, resentment, and anger after a group ends, without any means of dealing with and resolving these feelings. However, our contention that group members should not be left with unnecessary psychological turmoil does *not* mean that we think they should be comfortable and free of conflict when they leave. On the contrary, we're convinced that a certain amount of anxiety due to unfinished business can be a stimulus for continued growth. It is the leader's task to recognize when anxiety is counterproductive.

Group leaders have other tasks to perform when a group ends. They can minimize the post-group depression syndrome by pointing out that members often experience a sense of loss and depression after a group ends. Further, they need to prepare members for dealing with those they are intimate with. The group should be reminded that others in their lives may not have changed as they have and may not be ready for their changes. We routinely caution people in our groups to give people on the outside a chance to get used to their changes. Before the group ends, we do much role-playing to give members an opportunity to practice responding to others in different ways. In this role-play they have the advantage of receiving feedback from the rest of the group on how they come across. We also announce to our groups our availability for some individual sessions at no extra fee after the conclusion of a group, should members feel the need for such consultation. Finally, we spend time talking about where they can continue their personal work. Many group participants become aware of areas in their lives that they want to explore in more depth in individual sessions. Others may want to pursue specific types of groups or workshops. For this reason, we mention specific referral resources where participants can continue working on making the changes they've begun.

As a stage in the life of the group, termination has its own meaning and significance. Yalom (1975) observes that therapy groups tend to avoid the difficult work of terminating by ignoring or denying their concerns. Yalom sees it as the therapist's responsibility to keep group members focused on the reality and meaning of the ending of their group. He describes the termination of a group as a real experience of loss and suggests that therapists can assist members to deal with this reality by disclosing their own feelings about separating.

> The therapist, no less than the patients, will miss the group. For him, too, it has been a place of anguish, conflict, fear, and also of great beauty; some of life's truest and most poignant moments occur in the small and yet limitless microcosm of the therapy group [p. 374].

ISSUES RELATED TO FOLLOW-UP AND EVALUATION

What kind of follow-up should be provided after the termination of any group? What professional obligation does the group leader have to systematically evaluate the outcomes of a group? How can leaders assist members to evaluate the effectiveness of their group experience?

Gazda (1977) points out that a major criticism of the way leaders handle the termination of groups concerns the sudden ending of weekend encounter groups without any provisions for follow-up. According to Gazda, group leaders are responsible for the following follow-up services:

- planning a follow-up session for short-term, time-limited groups;
- becoming acquainted with professionals to whom they can refer group participants when they cannot continue a professional involvement themselves; and
- informing participants of referral sources where they can obtain the assistance they might need.

With Gazda, we question the ethics of failing to provide some type of follow-up for a group, particularly for marathon groups that meet for a few days and then disband. Follow-up can be done in a number of ways. Individual sessions can be arranged to discuss the degree to which members feel they have accomplished their goals. Questionnaires can be sent to members at some point after the termination of a group. A follow-up session can be arranged that includes the entire group.

In the week-long groups the three of us lead together, we have made it a practice to schedule a follow-up session around three months after the group ends. These sessions have been most valuable both for the group members and for ourselves. Through these sessions we get a more realistic picture than we would otherwise have of the impact of the group on the members' everyday lives; they enable us to see whether members have actually applied what they learned in the group. For their part, members can share what their reentry was like for them and discuss any problems they're having in implementing what they learned in the group in their transactions with others. They have a chance to express and work through any afterthoughts or feelings left over from the group experience, and they can report on the degree to which they have fulfilled their contracts since they left the group. They also have a chance to receive additional feedback and reinforcement from the other members. Even for groups that meet on a weekly basis, we think it's wise to set a time for a group follow-up session to discuss the experience and put it in perspective.

On the question of evaluating the results of a group, we admit that we find it difficult to objectively assess outcomes. Generally, we've relied on subjective measures; for example, after our groups terminate, we ask the members to write reaction papers in which they evaluate what the experience meant for them. We do think it's important to teach members how to recognize the ongoing changes they're making that are partially results of what they learned in the group. Members have a tendency to discount what they actually did in a group, and they may not be aware of the subtle changes they continue to make after the group ends. We think it's our responsibility to teach them how to evaluate the nature and degree of their changes. Also, we strongly believe that both members and leaders should assess the effectiveness of the group in an ongoing fashion. This can be done after each session. Members can ask: Am I getting what I want from this group? In what ways could this group be more effective? Am I applying in my everyday life what I'm learning about myself and others in the group? What changes need to be made in this group? We think this kind of assessment should be a topic for discussion at almost every session.

Now jot down some ideas about the kind of follow-up you would like to provide for a group.

_____

_____

_____

_____

In what ways would you attempt to evaluate the effectiveness of a group you were leading?

_____

_____

_____

_____

OTHER ISSUES IN GROUP WORK

In this section we briefly address a number of issues related to group work. As you consider each of these questions, attempt to clarify your own answers.

Group Size

The desirable size for a group depends on factors such as the age of the clients, the type of group, the experience of the group leaders, the number of group leaders, and the type of problems explored. An ethical issue can arise when group leaders settle on a certain size for reasons that are not related to therapeutic considerations. For example, from the standpoint of therapeutic and interactional value, the optimal size for a weekly therapy group might be eight people. However, the leader might accept 12 members or more because of the additional income. In your view, what are the ethics of deciding on the size of a group primarily on the basis of financial or practical motives, as opposed to what is therapeutically optimal?

_____

_____

_____

Leader Preparation and Presence

We've already discussed the group leader's responsibility to prepare the participants for a valuable group experience. The question also needs to be raised, what obligations do group leaders have to prepare *themselves* psychologically before they meet with a group?

One of our colleagues who leads three weekly groups allows at least an hour to get himself in focus before his group arrives. He reflects on what occurred in the group the week before, thinks about each person in the group, and asks himself how much in tune he feels with each person in the group. He also gives himself permission to reexperience past and current struggles and the feelings associated with these struggles, because he believes he functions best as a group leader when he can connect with other members by recalling and reexperiencing his own feelings. Without claiming that this is the best way for all group leaders to prepare themselves for their groups, we do advocate that every leader recognize the importance of a preparation period and find his or her own way to be psychologically ready for the group.

The question of psychological readiness is especially pertinent for group leaders who conduct several different groups in a single evening. For example, there are some group therapists who schedule three groups in an evening. They may lead one group for an hour and then go to another group while the first one meets as a leaderless group for another hour or so. In your view, is it possible for a leader to be psychologically present for as many as three groups in an evening? More generally, what ethical questions are involved when group leaders do not allow sufficient time to become ready for each group they lead?

_____

_____

_____

_____

Leaderless Groups

What questions are involved in allowing groups to meet without a professional leader? Gazda (1977) claims that the practice of allowing therapy and quasi-therapy groups to meet without the presence of a professional leader should be discouraged until there is more supportive research evidence. Yalom (1975), however, sees value in occasional or regularly scheduled leaderless meetings as adjuncts to traditional therapist-led groups. Yalom contends that these sessions can lessen dependence on the leader and foster a sense of autonomy and responsibility. Yalom does warn that proper timing is essential; that is, the therapy groups should develop some cohesiveness before leaderless meetings are considered. What is your view of leaderless groups?

1. What advantages do you see in the leaderless group?

_____

_____

_____

2. What disadvantages do you see in the leaderless group?

_____

_____

_____

3. What do you think about groups that meet for their entire life span without professional leaders?

_____

_____

_____

4. What do you think of groups that alternate therapist-led sessions with leaderless sessions?

_____

_____

_____

Socializing among Group Members

Does socializing among group members hinder or facilitate the group process? How does it affect the functioning of a group?

Our position is that any type of subgrouping or out-of-group socialization that thwarts the purposes of the group or interferes with its functioning is counterproductive and should be discouraged. There are times, for example, when cliques form outside of the group for purposes of "organized resistance." Members of these subgroups may talk about their hostility toward the group leader or certain other members yet be unwilling to talk about these feelings in the group. Although we're not opposed to socializing that doesn't get in the way of the primary purpose of the group, we think that Yalom (1975) makes a good point when he emphasizes that the therapy group teaches people *how* to form intimate relationships but does not *provide* these relationships. Yalom also points out that members who do meet outside the group have a responsibility to discuss the salient aspects of the meeting inside the group. What guidelines would you establish for your group on the issue of socializing among group members?

_____

_____

_____

_____

Sexuality in Groups

An issue related to extra-group socializing is that of sexual relationships among group members. Schutz (1971) says that he is not opposed to members having sex with one another, so long as they do not keep it a secret from the group.

He thinks that these sexual relationships, if they occur, can lead to important understanding and growth, but only if they are discussed in the group. In our own residential workshop groups, we state as a matter of policy that we're opposed to sexual involvements as a part of the group experience. We do so on the grounds that this type of involvement inevitably tends to get in the way of the work that members have contracted to do. Many members in our groups have expressed their appreciation for this position at the end of the group. They admit that it would have been very tempting to use the group as a place to have fun or develop romances instead of doing the difficult work of looking at the changes they wanted to make in their own lives. They appreciate our clear position, which encouraged them to think more carefully before entering into sexual relationships during the workshop.

1. In your view, what are the ethical aspects of sexual relationships among group members?

_____

_____

_____

2. As a group leader, would you state any policy regarding sexual relations among group members? Why or why not?

_____

_____

_____

3. How do you think that sexual relations among group members would affect the group if they were not discussed in the group?

_____

_____

_____

Take a moment now to list other questions or issues in group work that we haven't discussed and that you think are important. You can use your list to raise questions for discussion in class.

_____

_____

_____

_____

_____

ETHICAL GUIDELINES FOR GROUP LEADERS

Should there be formal ethical guidelines for group leaders who are licensed professionals and who are well trained in group approaches? Or should these practitioners be free to conduct a group in any way they see fit?

Group approaches seem to be increasing in popularity, and we believe there is a real need for special codes of ethics, or at least special ethical guidelines, for group practitioners. In addition, although professional group leaders are subject to the codes of ethics of their specializations, we think they have a responsibility to develop guidelines of their own that are appropriate to their particular types of groups.

Bass and Dole (1977) conducted a study to determine what professional psychologists and group specialists considered to be ethical and unethical practices in sensitivity groups for graduate students in psychology. From the responses given by their panel of 87 distinguished psychologists, Bass and Dole compiled a list of 37 practices judged to be highly unethical and 36 judged to be highly ethical. The "highly unethical" practices ranged from using groups for purposes that are not in the members' best interests to allowing supervisors to hear tape-recordings of group sessions without the members' permission. Although their study concerned a specialized type of group, Bass and Dole suggest that their results could be useful in developing guidelines for group practitioners generally.

To help you formulate your own position on ethical guidelines for group work, we'll present a list of guidelines that make sense to us, some of which have been developed by other writers and practitioners. Ask yourself the degree to which you think each of the guidelines is important. On the blank lines, rate each one on a five-point scale, with "1" representing "of little importance" and "5" representing "of great importance." You can also use the blank lines to write any qualifying statements that will make the guidelines fit for you.

1. Group leaders need to be aware of what their own needs are, what they get from leading groups, and how their needs and behavior influence their groups.

   _____

2. Group leaders should have the training and experience that are necessary and appropriate for the kinds of groups they lead.

   _____

3. Leaders need to clearly define for themselves the purpose and goals of their groups and then select methods that are appropriate to these ends.

   _____

4. It's important for leaders to be willing to do whatever they encourage members of their groups to do. For example, if leaders advocate risk taking for participants, they also should take risks.

   _____

5. It's important for group leaders to have a well conceptualized model of behavioral change (Gazda, 1977).

6. Group leaders must be well trained with regard to theory and appropriate procedures, and they must be aware of the range of effects these procedures can have on group members (Feinberg, 1977).

7. Group leaders must have a clear understanding of their values as leaders, and these values should be congruent with the ethics of their profession (Feinberg, 1977).

8. Leaders need to develop methods of screening that will allow them to differentiate between suitable and unsuitable candidates for their groups.

9. It is the responsibility of the leader to inform prospective participants of matters such as group goals and procedures, possible techniques, ground rules, expectations for participation, possible psychological risks, and any other factors that are likely to affect the participants' decision to become involved in the group.

10. Prospective group members should be informed that they have the "freedom of exit" from a group and that they have a right to resist suggestions from either the members or the leader (Gazda, 1977).

11. Group leaders need to be sensitive to group pressure that violates the self-determination of members, and they should intervene when scape-goating, projecting, or stereotyping threatens to undermine a member's sense of self.

12. The importance of confidentiality needs to be stressed to members before they enter a group, during the group itself when appropriate, and when the group terminates. It is the leader's responsibility to be explicit about the limits of confidentiality and the circumstances in which it would be necessary to disclose confidences.

13. Prospective group members should be informed of any research involving the group, and their consent should be obtained in writing.

14. It is a wise policy to ask participants to sign a contract in which they agree

not to discuss or write about what transpires in the sessions or talk about who was present (Bindrim, 1977).

_____

15. It is a good policy to tape-record group sessions with the knowledge of the participants and keep these tapes on file (Bindrim, 1977).

_____

16. When tape-recordings of group sessions are made, members should be informed that they can stop the recorder at any time if it is restricting their participation (Gazda, 1977).

_____

17. If group leaders use any data from their groups in their writing or instruction, they must disguise all data that might identify group members (Gazda, 1977).

_____

18. Leaders should be alert for symptoms of psychological debilitation in group members, which may indicate that their participation in the group should be terminated. Referral resources should be made available for persons who want further assistance.

_____

19. Participants should be prepared for translating what they learn in the group to their daily lives.

_____

20. Group leaders should arrange for follow-up sessions and make a serious attempt to evaluate the outcomes of each group.

_____

Now list other specific guidelines that you think are important.

_____

_____

_____

_____

_____

CHAPTER SUMMARY

Along with the impetus for group approaches to counseling and therapy comes a need for ethical and professional guidelines for those who lead groups. In this chapter we have focused on what we consider to be some of the most important issues in group work, and we have encouraged you to take your own position on these issues.

There are many types of groups, and there are many possible uses of groups in various settings. Our attempt has been to select the issues that are related to most types of groups. Some of these questions are: How does a leader's theoretical view of groups influence the way that a group is structured? What are some key elements in recruiting, screening, selecting, and preparing group members? What ethical, professional, legal, and practical issues concerning confidentiality are involved in any type of group? To what degree should participants be prepared for a group before the group begins? What are some ethical issues in the selection and training of group leaders? In what ways can group techniques be used or abused? What responsibility do group leaders have in terms of follow-up and evaluation? With respect to these and other issues, we have stressed the importance of formulating your own guidelines for ethical practice in leading groups.

ACTIVITIES, EXERCISES, AND IDEAS FOR THOUGHT AND DISCUSSION

1. In your own class, you can experience the initial session of a group. Two students can volunteer to be co-leaders, and approximately ten other students can become group members. Assume that the group is a personal-growth group that will meet for a predetermined number of weeks. The co-leaders' job is to orient and prepare the members by describing the group's purpose, by giving an overview of group-process concepts, and by talking about ground rules for effective group participation. If time allows, members can express any fears and expectations they have about being involved in the group, and they can also raise questions they would like to explore. This exercise is designed to give you practice in dealing with concerns that both group leaders and members often have at the beginning of a group.

2. This classroom exercise can be done in subgroups. One person develops a proposal for a group and presents this proposal to the people in the subgroup. The proposal should spell out the goals of the group, the rationale for doing the group, the people the group is intended for, the guidelines for participation, the screening and selection methods, the techniques that may be used, and the way the outcomes of the group will be evaluated. The members can give feedback and also ask questions about the proposal.

3. In subgroups, explore some of the following questions: (a) What are some of the major misconceptions people have about groups? (b) What are some ways of clearing up participants' misconceptions? (c) What are some of the psychological risks involved in group participation? What are some strategies for minimizing these risks? (d) How can you best determine who would be suitable candidates for a given group and who should be excluded?

4. This exercise is designed to give you practice in conducting screening interviews for potential group members. One person volunteers to conduct interviews, and another student can role-play a potential group member. Allow about ten minutes for the interview. Afterwards, the prospective client can talk about what it was like to be interviewed, and the group leader can share his or her experience. This exercise can be done with the entire class watching, in small groups, or in dyads.

5. Suppose you're expected as part of your job to lead a group composed of

people who are *required* to be part of the group and who really don't want to be there. How will the nature of the group affect your approach? What might you do differently with this group, compared to a group of people who requested the experience? This is a good situation to role-play in class, with several students role-playing the reluctant members while others practice dealing with them.

6. Assume that you're a group leader. A member comes to you to say that another member is gossiping about details that have been divulged in the group. The person who tells you this is quite upset over the disclosure of confidences. How will you deal with this situation? You can role-play this kind of case in small groups to demonstrate how you'd deal with the matter.

7. You're leading a counseling group with high school students on their campus. One day a member comes to the group obviously under the influence of drugs. He is incoherent and interruptive. How do you deal with him? What might you say or do? Discuss how you would deal with this situation in class, or demonstrate how you might respond by having a fellow student role-play the part of the adolescent.

8. Again, assume that you're leading a high school counseling group. An angry father who gave written permission for his son's participation comes to your office and demands to know what's going on in your group. He is convinced that his son's participation in the group is an invasion of family privacy. As a group leader, how would you deal with this angry father? To make the situation more real and interesting, someone in class can role-play the father.

9. Often group leaders neglect to pay sufficient attention to what happens to the participants when they leave a group. Assume that you're leading a group and that the group will soon end. What are some things you will do or say to increase the chances that the participants will apply what they've learned to their daily lives?

10. The issue of selecting a co-leader for a group is an important one, for not all matches of co-leaders are productive. For this exercise, form dyads and negotiate with your partner to determine whether the two of you would be effective if you were to lead a group together. You might discuss matters such as potential power struggles, competitiveness, compatibility of views and philosophy, your differing styles and how they might complement or interfere with each other, and other issues that you think would have a bearing on your ability to work together well as a team.

11. In small groups, discuss as many specific ethical guidelines for group leaders as you can come up with. Make your suggestions as concrete as possible. One person should record all the guidelines mentioned. After you've listed as many guidelines as you can think of as a group, spend some time deciding on which five items are the most important. Then the groups can reconvene as a class and compare results.

12. In small groups, explore your ideas about what you consider to be unethical behavior in group settings. Try to come up with specific behaviors and practices that you think are unethical. If time permits, discuss how you might deal with unethical behavior on the part of a co-leader or members of the group.

13. You become aware that certain members of your group are using one person in the group as a scapegoat. There is a tendency to gang up on this member and to dump feelings on the person. How will you deal with this situation?

14. What are your ideas about the kind of training you would like to see group

leaders receive before they lead groups? Assume that you're asked to design a training program for group leaders. What will the key features of your program be? In small groups, discuss the designs you and your fellow students come up with. Then the class can reconvene to share and compare results.

15. Form a panel in class to explore the topic of the uses and abuses of group techniques. The panel can look at specific ways in which group techniques can be used to enhance learning, as well as ways in which they can be misused.

16. Do this exercise in dyads. Assume that your partner has very little knowledge about groups. Your job is to inform your partner about groups in a way that is clear and easy to understand. It might be helpful to imagine that your partner is a neighbor who has an interest in groups but who also has many misconceptions about them. Your job is to give your partner a basic understanding of the values and limitations of groups.

The Counselor and Community Involvement 9

PRE-CHAPTER SELF-INVENTORY

For each statement, indicate the response that most closely identifies your beliefs and attitudes. Use the following code: A = I strongly agree; B = I slightly agree; C = I slightly disagree; D = I strongly disagree.

_____ 1. It's generally important to include members of the client's environment in his or her treatment.

_____ 2. Counselors ought to take an active role in dealing with the social conditions that are related to human suffering.

_____ 3. In failing to deal with political and social conditions, much of conventional psychotherapy simply perpetuates elitism, sexism, racism, and oppression.

_____ 4. Mental-health experts should devote more of their energies to prevention, rather than treatment, of emotional and behavioral disorders.

_____ 5. People with emotional or behavioral disturbances can generally be helped to a greater extent in their communities than in mental hospitals.

_____ 6. Most people are not motivated to take the preventive steps that would lead to a decrease in the occurrence of emotional disorders.

_____ 7. To effectively change behavior, long-term, intensive therapy is usually necessary.

_____ 8. Briefer therapies are usually employed because of economic considerations, and they generally offer second-class services to people who critically need adequate help.

_____ 9. Crisis intervention is usually "Band-Aid" therapy that doesn't really change the client's ability to meet new crises effectively.

_____ 10. The idea of a comprehensive community mental-health center is an excellent one.

___ 11. The use of paraprofessionals is a valuable and effective way of dealing with the shortage of professional help.

___ 12. A major function of professionals should be to train and supervise paraprofessionals.

___ 13. Paraprofessionals who receive adequate training and close supervision are capable of providing most of the direct services that professionals now provide.

___ 14. Lay volunteers from the community should be used as members of a mental-health team.

___ 15. Professionals have a responsibility to educate the community about the nature of psychological services.

___ 16. As a counselor, I want to find ways of getting actively involved in the community.

___ 17. Most people feel that a stigma is attached to getting any type of psychological help.

___ 18. Part of my job is to help people in my community become wise consumers of mental-health services.

___ 19. Counselors have a responsibility to be agents of change in their communities.

___ 20. Counselors have a responsibility to become informed about the mental-health services and referral sources available in the community.

INTRODUCTION

Working with individuals who come to them for counseling is only one way in which professionals can use their skills to promote mental and emotional health. It can be easy to neglect the fact that the aspirations and difficulties of clients intertwine with those of many other people in their lives and, ultimately, with those of the community at large. Many people would argue that professional helpers can foster real and lasting changes only if they have an impact on this social setting of people's lives.

Taking a community approach to mental health involves abandoning the view that the role of counselors is to sit back and wait for individuals to come to them for help. A broader conception of the counselor's role might include the following:

- actively reaching out to potential clients;
- initiating programs aimed at preventing problems rather than merely treating them;
- becoming an agent of change in the community;
- devising alternatives to traditional psychotherapy in order to reach more people and make better use of available resources;
- drawing upon the skills of paraprofessionals and laypeople to meet the many different needs of clients; and
- educating consumers about existing resources.

In this chapter, we explore these possibilities in the context of the counselor's responsibility to the community. We'll begin by looking at two recent approaches that emphasize the social setting of the counselor's work—Radical Therapy and the community mental-health movement.

THE CONCEPT OF RADICAL THERAPY

Like many other therapies, Radical Therapy is based on the assumption that therapy should produce *change,* not adjustment. For Radical Therapy, however, this change is social, personal, and political. Writers such as Agel (1971) contend that conventional psychotherapy fails to provide any real help for those who need it the most and that it becomes a self-serving profession. Agel takes a very cynical view of how therapy fails the common person:

> Wherever you look, therapy has failed. The only persons consistently helped are the therapists, whose lives are comfortable. State hospitals are collecting bins and processing plants; psychoanalysis serves a fancy elite group, and it's debatable if it helps even them. Other forms of therapy are hit-and-miss—the field is swollen with people selling their wares, but the wares are often shoddy and the marketplace is corrupt [p. x].

Agel goes on to describe how, in his view, conventional psychotherapy tends to breed sexism, racism, and oppression while failing to grapple with the underlying social and political dynamics of change. He contends that, since most therapists are men and most clients are women, therapy tends to reinforce sexist practices. Similarly, since most therapists are White and middle-class, members of minority groups and people in lower income groups often have a difficult time getting the counseling they need. The position of radical therapists is that people in the community need to become aware of how "self-serving" many of the so-called helping professions are. They can do so only if therapy is deprofessionalized and demystified.

In *Repression or Revolution? Therapy in the United States Today,* Glenn and Kunnes (1973) refer to therapists as "the priests and gurus and faith healers of our time, the experts whose words we accept as truth" (p. 4). They describe the profound influence of conventional psychotherapy on most aspects of life, including child rearing, marriage and family life, love and sex, education, and choice of life-styles. This influence is pernicious, they argue, because therapy makes "people crazy and bludgeons them emotionally, even while trying to help" (p. 2). Instead of challenging people to deal with their overall living situations, therapy deprives clients of their power. While granting that some therapists might be helpful, Glenn and Kunnes contend that conventional therapy, as a whole, fails to free people or cause any substantial change. Further, matters will not improve "unless therapy itself is totally changed in the light of social revolution" (p. 3).

Glenn and Kunnes criticize most community mental-health programs on the grounds that large sums of money are spent to pacify neighborhoods by professionals and institutions that do not have an inside view of the community's needs and problems. Mental health, they argue, should be the concern of the clients and local residents. Thus, day-treatment centers, mental-health clinics, halfway houses, and additional services should be run as community-based programs. The authors take a strong stand that community mental-health programs will be more effective and innovative if they become more concerned with social change and are controlled by the community itself.

At this point we ask you to take time out to clarify your own position with regard to a few of the issues posed by the Radical-Therapy viewpoint.

1. What is your view of the position that conventional therapy has failed and

that therapy must deal with the political and social factors that lead to problems in living?

_____

_____

_____

2. What are a few ways you can think of to involve the community in some of the services professional therapists now provide?

_____

_____

_____

3. One of the basic contentions of Radical Therapy is that psychological problems are the result of social conditions. This view seems to imply that individuals are not responsible for their conditions. Do you agree or disagree? Why?

_____

_____

_____

_____

4. How might the assumption that society, not the individual, is sick influence the way a therapist relates to his or her clients?

_____

_____

_____

_____

THE COMMUNITY MENTAL-HEALTH ORIENTATION

Many therapists who do not share the extreme view of Radical Therapy nevertheless see a need for new approaches to augment the process of individual therapy. Since only a relatively small number of people can be effectively reached by traditional therapeutic approaches, these practitioners support the idea of innovative measures that will make maximum use of the professional resources available. The need for diverse and readily accessible treatment programs has been a key factor in the development of the community mental-health orientation.

Whitlock (1978) describes the current "revolution" in community psychology:

The present revolution involves psychological counselors and the new professionals who are trained in crisis intervention, as well as other mental-health and allied professions. This revolution consists of discarding the constraints of the doctor-patient medical model and abandoning the idea that an emotional problem is a private matter between doctor and patient or between counselor and client. Personality disturbance is no longer a matter of private misery. Both the disturbance itself and the therapeutic efforts to alleviate it are related to the network of relationships in which an individual is involved [p. 9].

Goldenberg (1973) has observed that the community mental-health orientation represents a shift in focus from the individual to the well-being of the wider community. Rather than replacing individual approaches, the community orientation aims at supplementing psychotherapy by stressing the prevention of disorders and by offering a wide variety of programs for education and rehabilitation. This emphasis involves a change in the roles and functions of counselors and therapists, who must be equipped to offer a broader range of psychological services for a larger segment of the population.

Another major factor in the development of the community mental-health viewpoint is the notion that people can be helped more effectively in their communities than in mental institutions. Returning psychiatric patients to the community, it is hoped, will lead to their reintegration into society. On this issue, Bloom (1977) commented "The community-mental-health movement grew out of the conviction that mental hospitals were as much a cause of chronic mental disorder as a cure and that hospitalization was probably as often harmful as it was helpful" (p. 218).

It is our view that an increasing number of people are unable to cope with the demands of their environment and are receptive to the idea of professional assistance. As more people overcome the stigma attached to seeking psychological help, the demand for community services increases. In our opinion, psychotherapy can no longer afford to be tailor-made for the upper-middle-class group. People who are unable to afford the services of professionals in private practice are entitled to adequate treatment programs. Consequently, community clinics are needed to serve people of all ages and backgrounds and with all types and degrees of problems.

The need for community mental-health programs is compounded by such problems of our contemporary society as poverty, absent parents, broken homes, child abuse, unemployment, tension and stress, alienation, addictions to drugs and alcohol, delinquency, and neglect of the elderly. These are merely a few of the areas that pose a formidable challenge for the community approach to the prevention and treatment of human problems.

Operation Outreach

We are sympathetic to the "outreach" approach to mental health, which demands that counselors have the courage to leave their offices and work with people in various community settings. We think the following statement by Drum and Figler (1977) merits careful reflection:

Many helpers realized that services could not only be successfully provided outside of the office, but that in many cases they were more successful because they were now able to "draw the unreachables" and focus on some of the needs unique to people who lived in a certain part of the community or shared a common life-style [p. 25].

Brooks (1977a) also makes the point that professionals need to think of ways of actively reaching people who otherwise might not take advantage of available resources: "Counselors must leave their pleasant or semipleasant offices, and base their offerings in locations that are more readily accessible for the clientele being served" (p. 365). Thus, mental-health practitioners are asked to imagine themselves doing more outreach work in the territory of their clients. They might function on the steps of a tenement, in a data-processing lab, at a hospital bedside, in a school locker room, in a business setting, or in other places where their clients live, work, and play.

The outreach approach includes developmental and educational efforts aimed at the prevention of unnecessary life problems. Drum and Figler (1977) argue that clients should not have to experience real turmoil before they are willing to ask for the help they need. Rather, the outreach approach focuses on growth and developmental needs and aims at prevention, not just remediation. Preventive outreach entails programs that people can use to anticipate and thus deal more effectively with the hazards of living. Such programs might include psychological education, environmental engineering, education of the community concerning mental health, and consultation with human systems, among others. According to Drum and Figler, counselors who involve themselves in community programs will need to be skillful in planning, managing, persuading, suggesting, politicking, training, advocating, speaking to groups, writing, and organizing people. This shift in the counselor's role truly involves a real challenge!

Characteristics of Community Mental-Health Programs

The community mental-health orientation is based upon concepts from fields such as psychology, sociology, social welfare, education, mental hygiene, and public health. The characteristics of the comprehensive mental-health center, as described by Bloom (1977), Dugger (1975), and Goldenberg (1973), include the following:

- Focus is on the interaction a person has with others in the environment and on the impact of social forces on behavior. Emphasis of treatment should be on linking individuals with their communities through the use of new kinds of facilities, such as day-treatment and other out-patient centers.
- Treatment is available to a wide range of people with all types of problems.
- The term *comprehensive* implies a wide range of services, including consultation, direct care, education, and prevention.
- The center's programs should reach people who have previously been unreached, particularly those in the low-income groups.
- A major emphasis should be on the provision of services for children.
- A variety of treatment approaches should be offered, including crisis intervention, groups, therapeutic communities, and family therapy.
- Community control of the centers is important.
- Fees should be charged on an ability-to-pay basis.
- The center should develop a program of in-service education for the staff.
- Roles and leadership should be determined more by competence than by professional identification.
- Training and supervision of paraprofessionals is an important function of the center. Paraprofessionals can frequently assume roles previously limited to professionals.
- Periodic program evaluation is necessary to determine the degree to which the center is meeting the needs of the community.

Levels of Prevention

A central feature of the community mental-health approach should be prevention. We agree with Goldenberg (1973) when he writes: "Preventing behavioral disorders is one of the most innovative aspects of community mental health, although few programs with this purpose are operating" (p. 305). Some agencies have elaborate designs for prevention that look excellent on paper yet are never implemented. Despite the effort that goes into the creation of proposals, the demands of providing treatment for people already in crisis situations usually absorb the time that might otherwise be devoted to preventing emotional problems.

Three levels of prevention are generally described. *Primary prevention* is aimed at reducing the incidence of a disorder in a community through counseling and intervention methods employed *before* the disorder is evidenced. For example, people can be taught ways of dealing with stress in their lives. They can learn how to recognize their level of tension through the use of biofeedback devices and can learn to reduce it through relaxation exercises. Meditation is another example of a way to reduce the level of stress. Other activities that are aimed at primary prevention include developmental counseling, personal-growth groups, courses and workshops designed for enhancing skills in living, premarital counseling, child guidance, and other programs for those who are facing major changes in lifestyle.

Secondary prevention involves treating an existing disorder before it becomes severe and prolonged. Since intervention is more likely to be successful during the beginning stages of a disorder than after it has become ingrained, early detection is important (Goldenberg, 1977). Suicide-prevention centers, for example, are designed to diagnose personality patterns where suicide is likely and to intervene with supportive and reeducative measures.

Tertiary prevention is the maintenance of a maximal level of functioning after a chronic condition becomes evident. Like secondary-prevention programs, tertiary prevention is aimed at reducing the prevalence and duration of existing disorders. Some think that tertiary prevention should be the major goal of community mental-health programs. As Aguilera and Messick (1974) indicate, however, a great number of rehabilitation services still take place in institutions, with a minimum of community involvement.

Pause a moment now to reflect on ways of implementing preventive efforts. What part might you want to play in developing or implementing preventive measures?

1. Too often the people who seek psychological help are in a state of crisis. What are some ways of reaching these people before their situations become critical? How can people be encouraged to be open to prevention of emotional problems?

2. If you were asked to develop some specific programs aimed at preventing emotional and behavioral disorders, what are some of the features you'd include?

_____

_____

_____

_____

_____

CRISIS INTERVENTION AND COMMUNITY PSYCHOLOGY

There are many strategies in the community mental-health approach. In this section we discuss the crisis-intervention model as an illustration of one alternative to long-term individual therapy.

In *Understanding and Coping with Real-Life Crises,* Whitlock (1978) develops the thesis that crisis intervention is a significant dimension of preventive psychology. According to Whitlock, the community approach to mental health involves not only mental-health specialists and the "new professionals" who have been trained in crisis intervention but also other professional persons, such as physicians, nurses, school personnel, the clergy, probation officers, hospital staff, and police personnel. In the course of their work, these and other professionals frequently encounter people who are in the midst of emotional or life crises, and they should have appropriate training in order to deal with these situations.

The role of counselors as mental-health consultants and change agents in the community is advocated by Dworkin (1977) in his article on the "new activist counselor." He encourages counselors and other mental-health professionals to share their specialized knowledge with many of the primary caregivers in the community, so that these persons can learn ways of assisting people during the early stages of crises. Dworkin also indicates that this change of role can be very threatening for some mental-health professionals, because it means taking the mystique and magic out of psychotherapy, leaving the security of the office to enter the world of the client, and sharing skills with others.

Crisis Intervention as an Alternative Approach to Treatment

Several questions need to be asked in evaluating such alternatives to traditional, long-term psychotherapy as crisis intervention. These questions include:

1. Does psychotherapy have to be long-term to be effective? Can briefer therapies have the same impact as long-term therapies?
2. What are some of the advantages and disadvantages of long-term therapy? Of short-term therapy?
3. Is conventional therapy the most efficient way to provide psychological services? What is the best way to reach people who need immediate help?

Community mental-health facilities offer short-term counseling lasting anywhere from one to 20 sessions. Short-term crisis therapy is based on a different set of assumptions and has different characteristics from long-term psychotherapeutic approaches. The sole concern of short-term crisis intervention is to provide as much support and assistance as possible to clients or families who encounter a crisis. To do this, early detection is necessary, and brief, direct intervention methods need to be employed. The goal of these strategies is to restore persons to the level at which they were functioning before the onset of the crisis. A number of basic assumptions underlie this approach. The following have been summarized from Aguilera and Messick (1974) and Goldenberg (1973).

1. Short-term therapy is appropriate for people who are in panic states or who experience anxiety and depression, particularly if their condition is precipitated by a specific set of events.
2. Therapists who use crisis-intervention strategies must believe that these procedures are valid and appropriate. Crisis intervention must not be viewed as a second-best approach but as the therapeutic procedure of choice.
3. The focus of crisis intervention is on specific and limited treatment goals.
4. Accurate assessment of the client's crisis situation is basic to effective intervention. An early assessment of the major problems to be dealt with should be made, and generally there is very little deviation from this initial assessment.
5. Since crisis intervention is a here-and-now, action-oriented therapy, both therapist and client need to be aware of time limitations. Advice, direction, and information giving are often a part of this type of therapy. Intervention is directed mainly at removing symptoms and resolving the presenting problem. To accomplish this goal, the therapist must be willing to assume a directive role.
6. To be most effective, intervention needs to be focused on the material that is directly related to the crisis. Little attention is given to past experiences or to other factors that do not directly relate to the current crisis.
7. Therapy is terminated according to a predetermined schedule, but the possibility for later help or referral is kept open.

What advantages and limitations do you see in the crisis-intervention approach?

_____

_____

_____

_____

_____

Steps in Crisis Intervention

The crisis-intervention process can be described in terms of specific steps, although these should not be thought of as inflexible or definitive. Aguilera and Messick (1974) describe four phases of the technique of crisis intervention.

1. The initial phase consists of an *assessment* of the individual's problem. This assessment typically includes a consideration of factors such as:

- the major environmental stresses;
- the client's personal strengths and weaknesses;
- the precipitating events that resulted in the crisis;
- the reasons the client is seeking help;
- the ways in which the client is attempting to cope with the crisis;
- the degree to which clients might be dangerous to themselves or to others; and
- whether hospitalization or drug therapy should be used in conjunction with other brief therapy approaches.

2. The second phase consists of *making plans for therapeutic intervention*. The goal is to restore clients to their pre-crisis level of functioning, not to effect any major personality changes. During this phase the therapist is concerned with learning how the crisis has affected the client's life and the lives of those who are involved with the client. The therapist is also interested in finding out what coping skills the person has used in the past and what alternative ways of coping might be available. The therapist and client explore how other people and resources could be used as support systems during the current crisis.

3. The third phase consists of *intervention techniques* designed to alleviate the present stresses and achieve a resolution of the crisis. This phase generally lasts no more than five sessions. The nature of the intervention depends greatly on the experience and ingenuity of the therapist, who is free to employ a wide range of directive and supporting procedures. These techniques might include:

- helping clients understand the nature of the crisis;
- suggesting and exploring possible alternative ways of meeting the crisis;
- giving clients an opportunity to fully express their feelings;
- providing support and hope at a time when clients may feel trapped and unable to change their life situation;
- making appropriate referrals for supplementary forms of assistance; and
- helping clients find support systems in their immediate community.

4. The last phase is *resolution of the crisis*. Often counselors are too oriented toward resolution of problems and fail to allow clients enough opportunity to explore their problems or alternative ways of handling the situation more effectively. Even though crisis intervention is a short-term therapy, it is still essential for clients to be allowed to gain some understanding of their situation by expressing what they think and feel. They also need to learn how to use the resources available to them to reduce their anxiety. As their ability to cope with the crisis situation increases, therapists can reinforce any positive changes that occur, and they can discuss ways in which progress can continue to be made. At this time clients need assistance in formulating realistic plans, and they need to talk about how the present experience might indicate ways of dealing more effectively with future crises. The door needs to be left open so that clients feel that they can return for help if and when they need it at a later time.

Criticisms of the Crisis-Intervention Approach

How effective is crisis intervention? Some professionals are critical of crisis counseling on the grounds that it offers "instant therapy" and is aimed at giving easy solutions to complex problems of living. Certainly, there is a danger that crisis counseling can be practiced in such a way that the dispensing of advice and support become the central procedures. People come in when they are feeling miserable; as soon as they begin to experience symptom relief, they may quit, without really learning more effective coping skills to deal with future crises. It is also possible that an emphasis on getting clients out as soon as possible (preferably in fewer than six sessions) can lead to client dependency. If clients fail to gain any new insights or develop the coping skills necessary for self-management, they may become part of a revolving-door client population. We agree with Whitlock (1978) when he cautions against this danger:

> In helping persons face up to their problems realistically, counselors discourage any further infantilization or dependence upon them. Gently confronting clients with the reality of their situations provokes anxiety, and counselors must then communicate the message that they will not do anything for their clients that they can do for themselves [p. 23].

As Whitlock points out, clients need to be challenged to regain some of their sense of personal power to influence the outcomes of future crises. They need to realize that they aren't helpless in the face of crises. Unless crisis counselors exert care, they can reinforce the feeling of powerlessness by attempting to give solutions or in other ways offering instant "cures."

What is your view of the contention that much of crisis intervention is merely directed toward temporarily relieving disturbing symptoms? If you were doing short-term therapy with people who had chronic conditions, how might you prepare them to handle crises more effectively in the future?

_____

_____

_____

_____

_____

Dealing with Crisis Situations: Some Examples

We've suggested that short-term crisis intervention is one alternative to conventional psychotherapy. Not simply a second-best therapeutic approach, crisis intervention can be the preferred technique in some situations. Moreover, this short-term therapy allows counselors to work with more of the population and therefore results in a wider distribution of professional resources.

Now we'd like to involve you in thinking about the uses and applications of crisis intervention. The following are examples of crisis situations that you might encounter in a community mental-health center. Assume that your job involves working with a wide range of clients and problems. After reading each of the following cases, briefly write down your immediate response to this question: How adequately do you feel you could deal with this client, assuming you could see him or her for a maximum of six sessions?

John, age 8, is brought to the center by his parents because he is consistently getting sick and missing school. John's parents inform you that their physician referred him for *psychological help, saying that he had school phobia. In talking with John you detect that he is extremely anxious, very fearful of failing and of meeting others, and highly insecure when he is away from home.*

_____

_____

_____

_____

Cindy is 39 years old. She says that she has come to the clinic because she feels that her life is falling apart and she doesn't know where to turn. Her husband has left her and their four children, and she is in a panic state because she doesn't know how she will support herself and the children or how she will take care of them if she gets a job. In addition, she is frightened of her hostile feelings toward her husband for deserting her.

_____

_____

_____

_____

Chuck, a 24-year-old graduate student, comes to the clinic because of severe anxiety attacks that began when he received notice that he was on academic probation. He tells you that he simply must succeed and get his Master's degree. Since being placed on probation, he has been unable to focus on anything except his fear of not completing a program that means so much to him.

_____

_____

_____

_____

Evaluation of a Case

We'll now present a case and ask you to evaluate the way the therapist handles the client who is in crisis. We'll also ask you to decide what alternative approaches you might use if you were the client's therapist.

Michael, age 58, comes to the clinic because of severe bouts of depression and grief. Since his wife's death a year ago, Michael has steadily become less able to function effectively, and he is feeling more and more lost and alone. He tells the counselor that he hasn't been able to let go of his wife, that he is losing his own will to live, that he is unable to reach out to anyone else and make contact, that he doesn't eat or sleep well, that he is unable to find any joy or meaning in anything, and that he no longer really cares what happens to him. He knows that he must do something, or he'll "just rot away." He expresses his hope that he can be helped back on his feet once again.

Using a crisis-intervention model, the counselor takes the following approach with Michael.

1. At the initial session, she assesses Michael's problem. Her main concern is to answer such questions as:

- Why has Michael come to the clinic at this time?
- What are some of the specific events that have led up to his crisis?
- How much ego strength does Michael have?
- Is there a risk that he might attempt to end his life?
- Is there a possibility that he might need more intensive treatment at an in-patient facility?

2. During her next session with Michael, the counselor plans intervention measures. She decides that it's important for Michael to express and work through his unfinished grief. Since he has never fully grieved over his wife's death, memories of her dominate his thoughts. He continues to ruminate over all the things that he didn't do with her when she was alive and punishes himself for not doing what he feels he should have done. The counselor also decides that Michael needs to make contact with other people and begin to form new relationships. The main goals that will guide her during the sessions are to encourage Michael to see how he has not gone through the grief process, to help him express the feelings of loss that he has kept locked inside of him, and to design situations in which he will reach out and make some contact with other people.

3. During the remaining four sessions, the counselor uses the following intervention techniques to accomplish her therapeutic goals:

- She helps Michael to see how his present symptoms are related to the loss of his wife.
- She encourages Michael to talk about and experience his feelings of loss, guilt, anger, emptiness, and fear.
- She has Michael talk to his wife during a session to tell her directly all the things he has been keeping inside himself.
- She discusses with Michael some of the specific ways in which he behaves when he feels intensely anxious and depressed, and she suggests alternative behaviors.
- In conjunction with the series of six individual sessions, she asks Michael to join a weekly group so that he can have some experience of sharing with others and getting support from them.

4. During the final session, the counselor talks with Michael about the progress he has made and the specific steps he can continue to take in order to avoid becoming victimized by his depressive moods. Together they discuss how he can use the group-therapy sessions to cope more effectively with life.

1. What is your evaluation of the way the counselor worked with Michael?

_____

_____

_____

2. What would your goals be if you were to work with Michael for six sessions?

_____

_____

_____

_____

3. What are some specific interventions you would make to accomplish your goals?

_____

_____

_____

4. How would you feel about working with a client such as Michael?

_____

_____

5. What limitations do you see in the use of the crisis-intervention approach with Michael?

_____

_____

_____

THE USE OF PARAPROFESSIONALS

The question of how best to deliver psychological services to the people who are most in need of them is a controversial one. It is clear that there are not enough professionally trained people to meet the demand for psychological assistance. Faced with this reality, many people in the mental-health field have concluded that nonprofessionals should be given the training and supervision they need to provide some psychological services that only professionals have previously been allowed to provide. There has therefore been a trend toward the increased use of paraprofessionals in counseling and related fields.

One important reason for the increasing use of paraprofessionals is economic. Service agencies have discovered that paraprofessionals can indeed provide some services as effectively as full professionals for much lower salaries. However, as Goldenberg (1977) observes, this is not the only advantage to the use of paraprofessionals: "Many paraprofessionals are being trained for new service functions and roles that some psychologists believe they are better able than professionals to fulfill because of their special relationships, as residents, to the communities they serve" (p. 53).

A training model for paraprofessionals as educator consultants is described in *A Symposium on Skill Dissemination for Paraprofessionals* (Danish et al., 1978). The symposium touched on empirical studies that underscored an important point: Many jobs could be done equally well by helpers who were less highly trained than professional specialists. In some cases, paraprofessionals appeared to have greater success than professionals with institutionalized people who were once considered hopeless.

Not all mental-health professionals are enthusiastic about the potential of the paraprofessional movement. Some point to the danger that inadequately trained people might do more harm than good; others claim that the poor who need treatment will receive inferior service; still others fear that more and more paraprofessionals will be allowed to practice without the close supervision and intensive training they need. In addition, as Goldenberg (1977) points out, paraprofessionals represent a threat to the economic interests of some professionals. Despite the opposition of some professionals, however, there seems to be little chance that the trend toward the use of paraprofessionals will be reversed. We are in agreement with Goldenberg when he says "Professionals have a social responsibility to train paraprofessionals. If they fail to carry out this responsibility, the public will turn to individuals with little or no training and the results may in the long run prove to be most unfortunate for all" (p. 59).

Types of Nontraditional Mental-Health Workers

Currently, there are three general types of nontraditional mental-health workers.

1. Many community colleges offer two-year programs in the human services. Students in these programs receive specialized training that is aimed at preparing them to work in community mental-health centers, hospitals, and other human-services agencies. In addition, many colleges and universities have established four-year undergraduate programs in human services that stress practical experience, training, and supervision in mental-health work.

2. Lay volunteers from the community are also receiving training and supervision in therapeutic intervention with a wide range of clients. These volunteers work on hotlines, co-lead groups, and engage in other types of supportive activities. Many professionals contend that, although the use of community volunteers is not a cure-all for the problem of the shortage of available personnel, trained volunteers can make a contribution in augmenting the work of professional therapists.

3. The use of former patients is another promising way of meeting the increasing demand for mental-health services. Former addicts play a role in rehabilitating others who are addicted to drugs through Synanon programs. Alcoholics Anonymous is well known for its contributions in keeping alcoholics sober through the efforts of people who have learned that they can no longer handle alcohol. In many places former mental patients are helping others make the transition from state hospitals to their communities. Besides helping to alleviate the shortage of personnel in the mental-health field, these nonprofessionals may actually be more effective in reaching certain people, because they have experienced similar problems and learned to deal with them successfully.

The trend toward the increased use of paraprofessionals means that professionals will have to assume new and expanding roles. Rather than devoting the bulk of their time to direct services, such as one-to-one counseling, they may need to spend considerable time offering in-service workshops for paraprofessionals and volunteer workers. Other activities that could assume priority include educating the public about the nature of mental health, training and supervising the work of paraprofessionals, consulting, working as change agents in the community, designing new programs, conducting research, and evaluating existing programs.

OTHER WAYS OF BECOMING INVOLVED IN THE COMMUNITY

It is relatively easy for counselors to believe that they can effectively meet the needs of their clients through one-to-one sessions in the office. We have indicated in this chapter, however, that many problems demand a broader approach if real change is to occur. We suggest that you consider the responsibility you may have to teach clients to use the resources available to them in their communities.

What follows is a list of things you might do to link your clients to the community in which they live. Rate each of these activities, using the following code: A = I would do this routinely; B = I would do this occasionally; C = I would do this rarely.

____ 1. Familiarize myself with available community resources so that I could refer my clients to appropriate sources of further help.

____ 2. With my clients' permission, contact people who have a direct influence in their lives.

____ 3. Try to arrange sessions that would involve both a client and the significant people in his or her life so that we could explore ways of changing certain relationships.

____ 4. As a part of the counseling process, teach my clients how to take advantage of the auxiliary support systems in the community.

____ 5. Suggest homework assignments or use other techniques to get my clients thinking about ways that they could apply what they learn in the individual sessions to their everyday lives.

Now list other options you can think of for encouraging your clients to find other ways of meeting their needs besides individual counseling.

_____

_____

_____

_____

_____

The Professional's Role in Educating the Community

Too often counselors wait for clients to come to them in their offices. As a consequence many prospective clients never appear. There are many reasons why people do not make use of available resources: they may not be aware of their existence; they may have misconceptions about the nature and purpose of counseling; they may be reluctant to recognize their problems; or they may harbor the attitude that they should be able to take charge of their lives on their own.

For these reasons, we think that educating the public and thus changing the attitudes of the community toward mental health is a primary responsibility of professionals. Perhaps the most important task in this area is to demystify the notion of mental illness. Unfortunately, many people still cling to archaic notions of mental illness. They may make a clear demarcation between people they perceive as "crazy" and those they perceive as "normal." Some of the misconceptions about mental illness that are still widespread are these: that, once people suffer from mental illness, they can never be cured; that people with emotional or behavioral disorders are merely deficient in "will power"; and that the mentally ill are always dangerous and should be separated from the community lest they "contaminate" or harm others. Professionals face a real challenge in combating these faulty notions.

Psychotherapy is another area that needs to be demystified. Some of the misconceptions people have of psychotherapy include these: that it is some form of magic; that it is only for people with extreme problems; that therapists provide clients with answers; that therapy is only for weak people; and that people should be able to solve their problems without professional help. These misconceptions often reinforce the resistance people already have toward seeking professional help. Unless professionals actively work on presenting psychotherapy in a way that is intelligible to the community at large, many people who could benefit from professional help may not seek it out.

To illustrate how widespread ignorance concerning available resources can be, one of us regularly asks upper-division classes of students in human services and counseling whether they know where the college counseling center is located. Generally, only about 25% of the class members know where the center is; even fewer are aware of the kinds of services offered. If this lack of knowledge is common among people who will eventually be involved in community mental health, how much more common must it be among the general public! And if future professionals are not aware of available resources, how can they educate others to use them? Moreover, we've found that these students, who might be expected to be somewhat sophisticated regarding psychological counseling, often harbor misconceptions about therapy and resist seeking help when they need it for themselves.

Of course, the problem does not originate entirely with students. We've found that many college counselors are unwilling to do much public-relations work. They tend to resist going outside their offices and making themselves known to students through direct contacts. Some of these counselors assume that it's up to the students to take the initiative to find help if they want it. This same attitude is shared by many counselors who work in community agencies. They stay within the agency and do very little to develop a public-relations program that will make the community more aware of existing services and how to utilize them. It is hardly surprising that many people who need psychological help never get it if no one has launched an effective program to educate the public and deal with people's resistance to getting the help they need.

An Example of Educating the Community about a Program

Worthwhile projects often fail because the community has not been adequately prepared for them. As an example of a program designed to educate the community about psychological services, let's assume that your center offers several types of therapy groups. Your task is to inform people about the nature of these groups and to make the groups accessible to those who might benefit from them. As you think about how you would design your program of education, consider the following questions.

Have you thought through *why* you're offering a group, what specific type of group it will be, and who it is for? Unfortunately, many community workers haven't really clarified their objectives and offer groups mainly because they're in vogue. Thus, they frequently meet with more resistance than they would have if they had adequately prepared the community for the group. The questions that need to be addressed might include the following:

- Is the group designed for treatment or educational purposes?
- What are the specific goals of the group? What can participants expect to gain from it?
- Have potential members been prepared for participating in the group? Are they aware of its values and limitations? Are they informed about possible hazards and about their rights as group members?
- Have the group leaders assessed the need for the kind of group they are offering? If so, have they designed a program that will effectively address these needs?

As with other types of therapy, there are many misconceptions about groups that need to be identified and corrected if people are to take advantage of group offerings. Let's consider a few of these misconceptions.

1. "Group experiences consist of breaking down defenses, and then people are left vulnerable and psychologically damaged." Here your program of education could include explaining that, although some groups operate on the principle of stripping away defenses, a group can respect the fact that all of us have defenses and that these defenses are sometimes necessary. People are more inclined to surrender their defenses when they experience a sense of trust and caring in the group. Thus, people need to learn that confrontation can be done in a caring manner and that being challenged to take an honest look at themselves doesn't mean that group members will leave the group with psychological scars.

2. "Participants are often more unhappy after they experience a group, because their problems have surfaced." It's true that we might experience some pain as a result of recognizing and accepting some of our problems. In educating people about your group, you may need to teach them that group therapy, like any other therapy, is difficult work and involves considerable struggle. People who are contemplating any form of therapy need to be aware that they are likely to be increasingly vulnerable for a time as they begin to shed their protective masks.

3. "Only people who are sick get involved in group counseling." Perhaps

one of the most common misconceptions is that counseling is only for those who are seriously disturbed. This is unfortunate, because many people who don't see themselves as being "sick" close off possible avenues of understanding themselves and resolving problems. One of your challenges is to educate the community to the growth aspects of groups and to demonstrate that groups have other purposes besides curing emotional disorders.

4. "Groups encourage dependence, for they are really a form of brainwashing." Here you can work on informing the community that any type of therapy aims at fostering independence. In the case of groups, the point needs to be made that they are not designed to give people easy solutions and that a good group encourages participants to make their own decisions.

These four misconceptions are just a few examples of possible targets for a community-wide educational program. Although we've used groups to illustrate the point, other mental-health services need to be presented to the community in such a way that those who need them will be psychologically prepared to seek them out.

Education is only one area in which counselors can broaden their services to the community. To assist you in thinking of ways to get involved in your community, we'll list a number of options for you to consider. After reading each of these suggestions, briefly discuss how appropriate it would be for you.

1. You could give talks about your agency or center to local groups, clubs, classes, and other organizations where there are potential consumers.

   _____

   _____

   _____

2. You could learn about the sources of power in your community and contact these people. This may entail contacting local organizations, churches, physicians, schools, and so forth. You could tell these people what you do and ask for their ideas on how to reach the people who could most benefit from counseling.

   _____

   _____

   _____

3. You could offer noncredit short courses or workshops at a local adult school on such topics as learning how to cope with stress, techniques of meditation, developing friendships, and creative use of leisure time. These workshops could be of real value to people who might not otherwise make contact with a counselor.

   _____

   _____

   _____

4. You could offer courses or workshops through the extension programs of local colleges.

_____

_____

_____

5. You could conduct a survey in the community to find out what kinds of programs people want.

_____

_____

_____

6. You could give talks to community groups to help people become wiser consumers of psychological services.

_____

_____

_____

_____

Now list some other specific strategies that you might use in getting involved in the community.

_____

_____

_____

_____

_____

CHAPTER SUMMARY

The primary thrust of this chapter has been to suggest ways of going beyond the limitations of one-to-one counseling. We've suggested that counselors not only need to get involved in the community but also need to find ways of helping their clients make the transition from individual counseling to their everyday lives. In discussing the community mental-health orientation, we described crisis counseling as an example of one way to meet the increasing demand for psychological services. We suggested that it's important to think of ways to educate the community about available resources and to broaden the range of these resources. Too often mental-health professionals have not been creative in devising programs that are addressed to the diverse needs of the community. For this reason we discussed some alternatives to conventional therapy and the new roles implied by these alternatives for professional counselors and therapists.

ACTIVITIES, EXERCISES, AND IDEAS FOR THOUGHT AND DISCUSSION

1. Invite people who are involved in community mental health to speak to your class about the kinds of services they provide, the population they serve, and the current problems and trends in community mental health.

2. Several students can read books such as Agel's *The Radical Therapist* or Glenn and Kunnes' *Repression or Revolution? Therapy in the United States Today*. These students can form a panel to discuss the topic "Is conventional psychotherapy an adequate approach to meet the mental-health needs of the community?" Several other students who see value in conventional therapeutic approaches could also be part of the panel.

3. In small subgroups, explore specific ways of getting involved in your clients' lives beyond the office. What are some ways of becoming involved in the community or using community resources to assist you in working with your clients? After you've explored these issues, the class can reconvene to pool ideas.

4. In small groups, explore all the ways you can think of to develop a program that is geared to the prevention of emotional and behavioral disorders. If your group were to design a positive program geared to educating people in the community about keeping psychologically fit, what would your program look like?

5. Two students can volunteer to debate the issue "How does the effectiveness of short-term therapies compare with that of long-term therapies?" One student argues for the proposition that therapy must be on a long-term basis to be effective. The other student argues that briefer therapies not only are effective but are the appropriate and preferred form of treatment in many situations.

6. Several students who are interested in the use of paraprofessionals in the human-services field can investigate the issue and present their results in the form of a panel discussion. The discussion can focus on the advantages and disadvantages of the use of paraprofessionals, current trends, and other issues the panel deems important.

7. Assume that you're the director of a mental-health center in your community. Your project is funded by the government, and you're given the freedom to design and implement any type of program you think is appropriate and innovative. What would your program be designed to do? What would some of its innovative features be? What kinds of services would you offer to the community? What kinds of people would be working at the center? This exercise has many possibilities, a few of which include:
   a. It can be the basis of a reaction or position paper.
   b. It can be explored in class in small groups.
   c. It can be the basis for a panel discussion.
   d. Members of the class can interview mental-health workers or clinic directors.
   e. You can invite the director of a mental-health center to explore this issue with your class.
   f. Several students can work on this project as a team and present their findings to the class.

8. Design ways of informing and educating the community about what psychological services are, who they are for, and how people can make maximum use of the resources available to them.

9. As a slight variation or extension of the preceding exercise, prepare a ten-minute talk that would be appropriate to give to a community group. The purpose of your talk is to teach people how to be wise consumers of psychological services and to set a tone that would make them more likely to seek such services if they needed them. Several students can present talks, and the rest of the class can give them feedback on how they think a community group might respond.

10. An issue you may well face in your practice is how to get through the resistance that people have toward asking for psychological assistance. Ask yourself how you should respond to clients who have questions such as these: "What will people think if they find out that I'm coming for professional help?" "Shouldn't I really be able to solve my problems on my own? Isn't it a sign of weakness that I need others to help me?" "Aren't most people who come to a community clinic really sick?" "Will I really be able to resolve my problems by consulting a mental-health professional?" After you've thought through your own responses, you can share them in dyads or in small groups.

11. For this exercise, begin by working in dyads. One student assumes the role of a person in some type of crisis. The student who will role-play the client should be able to identify in some way with the crisis situation. The other student becomes the crisis counselor and conducts an intake interview that does not exceed 30 minutes. Alternatively, a crisis situation can be presented to the entire class, and several students can show what immediate interventions they would make. An example would be working on a hotline service with a teenage caller who is frightened because of a bad trip with LSD. Students who participate as counselors should be given feedback, and alternative intervention techniques should be discussed.

12. Assume that you want to become a change agent in your community and that one of your goals is to deal with social and political factors associated with the problems that people bring to your clinic. What are some things you can imagine doing? This is a good topic for brainstorming in class.

13. Groups of students can visit a private clinic, a day-treatment center, a state hospital, a family-guidance clinic, a free clinic, a comprehensive community mental-health center, and other human-services agencies. The groups can share their observations and reactions in class. This is an excellent way to directly experience the workings of a mental-health facility and to learn about the functioning of other agencies by hearing what other students observed.

14. How aware are you of the resources that exist in your community? Would you know where to refer clients for special help? How aware are you of the support systems that exist in your community? Individually or with other students, investigate a comprehensive community mental-health center in your area. In doing so, find the answers to questions such as these:

    a. Where would you send a family who needed help?

    b. What facilities are available to treat drug and alcohol abuse?

    c. What kinds of crisis intervention are available? What are some common kinds of crises that are encountered?

    d. Are health and medical services available at the center?

    e. What kinds of groups are offered?

    f. Is individual counseling available? For whom? At what fee? Long-term? Short-term?

    g. Where would you refer a couple who have a crisis in their marriage and are seeking marital counseling?

h. Are hotline services available?
i. What provisions are there for emergency situations?
j. What are the procedures for hospitalizing a client?
k. What do people have to do to qualify for help at the center?
15. As a class, see whether you can arrange for a field visit to a state mental hospital. Pay attention to the surroundings and to the type of treatment that is available to the patients. After your field trip, your class can explore such issues as whether patients in mental hospitals receive treatment or merely custodial care.

Learning to Work within the System 10

For each statement, indicate the response that most closely identifies your beliefs and attitudes. Use the following code: A = I strongly agree; B = I slightly agree; C = I slightly disagree; D = I strongly disagree.

_____ 1. I generally don't like to challenge the people I work for.

_____ 2. It's possible to work within the framework of a system and still do the things I'm convinced are most important to do.

_____ 3. When I think of working in some agency or institution, I feel a sense of powerlessness about initiating any real change in that organization.

_____ 4. It's important to continually ask myself "What makes me think I have the right to counsel anybody?"

_____ 5. I see myself as basically cooperative in working with colleagues.

_____ 6. I frequently have good ideas and proposals, and I see myself as willing to do the work necessary to translate these plans into actual programs.

_____ 7. If I'm honest with myself, I can see that I might have a tendency to blame external sources for a failure on my part to do more professionally.

_____ 8. I see myself as a fighter in a system, in the sense that I'll work to change things I don't approve of.

_____ 9. Although I might be unable to bring about drastic changes in an institution or system, I do feel confident that I can make changes within the boundaries of my own position.

_____ 10. I can see that I might fall into complacency and rarely question what I'm doing or how I could do my work more effectively.

_____ 11. Counselors who no longer raise questions or struggle with ethical concerns have stopped growing professionally.

____ 12. It would be unethical to accept a position with an agency whose central aims I disagreed with philosophically.

____ 13. Ethical concerns are not simply answered once and for all; to become an ethical practitioner, I must be willing to continually raise questions about what I'm doing.

____ 14. As a counselor, I'm part of a system, and I have a responsibility to work toward changing those aspects of the system that I think need changing.

____ 15. I feel a personal need for meaningful contact with colleagues so that I don't become excessively narrow in my thinking.

INTRODUCTION

Many professionals struggle with the issue of how to work within a system while retaining their dignity, vitality, and convictions. Although working in any organization can be frustrating, we've observed a tendency on the part of some counselors to put the blame too readily on institutions when their efforts to help others don't succeed. Although bureaucratic obstacles can certainly make it difficult to implement sound ideas, we assume that it's possible to learn ways of working within an institution with dignity and self-respect. Consequently, in this chapter we emphasize the need for honest self-examination in determining the degree to which the "system" is actually hindering you as you try to put your ideas into practice.

As counselors, we each need to determine how much responsibility we have for the outcomes of our projects. We also need to decide what our styles for working within a system will be and how we can be most effective. Some counselors who are dissatisfied with the system decide to subvert it in as many ways as they can. Others conform to institutional policies for fear of losing their positions. Some counselors find ways of making compromises between institutional demands and their personal requirements, while others find it impossible to retain their personal and professional dignity and still work within an institutional framework. It will be up to you to find your own answers to questions such as these:

- What stance will I take in dealing with the system?
- How can I meet the requirements of an institution and at the same time do what I most believe in?
- In what ways can I work to change the system?
- At what point does the price of attempting to work within an organized structure become too high? Can I work within an institutional framework and still retain my dignity?

AVOIDING RESPONSIBILITY FOR WORKING WITHIN A SYSTEM

We've alluded to the tendency to blame institutions for failing to implement effective programs. So often we hear the "If only it weren't for——" argument, which absolves the speaker of responsibility and diminishes his or her personal power at the same time. Take a moment now to reflect on some typical statements of this kind and apply them to yourself. How likely are you to resort to these statements as a way of deflecting responsibility to external sources? Rate each one, using the following code:

A = I feel this way often, and I can hear myself making this
        statement frequently.
B = I feel this way at times, and I might be inclined to say
        this occasionally.
C = I rarely feel this way.
D = I can't see myself using this statement as a way of absolving
        myself of personal responsibility.

_____ 1. You have to play politics if you want to get your programs through.
_____ 2. I can't do what I really want to do, because my director or supervisor wouldn't allow it.
_____ 3. If the community were more receptive to mental-health programs, my proposals and projects would be far more successful than they are.
_____ 4. I'm not succeeding because my clients aren't motivated.
_____ 5. I can't really say what I think, because I'd lose my job.
_____ 6. The bureaucratic system makes it almost impossible to develop innovative and meaningful programs.
_____ 7. If I were given more time off, I could develop exciting projects; as it is now, all my time is consumed by busywork.
_____ 8. I'm not free to pursue my own interests in my job, because the institution dictates what my interests will be.
_____ 9. The system makes it difficult to engage in the kind of counseling that would produce real change.
_____ 10. My own individuality and professional identity must be subordinate to the policies of the institution if I expect to survive in the system.

What other statements might you make in order to blame the system for the difficulties you encounter as a professional?

_____

_____

_____

_____

The Results of Evading Personal Responsibility

Counselors who put the blame on the "system" when they fail to act in accordance with their beliefs are bound to experience a growing sense of powerlessness. This feeling is sometimes expressed in words such as "I really can't change anything at all! I may as well just do what's expected and play the game." We think that the temptation to submit to this stance of professional impotence constitutes a real ethical concern. It is the kind of attitude that feeds on itself. When counselors surrender their own power, they assume the position of victims. They may soon develop the cynical attitude that any proposal they make will be frustrated, and they may seriously wonder whether anything they do really matters. Failing to see any significance in their work, they may begin to feel defeated and discouraged, and they may close off opportunities to make their work a source of vitality.

Another way of evading personal responsibility is to settle into a comfortable rut. We've seen many counselors who have found a niche in the system and who have learned to survive with a minimum of effort. In order to remain comfortable, they continue to do the same thing over and over for weeks, months, and years. They rarely question the effectiveness of their efforts or give much thought to ways of reaching a greater number of people more effectively. They neither question the system in which they're involved nor develop new projects that would give them a change of pace. We think that this kind of complacency is just as deadly a form of powerlessness as the defeated feeling of those who decide they can't really change things.

Defeatism and complacency are both attitudes that cheat the *clients* counselors are trying to serve. For this reason, we ask you to consider how ethical it is for counselors to give in to these feelings. We believe that counselors have a responsibility to look at their own tendency to become comfortable to the degree that they make the system work for them instead of those it is intended to serve.

ASSUMING POWER WITHIN THE SYSTEM

If counselors recognize that there are obstacles to overcome in any system, they may be able to acquire a sense of personal power to make significant changes. Our central aim in this chapter is to encourage you to define a style of working within a system that suits your personality. Although we cannot prescribe a universal method of getting along in an institution, we can present some strategies that we have found helpful and ask you to determine how appropriate these strategies are for you. In addition, we hope that you can think of additional ways of preserving your individuality while working as part of a system.

1. Your first opportunity to assert your individuality is in the job interview. Often people being interviewed for a position confine themselves to answering the questions that are asked of them. However, job interviews can be mutual exchanges in which you can explore the requirements and expectations of a position and assess its suitability for yourself. It's important to recognize that accepting a position with an agency entails agreeing to work within a certain philosophical framework. By asking relevant questions, you begin to assume a stance of power, for you are exploring how much you want a particular job and what price you're willing to pay for it.

What are some questions that you would want to raise in a job interview?

_____

_____

_____

_____

Under what circumstances, if any, would you accept a position even though you disagreed with the agency's policies or priorities?

_____

_____

_____

2. Our experience has been that most established organizations resist change but that small and subtle changes can be significant. If you devote most of your energy to trying to change the people who defend the status quo, your positive programs may become a lesser priority. You'll need to decide for yourself how much energy you're willing to expend on dealing with the resistive forces you encounter. If you attempt radical, system-wide changes, you might feel overwhelmed or paralyzed. If you focus instead on making changes within the scope of your position, you'll stand a better chance of extending your influence. For instance, a social worker whose goal is to correct fundamental inequities in the social-welfare system might soon feel discouraged and helpless. By directing his attention to ways of dealing more humanely with the people he comes into contact with, he may experience a sense of power and accomplishment as he makes less grandiose, but still significant, changes. To take another example, a school counselor might give up in exasperation if she directs most of her efforts to changing her colleagues' view of their role. If she concentrates instead on defining her own role so that she can do the kind of counseling she believes in, she may succeed in making a smaller but still meaningful change.

What experiences have you had in encountering resistance to ideas you wanted to put into practice?

_____

_____

_____

How do you think you would deal with a situation in which you felt that your power to make real changes was extremely limited?

_____

_____

_____

3. Another way to assume power to make changes is to learn the reasons for the policies of the organization you work for. Perhaps there are good reasons why certain policies have been established, even if they seem to restrict your freedom in your job. On the other hand, if a policy is not in the best interest of the clients, you can begin to challenge the assumptions on which the policy is based. You can suggest alternative policies, and you can find out whether others on the staff share your view. A sound understanding of the aims of the agency can strengthen your assessment of existing policies and make your suggestions more acceptable to those in charge. Consulting colleagues can put you in a better position to suggest changes than if you operate in isolation.

What would you do if the organization you worked for instituted some policies to which you were strongly opposed?

_____

_____

_____

What would you do if you strongly believed that some fundamental changes needed to be made in your institution, and your colleagues disagreed?

_____

_____

_____

4. Often people remain powerless because they don't make the effort to order their priorities and work on them systematically. We've found it helpful to determine what we *most* wanted to accomplish in a given position. We recognize that we don't have total autonomy while we're associated with a system, and so at times we're willing to negotiate and compromise. By ordering our priorities, we can decide which compromises we can make without sacrificing our integrity and which positions cannot be compromised in good faith. Knowing what we consider to be most important puts us in a much better position to ask for what we want. In conjunction with this, good communication with directors and supervisors is essential. We try to keep the people to whom we report informed about how we're using our time and why. Many times a proposal fails to be accepted, not because it's unsound, but because the person responsible for approving it has not been adequately informed of its rationale or design. Since supervisors or directors are the ones who will be on the receiving end of any complaints, they may thwart a plan or block certain activities because they haven't been convinced of their merit.

What are some things you most want to accomplish as a counselor?

_____

_____

_____

Which of these areas, if any, could you compromise on in good faith?

_____

_____

_____

What would you do if your supervisor continually blocked most of your activities, despite your efforts to keep him or her informed of the reasons for them?

_____

_____

_____

5. One essential element in learning how to work effectively within a system is to realize that you're a vital part of that system, that "the institution" is not something that can be divorced from you. This implies that your relationships with other staff members are a central part of the system. Ignoring this reality and attempting to function in isolation will probably diminish your effectiveness. More positively, colleagues can be nourishing and supportive, and your interactions with them can give you a fresh perspective on some of your activities. Furthermore, genuine relationships with your co-workers can be a way of gaining power to make changes with the help of others who share your cause.

Unfortunately, although interactions with others in the institution can be energizing, they can also be debilitating. Instead of developing support groups within an agency, some people develop cliques, harbor unspoken hostility, and generally refuse to confront the conflicts or frictions that keep the staff divided. Often there are hidden agendas at staff meetings, and only superficial matters are discussed while real issues are kept secret. We want to underscore the importance of finding ways to establish working relationships that enrich your professional life instead of draining your energy. It's strange that counselors, who are supposed to be experts in helping others to establish nourishing relationships, often complain that they miss meaningful contacts with their colleagues. If you feel isolated, you can decide to take the initiative and arrange for fruitful interactions with others on the staff. For example, you could suggest a regular meeting time during which several colleagues could share their concerns and experiences. In addition, we think that working with others on special projects is a good way to renew yourself and a source of inspiration that can suggest new directions.

How would you attempt to make contact with other colleagues if your staff seemed to work largely in isolation from one another?

If your staff seemed to be divided by jealousies, hostilities, or unspoken conflicts, what do you think you would do about the situation?

How might you benefit, both personally and professionally, from interactions with colleagues? What would you most want from them?

Although we've stressed the theme of learning how to work within a system, we recognize that there are circumstances in which leaving an organization is the only way to retain one's integrity without settling into a position of cynicism and powerlessness. What are some of the reasons that might lead you to leave an organization?

_____

_____

_____

_____

_____

TWO CASE EXAMPLES

The following two case examples are designed to illustrate some of the issues we've discussed in this chapter. Try to imagine yourself in each of these situations, and ask yourself how you would deal with them.

1. Sarah works in a community mental-health clinic, and most of her time is devoted to dealing with immediate crisis situations. The more she works with people in crises, the more she is convinced that the focus of her work should be on preventive programs designed to educate the public. Sarah comes to believe strongly that there would be far fewer clients in a state of crisis if people were effectively contacted and motivated to participate in growth-oriented educational programs. She develops detailed, logical, and convincing proposals for programs she would like to implement in the community, but they are consistently rejected by the director of her center on the grounds that the primary purpose of the clinic is to intervene in crisis situations. Because the clinic is partially funded by the government for the expressed purpose of crisis intervention, the director feels uneasy about approving any program that doesn't relate directly to this objective.

If you were in Sarah's place, what do you think you would do? Which of the following courses of action would you be likely to take?

_____ I'd probably do what the director expected and complain that the bureaucratic structure inhibited the implementation of imaginative programs.

_____ Rather than take the director's "no" as a final answer, I'd try to work toward a compromise. I'd do what was expected of me while finding some way to make room for my special project. I'd work with the director until I convinced her to permit me to launch my program in some form.

_____ If I couldn't do what I deemed important, I'd look for another job.

_____ I'd get several other staff members together in order to pool our resources and look for ways to implement our program as a group.

Other:

_____

_____

_____

2. George is a social worker in a school district. He is expected to devote most of his time to checking on children who are habitually truant and to doing social-welfare work with dependent families. Although he knew his job description before he accepted the position, George now feels that his talents could be put to better use if he were allowed to do intensive counseling with families as units. Referral sources in the area are meager, and the families he works with cannot afford private treatment. Although George has the training to do the type of family counseling that he thinks is sorely needed, his school administrator makes it clear that any kind of therapy is outside the province of the school's responsibility. George is told to confine himself to tracking down truant children, doing legal work, and processing forms. If you were in George's position, what do you think you would do?

_____ I'd present a written plan to the local school board, showing that family counseling is needed and that public facilities are inadequate to meet this need.

_____ I'd go ahead and do the family counseling without telling my administrator.

_____ I wouldn't make waves, because I wouldn't want to lose my job.

Other:

_____

_____

_____

SOME CONCLUDING IDEAS

In these chapters we've raised some of the ethical and professional issues that you will be most likely to encounter in your counseling practice. Instead of providing answers, we've tried to stimulate you to think about your own guidelines for professional practice and to initiate a process of reflection that you can apply to the many other issues you will face as a counselor.

If there is one fundamental question that can serve to tie together all the issues we've discussed, it is this: Who has the right to counsel another person? This question can be the focal point of your reflection on ethical and professional issues. It can also be the basis of your self-examination each day you meet with clients. You can continue to ask yourself: What makes me think I have a right to counsel others? What do I have to offer the people I'm counseling? Am I doing in my own life what I'm encouraging my clients to do? At times, if you answer these questions honestly, you may be troubled. There may be times when you feel that you have no ethical right to counsel others, perhaps because your own life isn't always the model you would like it to be for your clients. Yet this occasional self-doubt is far less damaging, in our view, than a failure to examine these questions. Complacency will stifle your growth as a counselor; honest self-examination, though more difficult, will make you a more effective helper.

We want to close our discussion by returning to the theme that has guided us throughout this book—namely, that developing a sense of professional and ethical responsibility is a task that is never really finished. There are no final or universal answers to many of the questions we have posed. For ourselves, we hope we never fall into the deadening trap of thinking that we "have it made" and no longer need to reexamine our assumptions and practices. We've found that the kinds of issues raised in this book have demanded periodic reflection and an openness to change. Thus, although we hope you've given careful thought to your own ethical and professional guidelines, we also hope that you'll be willing to rethink your positions as you gain more experience.

So where can you go from here? How can you maintain the process of reflection that you've begun in this course? One excellent way to keep yourself alive intellectually is to develop a reading program. We suggest that you begin by selecting some of the books that we've listed in the Annotated Reading List. We'd also like to suggest that you re-read this book from time to time. We hope that it has become more than an impersonal textbook and that, by writing your responses in the text, you've made it your own personal manual. It can be most valuable for you to re-read various chapters as you take different courses that deal with the issues we've considered. In addition, periodically reexamining your responses can stimulate your thinking and provide a measure of your professional and intellectual growth. We hope you'll find other ways to make this book meaningful for yourself as you continue your search for your own direction.

ACTIVITIES, EXERCISES, AND IDEAS FOR THOUGHT AND DISCUSSION

1. As a small-group discussion activity, explore the topic of how you see yourself in relation to the educational system of which you currently are a part. Discuss the implications your style as a learner may have for the style you'll develop when you work for some institution or agency. Some questions for exploration are: How active are you in the process of your own education? What specific things do you do to make your education more meaningful? Are you willing to talk with instructors if you feel that they aren't offering you a valuable course? Are you willing to suggest constructive alternatives if you're dissatisfied with a class or with your program? Do you often feel powerless as a student and thus assume the stance that there's nothing you can do to really change the things you think most need changing?

   After you've had enough time to discuss this issue in small groups, the class can reconvene and compare results. Are there any common characteristics in the learning styles of the class members? How might these characteristics affect the way you work in a system as a professional?

2. With another student, role-play a job interview. One person is the director of a counseling center, and the other is the applicant. After about ten to fifteen minutes, switch roles. Discuss how you felt in each position, and get feedback from your partner after both of you have had a chance to play each role. Some questions the interviewer might ask include:

   a. Why are you applying for this job?

   b. What are your expectations if you get the position?

   c. Since there are many applicants and only a few positions, tell me why we should select you for the job. What do you have to offer that is unique?

   d. Could you briefly describe your philosophy of counseling?

e. What do you most hope to accomplish as a counselor, and how would you evaluate whether you were accomplishing your goals?

f. What kinds of clients could you *least* effectively counsel? What kinds of clients would you be *most* effective with?

3. As a variation of the preceding exercise, several students can form an interviewing panel that has the task of selecting one applicant out of a field of six. Six students can volunteer to be interviewed for about ten minutes each. At the end of the hour, the members of the panel can talk about their impressions of each candidate. In addition, the people interviewed can state how they think they did during their interviews. The rest of the class can give additional feedback.

4. Invite an administrator of a mental-health facility to address your class on ways of working creatively within a system. You can also invite people in non-administrative positions to talk about how they have dealt with institutional barriers. Have they had to make compromises? Have they given up their identities to remain in their positions? Have they ever found it necessary to quit a certain job in order to keep their identities?

5. Several students can interview a variety of professionals in the mental-health field about the major problems they encounter in their institution. What barriers do they meet when they attempt to implement programs? How do they deal with obstacles or red tape? How does the system affect them? You can divide this task up so that a wide range of professionals and paraprofessionals are interviewed, including some who have been in the same job for a number of years and others who are just beginning. It would be interesting to compare the responses of experienced and inexperienced personnel. The students who do the interviewing can share their impressions and reactions without revealing the identities of the persons interviewed.

6. Make a written list of your priorities as a counselor. This list should include issues that you feel you could not compromise on, as well as issues on which you would be willing to compromise. Bring your list to class, and share your priorities with others in small discussion groups.

7. Proposals sometimes don't get off the ground because counselors don't give them adequate thought or do a poor job of presenting their ideas to those they work for. This exercise is designed to give you practice in planning and presenting a proposal. To begin with, members of the class list some programs they would be interested in implementing. Examples of such proposals include: conducting a parent-effectiveness group through a local elementary school; developing a realistic program to prevent drug abuse on a high school campus; forming a counseling group for single parents in a community mental-health center. Then the class should divide into committees of four people each who can work on a proposal they are all interested in. Each group should formulate a design of its program, including a means for evaluating outcomes. Afterwards the class can reconvene to discuss each program. Feedback can be given about the strengths and weaknesses of each proposal, and alternatives that were not mentioned can be suggested. If taken seriously, this exercise can give you good practice in learning how you come across as you present your ideas.

8. This exercise deals with the fundamental question, Who has a right to counsel anybody? Form small groups of perhaps three people. The students take turns briefly stating the personal and professional qualities that give them

something to offer people. The others give feedback. Afterwards, the students can each explore any self-doubts they have concerning their ethical right to counsel others.

9. Refer back to the multiple-choice survey at the end of Chapter 1 on attitudes and beliefs regarding ethical and professional issues. We suggest that you cover your initial answers and re-take the inventory now that you've come to the end of the course. Then you can compare your responses to see whether your thinking has changed. In addition, we suggest that you circle the ten questions that are most significant to you or that you're most interested in pursuing further. Bring these to class, and discuss them in small groups. Afterwards a survey can be conducted to get some idea of the issues that were most important to the students in your class.

10. As a final exercise, we'd like to request that you write to us about your experience in using this book and in your course. We also invite you to give us your reactions to some of our positions and assumptions. We hope you'll let us know what issues were most meaningful for you, and we welcome any suggestions you have for future revisions. If there are topics you think should be added, let us know what they are. Your comments can be most helpful to us, and writing them down may help you to clarify the meaning of your experience with this course and book. Address your letter to us in care of Brooks/Cole Publishing Company, Monterey, California 93940.

Annotated Reading List
and References

Agel, J. *The radical therapist.* New York: Ballantine, 1971. This book develops the theme that therapy means change, not adjustment. It consists of provocative essays dealing with radical therapy, mental illness, the limitations of traditional therapy, women and men, and community change. The book raises the basic question of whether real personal change is possible without changes in the social and political factors that contribute to the problems of humanity.

Aguilera, D., & Messick, J. *Crisis intervention: Theory and methodology.* St. Louis: Mosby, 1974. This book contains a clear discussion of brief psychotherapies, crisis intervention, and levels of prevention. Many examples of situational and maturational crises are given.

Alexander, F. *Psychoanalysis and psychotherapy.* New York: Norton, 1956. This book contains useful information on key concepts of the traditional psychoanalytic approach.

American Personnel and Guidance Association. *Ethical standards.* Washington, D.C.: American Personnel and Guidance Association, 1961. This booklet lists ethical principles relating to counseling, testing, research and publication, private practice, and professional preparation.

American Psychiatric Association. *Diagnostic and statistical manual of mental disorders* (2nd ed.). Washington, D.C.: American Psychiatric Association, 1968. DSM - II is the official system of classification of psychological disorders.

American Psychological Association. *Ethical standards of psychologists.* Washington, D.C.: American Psychological Association, 1967. This casebook on ethical standards and issues contains ethical guidelines for psychologists.

American Psychological Association. *Ethical principles in the conduct of research with human participants.* Washington, D.C.: American Psychological Association, 1973 (a). This document deals with ethical dilemmas in research with human participants. Ethical guidelines on some of the following issues are explored: informed consent, freedom from coercion, protection from stress, and confidentiality. Also examined are ethical issues related to the social context of psychological research.

American Psychological Association. Guidelines for psychologists conducting growth groups. *American Psychologist,* October 1973 (b),933. Tentative guidelines for growth groups are briefly described. These guidelines raise pertinent issues for group practice.

American Psychological Association. Ethical standards of psychologists. In *APA Monitor,* March 1977 (a), 22–23. This is an updated version of the APA's ethical standards relating to responsibility, competence, moral and legal standards, confidentiality, client welfare, and professional relationships.

American Psychological Association. *Standards for providers of psychological services.* Washington, D.C.: American Psychological Association, 1977 (b). A basic principle guiding the development of these standards is that all psychologists in professional practice should be guided by a uniform set of standards, just as they are guided by a common code of ethics. This document gives standards relating to providers, programs, accountability, and environment.

Arbuckle, D. *Counseling and psychotherapy: An existential-humanistic view* (3rd ed.). Boston: Allyn and Bacon, 1975. Part 3 deals with a number of professional and ethical issues in counseling and psychotherapy, some of which are: counselor control, diagnosis, testing, advice, confidentiality, counseling with members of minority groups, transference and countertransference, and the professional education of counselors.

Bandura, A. *Principles of behavior modification.* New York: Holt, Rinehart & Winston, 1969. Bandura develops the concept of the therapist as a role model and contends that clients learn new behavior largely from the kind of social modeling provided by the therapist.

Bass, S., & Dole, A. Ethical leader practices in sensitivity training for prospective professional psychologists. *Journal Supplement Abstract Service,* 1977, *7* (2), 47–66. This study describes the rating of group-leader behaviors as ethical or unethical by a panel of group specialists.

Berne, E. *Transactional analysis in psychotherapy.* New York: Grove, 1961. This book deals with social psychiatry and raises some issues about group approaches.

Bindrim, P. Confidentiality in group therapy sessions upheld by judgment rendered in California Superior Court. Group Psychotherapy Association of Southern California *Newsletter,* November/December 1977. This article raises the ethical concern about safeguarding confidentiality in groups. Bindrim describes procedures he routinely uses to make confidentiality legally effective.

Bloom, B. *Community mental health: A general introduction.* Monterey, Calif.: Brooks/Cole, 1977. This book deals with the meaning and practice of community mental health and the development of the movement. There are several useful chapters on crisis intervention, preventive intervention, and critical views of the community mental-health movement.

Brammer, L. *The helping relationship: Process and skills.* Englewood Cliffs, N.J.: Prentice-Hall, 1973. Brammer emphasizes communication skills designed to improve the helping person's ability to work with normal individuals. Issues discussed are: the nature of the helping process, characteristics of helpers, and specific intervention skills, particularly those needed for crisis intervention.

Brammer, L., & Shostrom, E. *Therapeutic psychology: Fundamentals of actualization counseling and psychotherapy* (2nd ed.). Englewood Cliffs, N.J.: Prentice-Hall, 1968. This general textbook in counseling deals with a number of professional issues, such as: diagnosis and testing in counseling, advice, the role of values in counseling, trends in counseling, and special relationship problems.

Brooks, B. Directions for tomorrow. In C. Hatcher and B. Brooks (Eds.), *Innovations in counseling psychology.* San Francisco: Jossey-Bass, 1977 (a). This article summarizes some trends in counseling psychology. Brooks discusses such issues as the counselor's role, the education of the community, accountability, interdisciplinary approaches, and professional ethics.

Brooks, B. Training models for tomorrow. In C. Hatcher and B. Brooks (Eds.), *Innovations in counseling psychology.* San Francisco: Jossey-Bass, 1977 (b). Trends in counselor education are examined, including accountability, competency-based programs, and systematic skills training.

Bugental, J. *The search for existential identity.* San Francisco: Jossey-Bass, 1976. This book consists of patient/therapist dialogues in humanistic psychotherapy and shows how Bugental works with six patients. His chapter on duality and openness is a moving summary of many of the things that Bugental has learned about human struggles from his work as a therapist and from his own life.

Burton, A. *Interpersonal psychotherapy*. Englewood Cliffs, N.J.: Prentice-Hall, 1972. A number of professional issues in counseling and psychotherapy are explored in this book, including the client/therapist relationship, goals in therapy, instrumental problems, and the use of techniques.

California Association of Marriage and Family Counselors. *Ethical standards for marriage and family counselors*. Los Angeles, Calif. (Undated.) This booklet is a statement of 17 principles that serve as guidelines for ethical practice for marriage and family counselors.

California Association of Marriage and Family Counselors. *Newsletter*. January 1978. This issue contains some updated information on the question of ethics governing the practice of marriage and family counseling.

Carkhuff, R., & Berenson, B. *Beyond counseling and psychotherapy*. New York: Holt, Rinehart & Winston, 1967. The client-centered, existential, behavioristic, and psychoanalytic models of therapy are discussed, together with some implications of these theoretical orientations for practice.

Christiansen, H. D. *Ethics in counseling: Problem situations*. Tucson, Ariz.: University of Arizona Press, 1972. Written primarily for school counselors, this book contains specific examples of ethical problems and questions. Topics include ethical problems concerning the counseling relationship, the school staff, parents, the public, drug use, school records, testing, and referrals. After each problem is briefly described, it is discussed by four counselors.

Cooper, G. How psychologically dangerous are T-groups and encounter groups? In R. T. Golembiewski and A. Blumberg (Eds.), *Sensitivity training and the laboratory approach* (3rd ed.). Itasca, Ill.: Peacock, 1977. This article deals with the incidence of psychologically disturbing outcomes in encounter-group experiences.

Corey, G. *Theory and practice of counseling and psychotherapy*. Monterey, Calif.: Brooks/Cole, 1977 (a). This book describes eight models of therapy and counseling that are applicable to both individual and group therapy. There are also chapters on the basic issues in counseling, ethical issues, and the counselor as a person. The book is designed to give the reader an overview of the theoretical basis of the practice of counseling.

Corey, G. *A manual for counseling and psychotherapy*. Monterey, Calif.: Brooks/Cole, 1977 (b). This student manual is designed to accompany *Theory and Practice of Counseling and Psychotherapy*. It consists of many exercises, activities, and self-assessment devices designed to make theories of counseling more meaningful and applicable to the student. Many of the exercises are appropriate for group-oriented classes.

Corey, G. & Corey, M. *Groups: Process and practice*. Monterey, Calif.: Brooks/Cole, 1977 (c). Much of this book deals with practical and professional issues special to group work. Separate chapters are devoted to basic issues in group leadership, ethical and professional issues, and applications of group procedures with different age populations.

Corey, G. *I never knew I had a choice*. Monterey, Calif.: Brooks/Cole, 1978. This book deals with existential concerns and issues in such areas as autonomy, work, love, sex, intimacy, loneliness, death, and meaning. Many of the questions discussed are brought up by clients in counseling. The book stresses the basis upon which we make choices for ourselves and the way these choices shape our lives.

Corlis, R. & Rabe, P. *Psychotherapy from the center: A humanistic view of change and of growth*. Scranton, Pa.: International Textbook, 1969. Resistance, transference, countertransference, physical contact with clients, diagnosis, and the goals of therapy are some of the issues discussed in this book.

Danish, S., D'Augelli, A., Brock, G., Conter, K., & Meyer, R. A symposium on skill dissemination for paraprofessionals: Models of training, supervision, and utilization. *Professional Psychology* 9 (1), February 1978, 16–37. This series of articles is based upon a symposium on the nature and importance of skills training for the paraprofessional.

Delaney, D. & Eisenberg, S. *The counseling process* (2nd ed.). Chicago: Rand McNally, 1977.

This book treats issues in counseling practice such as the goals of counseling, characteristics of effective helpers, values and their role in counseling, psychological assessment, working with reluctant clients, and counseling methods.

Dörken, H., and associates. *The professional psychologist today: New developments in law, health insurance, and health practice.* San Francisco: Jossey-Bass, 1976. This book presents an overview of many current developments in health services. Various articles deal with standards for psychologists, laws regulating psychological practice, issues relating to licensure and certification, health insurance programs and policies, the utilization of mental-health services, future trends in psychological practice, and issues facing professional psychology.

Drum, D., & Figler, H. Outreach in counseling. In C. Hatcher and B. Brooks (Eds.), *Innovations in counseling psychology.* San Francisco: Jossey-Bass, 1977. This article describes the evolution of outreach activities as an active approach oriented toward the prevention of mental-health problems in the community.

Dugger, J. *The new professional: Introduction for the human services mental health worker.* Monterey, Calif.: Brooks/Cole, 1975. This is an introduction to some basic issues for the mental-health worker, including the community mental-health movement, attitudes and values of the professional, cultural differences, crisis counseling, and community resources.

Dworkin, E. The new activist counselor. In C. Hatcher and B. Brooks (Eds.), *Innovations in counseling psychology.* San Francisco: Jossey-Bass, 1977. The central message of this article is that professionals should take the mystique and magic out of therapy and share their knowledge and skills with those they serve.

Egan, G. *The skilled helper: A model for systematic helping and interpersonal relating.* Monterey, Calif.: Brooks/Cole, 1975. This book presents a practical three-stage model for developing specific skills in counseling, from basic skills in listening to developing action programs for clients. It is a relevant and useful book that raises issues concerning the education of those in the helping professions.

Egan, G. *Interpersonal living: A skills/contract approach to human-relations training in groups.* Monterey, Calif.: Brooks/Cole, 1976. The author presents a contract approach to training in interpersonal skills. There are chapters devoted to issues and skills in self-disclosure, listening and responding, and challenging and confronting.

Egan, G. *You & me: The skills of communicating and relating to others.* Monterey, Calif.: Brooks/Cole, 1977. Designed for use in small groups, this book presents a systematic approach to training in interpersonal skills. It is essentially a less technical treatment of the subject matter of *Interpersonal Living* (Egan, 1976).

Ellis, A. *Humanistic psychotherapy: The rational-emotive approach.* New York: McGraw-Hill, 1973. This book gives a good overview of most of the basic concepts of the rational-emotive approach to psychotherapy. The chapters on the self-awareness and personal growth of the therapist and the goals of psychotherapy are especially relevant to some of the topics explored in this book.

Feinberg, S. Some questions about ethics and responsibilities in sensitivity training. In R. Golembiewski and A. Blumberg (Eds.), *Sensitivity training and the laboratory approach* (3rd ed.). Itasca, Ill.: Peacock, 1977. This brief article deals with reactions to sensitivity training, ethical guideposts, objectives, issues relating to group composition and screening procedures, the use of techniques, and general concerns.

Frankl, V. *Man's search for meaning.* New York: Pocket Books, 1963. Frankl deals with the role of values in therapy and discusses ways of searching for meaning in life. The first part of the book is a description of his experiences in a World War II concentration camp and his attempt to find meaning in this situation.

Frankl, V. *The will to meaning: Foundations and applications of logotherapy.* New York: New American Library (Plume Book), 1969. Frankl has a particularly good discussion of meaning and the role of meaning and values in psychotherapy. He also describes the concept of existential vacuum, as well as techniques and applications of logotherapy.

Gazda, G. Some tentative guidelines for ethical practice by group work practitioners. In

G. Gazda (Ed.), *Basic approaches to group psychotherapy and group counseling* (2nd ed.). Springfield, Ill.: Charles C Thomas, 1977. Gazda lists useful guidelines for group leaders and explores issues special to group work, including recruitment and screening of group participants, confidentiality, termination and follow-up, leaderless groups, and procedures for handling unethical practice.

Glasser, W. *Reality therapy.* New York: Harper & Row, 1965. Glasser outlines the basic concepts of reality therapy and shows how these principles apply to counseling with people in institutions, particularly people with behavioral problems. Among the basic issues discussed are the place of values and morality in counseling, the counselor as a role model, the nature of reality, and therapy as a teaching/learning process.

Glenn, M., & Kunnes, R. *Repression of revolution? Therapy in the United States today.* New York: Harper & Row, 1973. The authors present a harsh view of conventional therapy and abuses in professional practice. They explore community therapy, sexuality, marriage, alternative life-styles, and therapy and sexism. The book does raise basic issues concerning the values of therapy and alternatives to conventional approaches.

Goldberg, C. *Therapeutic partnership: Ethical concerns in psychotherapy.* New York: Springer, 1977. This book presents an ethically enlightened approach to the practice of psychotherapy based on informed consent and psychological contract. It joins two major themes, the search for an understanding of human existence through therapeutic encounter and the collaborative endeavors of client and therapist in establishing a therapeutic partnership.

Goldenberg, H. *Contemporary clinical psychology.* Monterey, Calif.: Brooks/Cole, 1973. This book contains several excellent chapters that are relevant for such professional issues in psychotherapy as professional preparation and practice, diagnosis and assessment, community mental health, crisis intervention, and brief psychotherapies.

Goldenberg, H. *Abnormal psychology: A social/community approach.* Monterey, Calif.: Brooks/Cole, 1977. This is a well written text with sections on trends in community mental health, the use of paraprofessionals, and human-services delivery systems. Goldenberg has a good discussion of psychodiagnosis and the classification of psychological disorders.

Goldstein, A. Behavior therapy. In R. Corsini (Ed.), *Current psychotherapies.* Itasca, Ill.: Peacock, 1973. Goldstein provides a very clear description of some of the basic assumptions underlying behavior therapy and deals with several professional issues related to this approach.

Gottman, J., & Leiblum, S. *How to do psychotherapy and how to evaluate it.* New York: Holt, Rinehart & Winston, 1974. The assumption of this book is that therapists should be scientists while they are doing psychotherapy. The authors provide guidelines for the ongoing evaluation of therapy.

Harper, R. *The new psychotherapies.* Englewood Cliffs, N.J.: Prentice-Hall, 1975. This is a good, although very brief, overview of group therapies, including transactional analysis, the encounter movement, and a variety of systems. The book also discusses family therapies, behavior therapies, and body psychotherapies, among others.

Hatcher, C., Brooks, B., and associates. *Innovations in counseling psychology: Developing new roles, settings, techniques.* San Francisco: Jossey-Bass, 1977. The authors look at new roles in which counselors move beyond traditional functions to become initiators of change and preventors of problems. They show how counselors are making use of recent knowledge concerning the effects of environment on behavior and they examine new developments in counseling of the elderly, minority-group students, and those with drug-related problems. They also investigate new settings such as community centers and urban free clinics.

Holroyd, J., & Brodsky, A. Psychologists' attitudes and practices regarding erotic and nonerotic physical contact with patients. *American Psychologist 32*(10), October 1977, 843–849. This article explores the ethics of sexual contact in the therapeutic relationship.

Ivey, A. & Authier, J. *Microcounseling: Innovations in interviewing, counseling, psychotherapy, and psychoeducation.* Springfield, Ill.: Charles C Thomas, 1978. This book updates extensive research on the microcounseling model. It also presents a detailed analysis of the interview, specific methods for teaching and researching interviewing skills, and an explication of videotape methods used in microcounseling.

Jorgensen, F. & Lyons, D. Human rights and involuntary civil commitment. *Professional Psychology*, 1972, 3(2), 143–150. The authors argue that candidates for civil commitment should be afforded the same due-process protection as those facing criminal conviction.

Jorgensen, F., & Weigel, R. Training psychotherapists: Practices regarding ethics, personal growth, and locus of responsibility. *Professional Psychology* 1973, 4(1), 23–27. The article contains interesting information from a survey of training directors on graduate training practices. It deals with the value given to professional and ethical issues.

Jourard, S. *Disclosing man to himself.* Princeton, N.J.: Van Nostrand, 1968. Part II of the book, *Psychotherapy for Growing Persons*, raises many significant issues in counseling and psychotherapy. Jourard has many insightful views on these issues, and he provides some excellent material for discussion.

Jourard, S. *The transparent self* (rev. ed.). New York: Van Nostrand, 1971. Jourard has many provocative things to say concerning the role of the therapist and the importance of self-disclosure. He also deals with sex roles, education, drugs, privacy, encounter groups, and other professional issues.

Kaplan, H. S. *The new sex therapy.* New York: Brunner/Mazel, 1974. Kaplan has an excellent chapter devoted to professional issues in sex therapy that explores the following topics: conjoint treatment of couples, the use of co-therapists, and transference and countertransference in sex therapy.

Kempler, W. Gestalt therapy. In R. Corsini (Ed.), *Current psychotherapies.* Itasca, Ill.: Peacock, 1973. Kempler presents his version of Gestalt therapy in this article. Of particular interest is his treatment of the topic of the therapist as a person and the client/therapist relationship. Also valuable are his discussions of the role of diagnosis in Gestalt and the dangers of labeling.

Koch, J., & Koch, L. A consumer's guide to therapy for couples. *Psychology Today*, March 1976, 33–40. The authors describe some of the pitfalls in selecting a counselor, issue some cautions for consumers, and give guidelines on how to find a marriage counselor.

Kopp, S. *If you meet the Buddha on the road, kill him!* New York, Bantam, 1976. This book describes what psychotherapy is like for patients and stresses the involvement of the therapist in the process.

Krasner, L. The reinforcement machine. In B. Berenson and R. Carkhuff (Eds.), *Sources of gain in counseling and psychotherapy.* New York: Holt, Rinehart & Winston, 1967. Krasner develops the thesis that therapists, regardless of their orientation, have the power to influence and control the behavior and values of their clients. He contends that therapists who refuse to recognize their power are behaving unethically.

Laing, R.D. *The politics of experience.* New York: Pantheon, 1967. A critic of traditional psychodiagnosis, Laing warns that a psychiatric label may result in a self-fulfilling prophecy for both the client and the therapist. Labels influence the way hospital personnel view and treat patients, which in turn affects how patients view themselves and how they behave.

Lakin, M. *Interpersonal encounter: Theory and practice in sensitivity training.* New York: McGraw-Hill, 1972. Lakin explores professional issues related to training groups and encounter groups, including policy issues in training groups, psychological risks, pre-group concerns, selection and recruitment, ethical questions related to the process of training groups, and problems in evaluation.

Lewinsohn, P., & Pearlman, S. Continuing education for psychologists. *Professional Psychology* 3(1), Winter 1972, 48–52. This article explores continuing education as a way of upgrading personal and professional competence.

Lewis, J. *To be a therapist: The teaching and learning.* New York: Brunner/Mazel, 1978. The author describes a program for teaching and learning psychotherapeutic skills, regardless of one's theoretical orientation.

Lowe, C. M. *Value orientations in counseling and psychotherapy: The meanings of mental health.* San Francisco: Chandler, 1969. Some of the topics explored in this book are: the therapist and the client in a world of changing values, moral aspects in counseling, moral myths and their meaning, moral messages of psychotherapy, relating therapy and the law, and the therapist and the new morality.

Lowry, T., & Lowry, T. Ethical considerations in sex therapy. *Journal of Marriage and Family Counseling, 1*(3) July 1975, 229–236. One of the issues discussed in this article is overt sexual activity with clients.

Maslow, A. *Toward a psychology of being* (2nd ed.). New York: Van Nostrand, 1968. This book deals with issues such as growth and motivation, creativity, values, and the self-actualizing person.

Maslow, A. *Motivation and personality* (2nd ed.). New York: Harper & Row, 1970. The chapter on self-actualizing people provides a useful frame of reference for developing general goals for counseling and psychotherapy.

May, R. *Psychology and the human dilemma.* Princeton, N.J.: Van Nostrand, 1967. May describes the roots of contemporary problems of living, such as the loss of significance and the anxiety of living in a world that encourages anonymity. May raises value issues that are relevant to psychotherapy and discusses the social responsibilities of psychologists.

May, R., & Ellenberger, H. F. (Eds.). *Existence: A new dimension in psychiatry and psychology.* New York: Basic Books, 1958. Readers can get a good idea of the areas of focus in an existential approach to therapy from the cases described in this book.

McWaters, B. (Ed.). *Humanistic perspectives: Current trends in psychology.* Monterey, Calif.: Brooks/Cole, 1977. This book is a collection of essays on various views of humanistic psychology in general areas such as broadening images of self, new modes of being together, and emerging sociocultural forms. Each author briefly answers the question: What are the major issues facing psychology today?

Meyer, R., & Smith, S. A crisis in group therapy. *American Psychologist, 32*(8), August 1977, 638–643. This article indicates that federal courts may not recognize privilege in group therapy and calls attention to the implications of this possibility.

Mintz, E. *Marathon groups: Reality and symbol.* New York: Avon, 1971. The nature of marathon groups, the process of these groups, and suggestions for group leaders are dealt with in an interesting manner. Mintz also discusses guidelines for screening and selecting participants.

Mosak, H., & Dreikurs, R. Adlerian psychotherapy. In R. Corsini (Ed.), *Current psychotherapies.* Itasca, Ill.: Peacock, 1973. The core concepts of Adlerian theory and practice are summarized well in this chapter.

Patterson, C. H. *Counseling and psychotherapy: Theory and practice.* New York: Harper & Row, 1959. Patterson has a section on ethics and counselor needs, values and psychotherapy, and issues in training in counseling and psychotherapy. Also examined are issues such as diagnosis, use of counseling techniques, the role of theory, and the client/therapist relationship.

Perls, F. *Gestalt therapy verbatim.* Moab, Utah: Real People Press, 1969. Perls gives an informal, easy-to-read description of most of the basic concepts of Gestalt therapy. Of particular interest are topics related to goals of therapy, the issue of responsibility, the client/therapist relationship, diagnosis, and functions and roles of the therapist.

Peterson, J. *Counseling and values: A philosophical examination.* Scranton, Pa.: International Textbook, 1970. Some of the topics discussed in this book are: values and the counseling process, the issue of counselor neutrality, goals in counseling, and the degree and direction of counselor influence. There is also a chapter on the counselor and religious issues.

Plotkin, R. Confidentiality in group counseling. *APA Monitor,* March 1978, 14. This article raises some very important ethical, legal, and professional issues concerning the obligation of group members to maintain the confidential character of disclosures made in their group.

Polster, E, & Polster, M. *Gestalt therapy integrated.* New York: Random House, 1973. An excellent treatment of some advanced concepts underlying the practice of Gestalt therapy, this book describes clearly the nature of Gestalt therapy and emphasizes the human role and function of the therapist. The authors make the point that therapists who ignore their personal qualities as instruments in therapy become mere technicians.

Portwood, D. A right to suicide? *Psychology Today,* January 1978, 66–74. The author pleads for an objective discussion of a taboo topic—the right of the aged to choose their own time to die.

Rogers, C. *Counseling and psychotherapy.* Cambridge, Mass.: Houghton Mifflin, 1942. This is one of the pioneering books in the counseling field, and it presents much of Rogers' initial thinking. It deals with issues such as the use of techniques in counseling, problems faced by the counselor, and structuring the client/counselor relationship.

Rogers, C. *Client-centered therapy.* Boston: Houghton Mifflin, 1951. Rogers discusses issues such as transference, diagnosis, the applicability of client-centered therapy, the importance of the attitude and orientation of the counselor, and the therapeutic relationship.

Rogers, C. *On becoming a person.* Boston: Houghton Mifflin, 1961. This book explores many of Rogers' viewpoints on the nature of the helping relationship, the process of counseling, and the client/counselor relationship. It is especially useful on the topic of the importance of the counselor's personality in influencing client change.

Rogers, C. *Freedom to learn.* Columbus, Ohio: Charles E. Merrill, 1969. Rogers has an excellent section on values and the valuing process. He discusses the process of valuing with implications for both education and psychotherapy.

Rogers, C. *Carl Rogers on encounter groups.* New York: Harper & Row, 1970. This book deals with the basic process of the encounter group, discusses how groups can facilitate changes in both individuals and organizations, and raises issues on the uses and applications of groups.

Rogers, C. *Carl Rogers on personal power: Inner strength and its revolutionary impact.* New York: Delacorte, 1977. In this book Rogers extends his earlier thoughts to areas such as marriage and family life, education, and international relations. The focus is on interpersonal relationships and the social system.

Ruitenbeek, H. *The new group psychotherapies.* New York: Discus/Avon, 1970. A comprehensive overview of newer approaches in group therapy, marathon groups, and a variety of styles of conducting encounter groups.

Schacht, T., & Nathan, P. But is it good for the psychologists? Appraisal and status of DSM III. *American Psychologist,* December 1977, 1017–1025. This article discusses some of the problems of the medical model of mental illness. The implication is made that social, political, and professional influences on diagnosis may be a part of the mental-health professions for some time.

Schofield, W. *Psychotherapy: The purchase of friendship.* Englewood Cliffs, N.J.: Prentice-Hall (Spectrum), 1964. The author deals with anxiety, the issue of diagnosis, and the nature of the therapeutic process.

Schutz, W. *Here comes everybody.* New York: Harper & Row, 1971. This is a good treatment of the "open encounter group" that can be highly recommended for group leaders and participants, as well as those who want a sample of various types of growth groups. Schutz discusses the types and techniques of groups and has a good section on the group leader.

Shaffer, J., & Galinsky, M. D. *Models of group therapy and sensitivity training.* Englewood Cliffs, N.J.: Prentice-Hall, 1974. This is an excellent overview of the various models of groups, including the psychoanalytic and existential-experiential models, psychodrama, Gestalt, behavior therapy, T-groups, the encounter group, and theme-centered groups. The final chapter on integration and perspectives is excellent.

Shah, S. Privileged communications, confidentiality, and privacy: Privileged communications. *Professional Psychology, 1*(1), November 1969, 56–69. The nature of privileged communication and basic issues related to this legal concept are examined in detail. The distinctions among the three related concepts of confidentiality, privileged communications, and privacy are clarified.

Shah, S. Privileged communications, confidentiality, and privacy: Confidentiality. *Professional Psychology. 1*(2), Winter 1970 (a), 159–164. General considerations and specific issues regarding confidentiality are examined. The article raises the question: Whose agent is the psychologist?

Shah, S. Privileged communications, confidentiality, and privacy: Privacy. *Professional Psychology 1*(3), Spring 1970 (b), 243–252. The right to privacy is discussed as an affirmation of the individual's freedom from unreasonable intrusions by others.

Steinzor, B. *The healing partnership: The patient as colleague in psychotherapy.* New York: Harper & Row, 1967. Steinzor deals with many practical concerns facing the practitioner, such as the matter of fees, the nature of the therapeutic relationship, issues relating to transference, and joy and suffering in psychotherapy.

Stolz, S., and associates. *Ethical issues in behavior modification.* San Francisco: Jossey-Bass, 1978. This is a report of the American Psychological Association Commission that examined and clarified the ethical issues involved in behavior modification. The book is organized around settings where behavior modification is in use: out-patient settings, institutions, schools, prisons, society, and so on. Recommendations are given concerning the use and misuse of behavior modification.

Suinn, R. & Weigel, R. (Eds.). *The innovative psychological therapies: Critical and creative contributions.* New York: Harper & Row, 1975. This is a good book of readings on a range of topics, including behavior therapy, therapeutic programs, and paraprofessionals. One section consists of eight articles on group procedures.

Szasz, T. *The myth of mental illness: Foundations of a theory of personal conduct.* (Rev. ed.). New York: Harper & Row, 1974. Szasz has challenged the medical-model concept as it is applied to psychotherapy. His thesis is that mental illness does not exist in the sense in which physical diseases do, and he challenges the idea that people should be excused for their behavior on the grounds that they are mentally ill and therefore not responsible for their acts.

Tolchin, G., Steinfeld, G., & Suchotliff, L. The mental patient and civil rights: Some moral, legal, and ethical considerations. *Professional Psychology*, 1970, *1*(3), 212–216. The article calls attention to the legal and ethical aspects of the loss of basic human rights when one is hospitalized.

Torrey, E. F. *The death of psychiatry.* Radnor, Pa.: Chilton, 1974. Written by a psychiatrist, this book develops the thesis that psychiatry and the medical-model approach to human problems are outdated and that a new approach is needed to understand problems of living.

Van Hoose, W., & Kottler, J. *Ethical and legal issues in counseling and psychotherapy.* San Francisco: Jossey-Bass, 1977. The authors deal with a variety of professional issues, such as: incompetent and unethical behavior, psychotherapy and the law, legal regulations of professional psychology, ethics in group work, the marketing of therapeutic services, issues in behavior therapy, issues related to diagnosis and assessment, value problems in psychotherapy, and ethical principles in the practice of therapy.

Whitlock, G. *Understanding and coping with real-life crises.* Monterey, Calif.: Brooks/Cole, 1978. This is a very useful book that emphasizes the *practice* of crisis intervention. Also dealt with are issues such as the training of crisis counselors, the stages of crisis intervention, and crisis intervention and community mental health. Specific crises are examined in separate chapters, and experiential exercises are given to provide learning opportunities.

Wrenn, G. Two psychological worlds: An attempted rapprochement. In J. Krumboltz (Ed.), *Revolution in counseling.* Boston: Houghton Mifflin, 1966. Wrenn discusses how it is possible to combine humanistic goals with behavioral techniques.

Wrenn, G. *The world of the contemporary counselor*. Boston: Houghton Mifflin, 1973. This book presents a good overview of a range of issues in counseling, including changing values related to authority, women, work, sex, drugs, education, philosophy of life, and youth. Wrenn has two chapters on the topic of counseling and caring in which he discusses contemporary developments in counseling, counselors' expectations about their roles, counselor selection and education, and the nature of caring.

Yalom, I. *The theory and practice of group psychotherapy* (2nd ed.). New York: Basic Books, 1975. This is an excellent, comprehensive text on group therapy. Detailed discussions are devoted to the curative factors in groups, the group therapist, procedures in organizing therapy groups, problem patients, research on the encounter group, and training of group therapists.

Index